NO QUARTER:
The Ravings of
WILLIAM NORMAN GRIGG

The
LIBERTARIAN
INSTITUTE

No Quarter:
The Ravings of William Norman Grigg
Copyright © 2019 by The Libertarian Institute
All rights reserved.

Cover Design: Scott Alberts.

Published in the United States of America by

The Libertarian Institute
612 W. 34th St.
Austin, TX 78705

LibertarianInstitute.org

ISBN-13: 978-1-7336473-0-4
ISBN-10: 1-7336473-0-9

All proceeds from this book will go to the Grigg family.

Table of Contents

No Quarter

Foreword

The great writer William Norman Grigg deserves a legacy, and as luck would have it, he happened to put together a selection of his work for publication in book form several years before his tragic death in the spring of 2017. Though the book project was put on a back-burner for several years, his death adds a new urgency to expanding the reach of Will's work.

And here it is. Each of the 65 documents in the main corpus of this book were personally selected by William Norman Grigg before his death for inclusion in this volume. Will often complained to me that his manuscripts were bowdlerized by *The New American*'s editors. (Don't worry, I had to look the definition of the word "bowdlerized" up as well, the first time I heard him say it.) But these manuscripts are unedited, except by Will, which is to say they are literary masterpieces. This is Will Grigg, off the chain.

One caveat about these manuscripts: The various tracts in this book do not give justice to Will's outstanding research skills, as the hyperlinks he provided in these mostly online columns do not fit into the format of this print volume.

The articles herein begin with some manuscripts Will wrote for the web on his "Birch Blog" (most of which were rejected outright for publication in John Birch Society publications, as they gradually rejected the punchy for the prosaic), followed by mostly his Pro Libertate blog items. The documents are in chronological order, and the reader will see an evolution of Will's thinking, as he transformed from a classical liberal, to libertarian, to a largely anarchist/voluntaryist worldview.

My Friendship with Will Grigg

I first met Will Grigg sometime in 1993, when he came into the John Birch Society office in Appleton, Wisconsin for a visit. He'd written several great articles for the flagship magazine, *The New American*, as a freelance writer. He'd already made a name for himself with his vocabulary, which the magazine had been forced to dumb down somewhat in order to package to the general readership. I shook his hand on a tour of the little office at 770 Westhill Boulevard, and then attended a meeting in CEO G. Vance Smith's corner office upstairs. By the time I got to the office, someone had already quipped that he was "Thesaurus Rex." It stuck. But Will Grigg was not like some of the people I'd known in high school and college who deliberately used obscure words to demonstrate their supposed great intellect. Will wasn't showing off. He used the *best* word to describe the situation he was speaking about. And he was gracious when I—or others—were unfamiliar with the vocabulary he was using.

Will was quickly hired as a "research associate" after that first meeting, and assigned to my staff, sort of. I was the Director of Research for both *The New American* and the John Birch Society (and its other affiliates) at the time, but it made little sense to have this genius do any of the mundane library work of my research staff. Smith quickly promoted Will to "Senior Editor" for *The New American*, where he served officially within the editorial department but had an office in the research area. It was a lucky break for me.

Shortly after Will was hired, the JBS managed a successful fundraising campaign that allowed them to purchase the building next door and construct a tunnel connecting the basements of the two buildings. The research and editorial offices were relocated to the new building at 700 Westhill Boulevard, and—even though we were still in the basement—it was an ideal set-up. Nerds like Will Grigg and I had everything we could want in our new offices. We had our own little office space, a library of 30,000 books (many of them rare), 130 file cabinets full of news clippings on various topics and persons, the Internet, Lexis-Nexis, and subscriptions to more than 120 periodicals coming into the building.

I love being a classroom social studies teacher today, but being in the research department was the best job of my life. And one of the biggest perks was that my desk was right next to Will's little office for seven years. Will and I were paid to read, and to write occasionally about what we'd read. I couldn't have imagined a better job, and still can't imagine a better one. And because the JBS was poorly managed, we had no real supervision from the other building. We could do and write almost whatever we wanted, and we both wanted to write about—and in support of—liberty.

To be sure, I was the junior partner in this partnership of liberty with Will. Even when I fully understood what Will was saying, I'd jokingly play the Gilligan to his Professor. Will would often use his broad vocabulary to describe something, noting that "Clinton has really become ostentatious about promoting a police state," to which I'd jokingly repeat deliberately using smaller, more common words: "Yeah, and he's being really obvious about it too." He'd usually reply with a smile "Okay, Gilligan."

But it was fun even when I didn't possess an understanding of the vocabulary he was using. One example of his wit was his description of the apprehension of the Unabomber, Ted Kaczynski in "The Insider Report," the informal weekly internal newsletter management imposed on the research and editorial staff. Will had written that the environmental terrorist Kaczynski—who had been apprehended unbathed—had experienced "personal biodiversity while living in a yurt made of his own offal." I read it and laughed, even though at the time I didn't know what a "yurt" or "offal" was (though I had a pretty good idea from the context). So I looked them up in a dictionary . . . and laughed again, even louder.

Of course, there were two senior editors and three researchers who wrote for "The Insider Report," but Will Grigg wrote the majority of the content. And he wrote the best content. Will quickly became the most prolific writer for *The New American*, and the writer the majority of readers looked forward to reading most. He possessed a quick and insightful mind; he could think to the root of a problem in an instant, in cases where it would take me an hour or even days. He was the only genius I've ever gotten to know really well.

And like most geniuses, Will had issues with some of the mundane details in life that most of us humans solve as a matter of course. He didn't dress himself fashionably, to say the least. His little office was reliably a pigsty, with more of a piling-system than a filing-system on his desk and floor. It wasn't unusual to see a Taco Bell wrapping in between clippings of *Washington Post* and *New York Times* stories in his office. Will was a self-described "techno-klutz," and I can't remember how many times I had to go into his office to rescue a file he'd accidentally deleted on his office computer.

Will was an open nerd, a vocal Trekkie and a bookworm, but he was also the coolest thing we had ever known. By 1994, the JBS had a full-time staff of about 90—more or less equally divided between sales staff ("field staff") spread out across the country and office personnel in the two Appleton buildings. All the guys in the office under 50 years of age (and a few of the geezers), just wanted to hang around Will to see what outrageous thing would come out of his mouth next. Will had made the "Insider Report" the hottest commodity on the staff; everyone wanted to read it, including the field staff who received it in their weekly packets. The field staff would want to visit him first when they journeyed to Appleton.

Though he had a way of making all the guys laugh, he was awkward around women. The women in the office tolerated him at best, regardless of their age and political viewpoint. Then I got two new female interns from Utah, the Mormon area of the country. One of them was named Korrin Weeks. She was an attractive and shapely young lady who'd majored in physical education in college, and the two of them were inseparable from the moment she was assigned to my department. Will had grown up in the LDS church, a point of similarity with the CEO G. Vance Smith; Smith's familiarity with these families are probably part of the reason I was assigned these two particular interns.

Will and Korrin married after a short engagement, and they remained together happily until the end. Both ended up leaving the Mormon church several years later for what could be described a fundamentalist, Bible-only faith largely because Will became convinced Jesus was God in the flesh (a doctrine rejected by the Mormons). It wasn't an easy decision for either of them; Will had never expressed anything but love and admiration for his adopted mother and father, who were LDS Church members. He didn't want to disappoint them, but faith in the true God in the end became his primary concern.

Will's one materialistic craving was books. He was constantly carrying around an armload of them, read them quickly, and remembered almost everything in them. As long as he had $50 to spend on new books, he was a happy man. Will would often moonlight as a guitarist to make a few extra bucks for those books, an instrument he played very well. Even before coming out to Appleton, local music shops would recommend Will to play with the Beach Boys and other headlining acts on tour when they needed an extra guitar in the band. In Appleton, his band was called "Slick Willie and the Calzones," and their chief product was to produce an album of songs about the local Green Bay Packers.

Growth of *The New American*

As soon as Will joined *The New American*'s staff, circulation took off. In April 1994, they published the "Toward a Police State" issue. That single issue that added 10,000 new regular subscribers during several reprints that sold more than 400,000 copies. The magazine circulation had been stable at 15,000 for several years, but it tripled over the next few years to more than 50,000 regular subscribers (with several special issues receiving several hundred thousand in paid circulation).

In the years following the "Toward a Police State" issue, Will repeatedly credited me for proposing and outlining the issue in Editor Gary Benoit's office. I don't remember calling that meeting, but if I did, it was because Will had already published most of the pieces of the puzzle in separate articles after covering the Ruby Ridge and Waco sieges in 1993.

No Quarter

The John Birch Society—or more accurately *The New American* magazine—became the Tea Party of the 1990s, the major grassroots opposition to Clinton administration proposals for new gun laws and other attacks against the U.S. Constitution. It stood in stark contrast to the Washington, D.C.-based mail order operations operated by Richard Viguerie; it gave ordinary people something to *do* about big government. It wasn't just circulation of *The New American* that increased, even the reliably declining JBS membership rolls enjoyed a modest bump in the mid-1990s.

The Balkan wars in the mid-1990s served as an occasion for the JBS to drift into a more liberty-minded direction. From its founding, the JBS had been a coalition organization of sorts. Rank-and-file members always saw the JBS as monolithic with unchanging principles, but founder Robert Welch welcomed free trader Ludwig von Mises and protectionist Dan Smoot into the organization in order to fight communism. Civil libertarians and "national security" conservatives, religious conservatives and libertine libertarians also flowed in-and-out of the organization over the decades. The JBS published essays against the civil rights movement and Brown v. Board of Education, but also essays by Austrian school economist Hans Sennholz defending the decision.

Opposition to Clinton's undeclared war in Serbia, Bosnia and Macedonia began on a constitutional basis, and Will and I overcame typical "national security" conservative objections to follow the commander-in-chief during a time of war. There really wasn't anyone on staff that provided obstacles to publishing critiques of the war.

The Balkan War was in marked contrast with the later Iraq War controversy within the JBS, which replayed Robert Welch's opposition to the Vietnam War. Will powerfully utilized Welch's criticism of the Vietnam War as reason the JBS should vigorously oppose the Balkan War. But the internal JBS bureaucracy blunted that opposition in both the Vietnam and Iraq cases.

The New American began publishing a regular stream of anti-war pieces against the Balkan War, which would inevitably turn into a river authored primarily by Will. In this effort, Will and I were strongly influenced by the heroic libertarian writers Justin Raimondo and Lew Rockwell, who had begun building powerful websites of their own, Antiwar.com and LewRockwell.com, respectively.

Will proved to be an amazing machine of writing during this time. He could produce a 1,500-word essay in a couple of hours that wouldn't even need a touch of editing and was a work of art. I was the opposite; it would take me nearly a week to produce the same length essay, and I would need a heavy dose of editing to smooth over my turgid prose. I didn't become a good writer until after I had left the JBS staff and became a newspaper editor in my own right; my primary role on *The New American*'s staff was to provide raw research to writers.

Research was my one talent; I got many of the other writers for the magazine to write more in a liberty-minded direction—the direction that Will had already decided upon—by providing them photocopies of articles with highlights of quotes to use. Of course, I provided these clippings to Will as well. And he used them. But it was different with Will. He had tons of his own research that was far beyond what I had provided him. I always felt that I strongly influenced the other writers in how their final article was written. I could get into their minds; I knew which quotes the writers would use in their pieces before I sent them off. With Will, my research role was negligible because he had so much more to offer than the rest of us mere mortals. When it came to research, I sent him good stuff, but he more often than not had better stuff. My expertise was research, but he was a better researcher than me.

During my tenure in the research department, Will and I often battled organizational sclerosis of authoritarian ideology that was the legacy of Robert Welch's broad coalition. One anecdote of this was a series of articles written in 1999 about "20th Century Heroes," published the following year in book form. The magazine profiled a number of genuine 20th century heroes, from journalist John T. Flynn to Christian writer C.S. Lewis to economist Ludwig von Mises to dissident Cardinal Mindszenty. But among the 25 profiles published of prominent people included an increasing list of dictators, including Chaing Kai-Shek, South Korean strongman Syngman Rhee and Augusto Pinochet of Chile. JBS Founder Robert Welch had been pen pals with the Chaing and Rhee. But I didn't understand why, if we were going to pick the best two dozen people of the 20th century to promote freedom we'd have to choose dictators whose chief virtue was not being a communist.

What followed next was perhaps the only time I was right on an issue and Will was wrong. The magazine staff approached me to write a puff piece on Spain's Francisco Franco. I said I didn't want to write it, and that if I did write something on Franco, it wouldn't remotely resemble a "heroes" piece. So Will was asked next to write the piece. He agreed, and wrote a piece about the very best part of Franco's reign—the part when he defeated the genocidal anti-Catholic republican forces. It was factually correct, but it had left out all the parts of Franco's bloody history. He later wrote to me that "Tom, with the benefit of more than a decade's worth of reflection, and hopefully a modicum of intellectual growth, I can see that I was entirely wrong to write a hagiography of Franco." But a profile of Portugal's Antonio Salazar was also already in the works as Will's Franco profile hit the newsstands, and the magazine was considering writing similar additional paeans to Nicaragua's Somoza and the Shah of Iran. I convinced Will that we should draw a line if we didn't want to be the JBS to mean the Jack-Boot Society. The two of us called an editorial meeting where we confronted Editor Gary Benoit and other editorial staff with the slogan "no more dictators." Will did all the talking, repeating the slogan several times, and the Somoza/Shah pieces were canceled.

The "no more dictators" meeting was one example of how Will and I battled and maneuvered within the confines of the JBS ideological labyrinth, winning most of our battles eventually. We still weren't able to stop the quinquennial cover story condemning rock music, or the periodic stories claiming the South was right to secede from the Union in 1861. Despite those annoyances, I believed the organization was moving in the right direction. And we had other creative outlets as well; Will and I co-hosted a weekly hour-long cable-access television program in Appleton in 1999–2000 which some activists redistributed in other cable markets (Chicago and the Boston area in particular).

But by the time George W. Bush became President in 2001, I had already decided 12 years in Appleton was long enough. I left the staff and continued as a freelance writer from my old homeland south of Boston. Will stayed on the staff as JBS leaders slowly increased pressure to tone down criticism of wars that had been published with unvarnished invective against the Clinton administration.

Decline of *The New American*

Leadership guessed that part of the reason the organization had stopped growing was GOP party loyalty among membership prospects. The mostly GOP membership of the JBS had forwarded a handful of complaints about insults against Dubya, mostly delivered at the hands of Will's acidic keyboard. I've heard it said that the JBS tempered its anti-war position in 2001–05 period, but this is patently untrue. Leadership was attempting proper marketing and branding of the JBS message in *The New American*. They never properly managed the brand, however; strong opinions about Bush did far less damage to the organization's popular credibility than publishing cover stories attacking rock music (at the same time its senior editor was playing guitar in night clubs across Wisconsin and Michigan's Upper Peninsula). Will largely retained a free hand to write as he pleased while the rest of us were indirectly asked not to use negative adjectives to describe the Republican attack on the Bill of Rights. During the immediate post-9/11 period, however, the JBS and *The New American* remained adamantly anti-war.

After I left Appleton in 2001, I only saw Will face-to-face only one more time, in a brief visit to Appleton in 2005. We had fairly regular telephone conversations, shared several hundred email messages, and 117 pages of Facebook Private Messages. We always shared a strong kinship, but it was nothing like sharing office space with him.

But the flair of the JBS position was blunted. Will and I occasionally bristled over the prosaic language that had been substituted for fiery drafts condemning the Bush attack against the Constitution and Bill of Rights. We'd both occasionally offload pieces we had written to LewRockwell.com or Antiwar.com that *The New American* didn't want to publish. The JBS had stagnated, and magazine circulation dropped precipitously.

Then in 2005, Vance Smith was deposed in an organizational coup engineered by the staff. I had no idea it was coming, and I wrote to Will from the Boston area afterwards that "I feel like I must have been really, really crunchy cereal (like the TV commercial) all day during my tenure in Appleton."

When I heard that the new leadership was former field staff coordinator Art Thompson and my old office supervisor Alan Scholl, I wasn't optimistic. Alan wasn't very bright, but he meant well. He was the one supervisor I had in Appleton who tried to meet regularly with me and give me some direction. We had worked reasonably well together, but he wasn't leadership material. I had more apprehensions about Art Thompson, whom I knew less well. My first perception of him that he was very impressed with his own intellect but gave little evidence of any actual knowledge or critical thinking. He had strong opinions about subjects he knew little about, and easily dismissed more informed, nuanced views on topics. My initial snapshot impression turned out to be a dead-on assessment.

The problem with the new JBS leadership, in my view, was not that they were malicious. Rather it was that they were intellectual dullards. Will was more optimistic at first, arguing that Alan had gone back to school at the University of Phoenix to earn a master's degree. Will was even given a direct portal to publishing on the web with the "Birch Blog," without any editor getting in the way.

But his optimism didn't last long. The new leadership doubled down on the Smith idea that the JBS should tone down its language against Bush. By 2006, the "marketing" strategy meant turning any vigorous criticism of the Bush regime into a sterile recitation of facts. Will was the still only one who could get away with making any significant criticism in print; at first he seemed untouchable. I was constantly amazed at what he could get away with in print and on the web with his "Birch Blog"; whenever I had submitted something similar, it was sanitized by the editorial department. I had emailed Will of declining circulation of *The New American* that "we failed because TNA is fundamentally an opinion magazine that fails to render its opinions openly and concisely. . . Instead, we are writing 'news' articles that aren't news because nothing in them is new. What we've got is a dozen high school term papers regurgitating the work that all the real reporters have done." Except, of course, for the work Will had done.

More importantly, JBS leadership had decided to launch a new campaign against "illegal" immigration to coincide with a growing Republican Party fall election campaign. Art and Alan had convinced themselves that the non-denominational Christians at their local churches would sign up for the John Birch Society by the hundreds of thousands if only the JBS would parrot what the sinking GOP was saying (so long as they appended conspiracy theories about "Aztlan" or "Cloward-Piven"). The JBS would "ride the wave" of sentiment against "illegal" immigration, we were told. Will and I were astonished that this would be their choice of campaigns. We both knew it made no sense to pair up with the party that had done so much damage to the Bill of Rights, promoting torture (8th Amendment), detention without trial (6th amendment) or due process (5th amendment), denial of counsel (6th amendment), and warrantless surveillance (4th amendment), to name the most blatant examples.

As time passed under the new leadership, Will faced increasing censorship of his wit and on a variety of topics. Will would post many insightful pieces on his "Birch Blog" only to find them increasingly deleted by the end of the day. In early 2006, he would often email me in the morning with a message about a recent post: "read it, and pass it along, before it gets expunged!" Sometimes I made it to the Birch Blog post before it was taken down, and other times I didn't. As a reader of this volume, you can read the best of those excellent expunged items.

What, Will continually asked me through email messages and in phone conversations, is the value of a "freedom" organization that won't lift a finger to defend freedom at a time when freedom is most threatened? We both did our best to reverse the course of the organization. I wrote numerous letters internally offering advice ever-more-urgently, while Will took his concerns public with his "Birch Blog" on the web. No one listened back in Appleton. Will relocated to his home in Idaho with his family in early 2006, and I advised him to curb the public criticism of his employer. I warned that he risked losing his job.

But following orders was never Will Grigg's style. Will had foreseen and forewarned the leadership what results they could expect from focusing upon backing the GOP immigration campaign, but Will's repeated pleas fell on deaf ears. By mid-2006, Will had been fired by *The New American* (or he had resigned, according to Appleton). I saw it coming months in advance. The net result of the 2006 JBS anti-immigration campaign—a campaign still in progress, and still receiving the same results—was no new "wave" of interest in the organization, and a general decline in membership and subscriptions to *The New American*. And the GOP went down in flames at the polls during the November midterms (they lost both the House and Senate that year).

By way of contrast, the following year—2007—became the birth year of the Ron Paul movement. Had the JBS followed Will's advice, the JBS would have been set up to amplify his agenda of restoring the Bill of Rights and ending our undeclared and unconstitutional wars. The nation had longed for a truth-teller, and Ron Paul succeeded in igniting the nation's interest where the JBS leadership had failed. New "Campaign for Liberty" chapters sprung up across the nation while the JBS remained on financial life-support, sustained financially by bequests as its aging but loyal membership died off.

Some other people made efforts to keep Will on the staff—especially the other Senior Editor Bill Jasper—but too many over-sized egos were bruised by Will's biting and public criticism to prevent him from being cut loose.

After *The New American*

Will's separation from *The New American* came at the worst possible time for him personally. Though he converted the "Birch Blog" into his own "Pro Libertate" and became a regular contributor to LewRockwell.com, both Will and Korrin suffered prolonged stays in the hospital that racked up huge medical bills and prevented him from getting a standard 9-to-5 job. When Will wasn't sick himself, he was often the sole adult caretaker of his five (later six) young children.

As a side note, I filled in at *The New American* as the new most-prolific-writer in my freelance role in 2007, but no one could replace Will. He never criticized me or his other friends at the JBS for continuing with the magazine. My relationship with *The New American* magazine didn't end until 2015, when I concluded I didn't want my name to fall directly below the openly racist Selwyn Duke who had been added to the contributor's list.

Full-time employment didn't come for Will after *The New American*, and he would have had to refuse most offers anyway. Korrin's illness had proven chronic, and he had to stay home with the little ones. Having "John Birch Society" on your résumé was also a tough mark to overcome in journalism. He took a variety of contract jobs over the years, editing a couple issues of Gary Franchi's *Republic* magazine, sent in stories to *The American Conservative*, and several other publications. The tag line for the "contribution" button on "Pro Libertate" might as well have said "Your tips are my salary." He so often would remark to me over the next few years how a donation of $500 or $1,000 had been sent just in time to buy new tires for the family van, or to pay the rent on his apartment. The people making those donations will never know how gratefully they were received, or how much they helped. I was also going through some tough times economically, but nothing like the deprivation Will and Korrin experienced. The donations were not enough to last, however. Will's family eventually moved into an apartment provided by the generosity of a friend, and had accepted the voluntary help of nearby family and friends.

Will continued his journalism, but he spent more time with the domestic chores of day-to-day life. He increasingly focused upon the single topic of police abuse. It annoyed me that Will seemed to focus so heavily on that single subject. I wasn't annoyed because we disagreed on the issue of police (he had gradually become an anarchist while I remained a classical liberal), but because I felt cheated of his opinion on the wide range of issues upon which he had commented so insightfully from 1993–2007. Despite disagreeing with his opinion opposing the mere existence of a police force, I thought his work on the militarization of and brutality of police was and remains vitally important.

And Will became the best at focusing his journalistic spotlight on individual abuse cases. He did so just as the JBS was reviving its ill-timed "Support Your Local Police" campaign. Will criticized the JBS for blind support of police at a time more than 1,000 Americans every year were being killed by police, a rate several dozen times higher than any other industrialized nation. He had no use for anyone still in leadership at the John Birch Society, and felt that they spent too much time on the wrong side of the liberty issue. But I took—and still take—a more charitable view of the JBS leadership and the organization's role in the struggle to restrain runaway government. I was also keenly aware I had foolishly drafted and pushed for a flier to support the LAPD in the wake of the Rodney King riots, against the urging of Bill Jasper, who had first-hand knowledge of some peaceful pro-lifers whose skulls had been cracked by LAPD personnel.

Will and I both became stridently against federal government limitations on immigration after the JBS began a campaign to impose them. I was much more of a late bloomer. I had written an "Immigration Myths v. Facts" bullet-point piece in favor of enforcing immigration laws as late as 2006 for *The New American*. But Will—who believed he was half Mexican and half Irish until he met his birth mother Vonda in 2013—would never have any of that nonsense. When a JBS member approached me in about 2009 to write more hard-core anti-immigration stories, I did some research and came to the opposite conclusion. I was already teaching U.S. History at the high school level and assigning the Virginia and Kentucky resolutions as readings to my students; in those documents James Madison and Thomas Jefferson argued federal immigration controls were flatly unconstitutional.

During the time when Will had left *The New American* and I was still writing for it freelance, from 2007–2015, it was my turn to play the "what can I get away with?" game over the JBS leadership. Will had played it so well during his tenure, and we enjoyed a few laughs over what I had sent over. I sent numerous pieces over lauding the technique of nullification and the Virginia and Kentucky resolutions at a time they were promoting federal immigration enforcement. Nobody in JBS leadership had a clue that they were publishing pieces that flatly contradicted their own campaign. It was the same on other issues. Most Birchers are unreconstructed Southerners on the Civil War, but they published my nullification piece citing the southern states complaining about northern nullification of fugitive slave laws as the sole reason for secession, and even published a pro-reconstruction piece packaged in the form of how America's first gun control laws came out of the Reconstruction-era "black codes." Both became among the most-trafficked stories for the magazine online, even though they ran counter to the organization's campaigns and ideological sclerosis. Will thoroughly enjoyed the irony.

I had hoped at first that these pieces would change the direction of the organization's leadership away from its self-destructive course, and when that failed, I hoped to lay a trail of breadcrumbs for whomever was left to follow out of the morass. When the monthly *JBS Bulletin* sent to members became digitized, I noted that it had long been a complete waste of trees, and Will quipped "now it has become a complete waste of bandwidth." When Art Thompson's unintelligible and poorly researched ramblings moved from polluting the first two pages of the *JBS Bulletin* to a weekly vlog on YouTube, Will frequently expressed incredulity in email messages or Facebook PMs about Thompson's complete lack of focus and strategic vision.

Will's fortunes seemed to have experienced a turnaround with the foundation of the Libertarian Institute in 2016. The organization had a strong foundation with a number of thoughtful contributors right out of the gate, with Will, Scott Horton and Sheldon Richman headlining. Will experienced a brief revival in his writing volume with the Libertarian Institute, but time had run out for him.

The end for Will came with hospitalization for a serious infection, followed by a heart attack at the beginning of Holy Week in 2017. The Libertarian Institute promoted a GoFundMe for Will's medical bills to the hilt, and then again to benefit his family after his death. Antiwar.com, the Foundation for Economic Education and Lew Rockwell generously helped promote the fundraiser as well. I sent a tiny donation by way of PayPal while he was in the hospital with the message: "Get better. That's an order!" But again, following orders wasn't really Will's style.

Most people knew Will Grigg only by his writing. I was privileged to know him as a friend as well. His learned elucidation of liberty and personal example of Christian faith inspired many who didn't know him, his friends more, and his wife and children most of all. Thus, his departure left a hole in the liberty movement, and a bigger hole in his young family.

Will Grigg can't be replaced. But he'd be urging all of his fans, friends and family members to heal up from the loss and renew the fight, until their last breath.

As Will so often said, *Dum spiro, pugno*!

Thomas R. Eddlem

Easter, 2017
Taunton, Mass

2001

Will the Laws Fall Silent?

September 13, 2001

This essay was written for the JBS website a few days after the attacks of September 11, 2001. Readers may notice that the policy prescriptions offered here diverge, in some subtle but critical ways, from views I have expressed more recently. As a friend of mine once said, my opinions will sometimes change because I reserve the right to become more sensible on any subject.

As America braces for a war of uncertain length against an unspecified enemy, many have embraced the ancient legal maxim *inter arma, enim silent leges*— "In time of war, the laws fall silent."

In a sense this is an understandable reaction to the depraved lawlessness displayed by the foreign enemies who killed several thousand Americans in the attacks of September 11th. While we certainly must track down and eradicate those directly responsible for that attack, we must also remember that our laws— the Constitution that frames our system of government, and the heritage of Christian laws that inspired our nation's charter of government—define us as a people. If we allow those laws to become "collateral damage" in the "war on terrorism," we will suffer losses even greater than those we endured on that terrible Tuesday morning.

Under the Constitution, the federal government is allocated a few specific responsibilities, the most important of which is to secure our nation's borders and protect our citizens from foreign attack. It does not diminish the guilt of the perpetrators of the September 11th assault to observe that the success of that terrorist strike represents a failure on the part of our federal government to carry out its most important role. That failure is now being invoked to justify lifting the constitutional restraints upon the central government's power. Even more ominously, we are being told that the present crisis can only be dealt with in the framework of "collective security," as administered by the United Nations and its subsidiary bodies.

Following the 1995 Oklahoma City Bombing, then-Congressman Charles Schumer told a reporter that new restrictions on freedom would be necessary in order to deal with the threat of terrorism. After all, he insisted, "in wartime, it's different than peacetime. In terrorism time, it's different than peacetime." It's hardly surprising that those sentiments would be expressed by Schumer, a fervent advocate of "gun control" and federal surveillance of "right wing" domestic dissidents. It might be considered surprising, however, to see even more expansively statist views being expressed by the *Deseret News* of Salt Lake City, Utah, a reliably pro-Republican newspaper.

"Americans need to rally around President Bush and the federal government," declared a September 14th *Deseret News* house editorial. "Some Utahns have become almost consumed in recent years with their distrust of Washington and various federal agencies. That must be put aside for now. . . . Utahns of every stripe ought to be ready to respond to whatever their president asks."

If one assumes that the most important task before us is to punish the guilty, rather than to prevent further assaults upon our country, then it might make sense to embrace a vision of president as war dictator, and to suppress criticism of our central government. But under the Constitution's mandate to "provide for the common defense," our most urgent task is to take immediate steps to protect the citizenry. Finding and annihilating the foreign enemies who attacked our country, while necessary, will do little to enhance our national security in the long run unless the failed foreign and security policies that led to the disaster of September 11th are changed.

Within hours of the September 11th attack, congressional leaders of both parties emphasized their unanimous and unlimited support for the President. On September 14th the Congress passed—with one single negative vote—a joint resolution to "authorize the use of the United States Armed Forces against those responsible for the recent attacks against the United States." That resolution cited the War Powers Resolution, not the constitutional provision for a congressional declaration of war. Further, Congress chose not to approve a joint resolution introduced by Congressman Bob Barr that contained an explicit declaration of war.

In brief, Congress—as it did in 1965 with the Gulf of Tonkin Resolution— ignored its constitutional role, choosing to ratify the President's decision to commit our nation to war, rather than re-asserting its authority to declare war.

Indeed, the Bush administration has behaved as if congressional approval were a mere formality. On the day following the attack, President Bush told reporters: "Now that war has been declared upon us, we will lead the world to victory." White House correspondent Fred Barnes notes that as the reporters were ushered out of the Oval Office, "Bush was asked if he would seek a declaration of war. Bush didn't answer, flinch, or look up. He sat stonily."

This is not a trivial matter. University of Pittsburgh law professor Jules Lobel points out that the use of force resolution "is not directed against anybody. For example, if the President believes Libya, Iraq, Iran and Pakistan were involved in harboring these terrorists he could attack all of them." The BBC reported on September 16th that the Bush administration aims "to uproot perceived terrorist networks spanning 60 countries in America's war against those who carried out Tuesday's suicide plane attacks in New York and Washington."

So, without a declaration of war, President Bush has announced his intention to "lead the world" in a war that could involve military action in nearly one third of the world's existing nations. That undeclared war could last for decades, thereby consuming our wealth, devouring the lives of our young men, and deepening the bonds of our "interdependence" with the UN and its auxiliaries.

These are precisely the dangers that our constitutional provisions for war-making were intended to address. It is through war that the power of the State is most dramatically magnified. That is why the power to declare war was vested in the branch of the federal government most accountable to the people whose wealth, liberties, and lives would be directly affected by war.

Alexander Hamilton, who was a proponent of a strong chief executive, wrote in 1793: "It is the province and duty of the Executive to preserve to the Nation the blessings of peace. The Legislature alone can interrupt those blessings, by placing the Nation in a state of War." Writing a year later, Hamilton emphasized that "war is a question, under our constitution, not of Executive, but of Legislative cognizance. It belongs to Congress to say—whether the Nation shall of choice dismiss the olive branch and unfurl the banners of War."

Madison's *Notes* of the 1787 Convention document that the Framers understood that a President's duty to "preserve . . . the blessings of peace" included an ability to "repel sudden attacks"—or, in the words of Roger Sherman, "to repel and not to commence war." September 11th represents the first time in our history that a President has had to deal with a sudden attack upon our homeland (Hawaii, at the time of Pearl Harbor, was not a state).

President Bush was within his constitutional mandate to mobilize military and law enforcement personnel to prevent further attacks. But without a congressional declaration—or, for that matter, a specific enemy—the President, with the support of Congress and the media, committed our nation to what is expected to be a long, costly, and bloody foreign war.

The Uses of War

War swiftly dissolves both the legal and moral restraints upon government power. The American war that began with the Japanese attack upon our naval forces in Pearl Harbor ended with the atomic strikes that vaporized tens of thousands of civilians at Hiroshima and Nagasaki. It is difficult to imagine that Americans prior to Pearl Harbor would have countenanced such wholesale slaughter of civilians. It is impossible to imagine what measures the public will be willing to support in the wake of a terrorist attack that killed thousands of American civilians in the heart of our most prominent city. But Americans must remember that the powers we are willing to allow our government to exercise against our foreign foes may someday be used against us as well.

It must also be remembered that social revolution is a predictable consequence of war. Indeed, this is why statists of all varieties regard war as something to be exploited (and even encouraged), rather than prevented. Norman Dodd, director of research for the Special Congressional Committee to Investigate Tax-Exempt Foundations (the so-called "Reece Committee"), has described how the Carnegie Endowment for International Peace eagerly supported America's entry into World War I as a means of bringing about a social revolution.

In an interview with investigative reporter William H. McIlhany, Dodd recounted the findings of Kathryn Casey, who had examined the minutes of Carnegie trustees in the years prior to World War I. In the minutes, the trustees discussed the following question:

> "Is there any means known to man more effective than war, assuming you wish to alter the life of an entire people?" And they discussed this and at the end of a year they came to the conclusion that there was no more effective means to that end known to man. So, then they raised question number two, and the question was, "How do we involve the United States in a war?"

When the trustees convened a meeting following America's entry into the war in 1917, Dodd continued, they "had the brashness to congratulate themselves on the wisdom of their original decision because already the impact of war had indicated it would alter life . . . in this country. They even had the brashness to word and to dispatch a telegram to [President Woodrow] Wilson, cautioning him to see that the war did not end too quickly." Since there is little prospect that the open-ended war on terrorism in which our country has become embroiled will end "too quickly," it stands to reason that the conflict will present unprecedented opportunities for social reconstruction.

The war on terrorism will also be used to preserve and expand the power of globalist institutions, particularly the United Nations, which until September 11th were under sustained political assault. One ominous portent was the decision of Representative Tom DeLay (R-Texas) to withdraw his proposed "American Servicemen's Protection Act," which was intended to exempt U.S. servicemen from prosecution by the UN's proposed International Criminal Court. The Bush administration opposed DeLay's measure as an intrusion upon the President's power to conduct foreign policy, and the Congressman withdrew the measure following the terrorist attack as a way of expressing support for the President.

In the early years of the Cold War, congressional critics of U.S. involvement in multilateral alliances and institutions found that President Truman and his foreign policy trust could cite the Soviet threat to justify nearly any foreign entanglement or assertion of presidential power. Senator Robert Taft, whose anti-Communist credentials were impeccable, complained in 1947 that he was "more than a bit tired of having the Russian menace invoked as a reason for doing any—and every—thing that might or might not be desirable or necessary on its own merits."

By 1950, as congressional inquiries into subversion documented the extent to which our foreign policy institutions had been infiltrated by Communists and their allies, political opposition was building to American involvement in the United Nations. Writing in the June 1996 issue of *The Atlantic Monthly*, Benjamin Schwartz of the World Policy Institute observed that Harry Truman's "secretary of state Dean Acheson put things in proper perspective: describing how Washington overcame domestic opposition to its internationalist policies in 1950, he recalled in 1954 that at that critical moment the crisis in Korea 'came along and saved us.'"

Tens of thousands of American servicemen were killed in the Korean conflict. They fought as part of a UN military force, under rules of engagement that denied them victory, and under a UN chain of command in which our battle plans were made transparent to the Soviets and the Communist North Koreans. But from Acheson's perspective, these losses were necessary in order to "save" the designs of the internationalist Power Elite.

Acheson is in many ways typical of that Power Elite, which is infinitely resourceful in creating or exploiting crises to magnify its power. The most visible element of the Power Elite is the New York-based Council on Foreign Relations, to which Acheson (and nearly every other Secretary of State, including Colin Powell) has belonged. On September 14th the CFR held a televised forum featuring the "U.S. Commission on National Security in the 21st Century," which submitted its report to President Bush earlier this year. The forum featured a frank discussion of the ways in which the September 11th attack and its aftermath can be used to enhance the drive to create a UN-administered new world order.

During a question-and-answer period near the end of the program, a Harvard scholar declared that America is "facing the reality of a new world order" in which we must collaborate with other governments in counter-terrorism efforts. Responding to this statement, Commission co-chair Gary Hart expressed the hope that the Bush administration could "use this disaster to achieve that end, or at least explore the possibility to take some of these countries we have held at arm's length and challenge them to help us."

James Sasser, a former ambassador to Red China, elaborated upon that point, noting that as a result of this assault, the United States might be led into an anti-terrorism coalition with Russia, Red China, Iran, and similar states. "Can we not use this as a catalyst to reach out and develop intelligence in conjunction with these other regimes?" asked Sasser. This suggestion was warmly embraced by former House Speaker Newt Gingrich, a member of the CFR-dominated Commission.

So, in the name of "collective security," the United States is to enter into a coalition with the most notorious state sponsors of international terrorism. This Orwellian proposition, which provoked not a single critical comment from the CFR forum's participants, is typical of the "wisdom" of our foreign policy elite.

NATO's ruling Council has already invoked Article V of the North Atlantic Treaty, thereby designating a terrorist attack upon any of its members to be an attack upon all of them. And Beijing has already indicated that it would gladly cooperate in an anti-terrorism coalition, as long as it is organized through the United Nations. The logic of "collective security" against terrorism dictates that in exchange for the help of our dubious allies in finding and punishing those who attacked our nation, we must be willing to reciprocate should any of those nations be attacked.

This may mean using U.S. power not only to punish attacks upon our NATO allies, but also to put down any movement that threatens Beijing, Tehran, or any of our other new "allies" in the grand coalition. It may also lead to expanding our intelligence and law enforcement collaboration with Moscow and Beijing. It will almost certainly mean further empowerment of both NATO and the United Nations.

And what will be done once the crisis has passed, assuming that it ever does? Would these new arrangements be dissolved or institutionalized? Will the new powers assumed by the President devolve back to Congress? Will our global crusade against terrorism eradicate that menace, or exacerbate it as we acquire an even larger roster of foreign enemies?

What Is to Be Done?

Since the attack of September 11th, The Powers That Be have recited the mantra that the terrorists responsible for the slaughter hate us for our virtues—our freedom, prosperity, and global influence. Some have insisted that the example of a multi-ethnic, multi-religious society is abhorred by the radical Islamists who are presumed to be behind the assault.

But it's worth remembering that Switzerland is a free, prosperous, multi-ethnic, multi-religious society as well—and that despite its much greater geographic vulnerability, it has never been a terrorist target. That nation has chosen to exercise its global influence through finance and neutral diplomacy, rather than through military intervention. By refusing to insinuate itself into foreign quarrels, it has eschewed the role of "superpower"—and preserved its own domestic tranquility. Switzerland was admired by our Founding Fathers as much for its resolute independence as for its stable, long-lived institutions of ordered liberty, and its example is now more relevant than ever.

The familiar arguments against "isolationism" should be casualties of the September 11th attack, which was the predictable—and tragic—product of our government's interventionist foreign policy. For several days after the attack, our country was, to a remarkable extent, isolated from the world, as our airlines were grounded and our borders were sealed. The financial and commercial networks through which Americans conduct business with people abroad were disrupted, or shut down altogether. It's not clear yet if our sense of normalcy can ever be completely restored.

But there are necessary steps that can be taken immediately to address our most critical national security needs:

Rather than pouring tens of billions of dollars into an open-ended foreign war, Congress should radically increase the budget of the Immigration and Naturalization Service, and vastly expand the manpower of the Border Patrol.

Congress should rescind the counter-intelligence guidelines created by Attorney General Edward Levi in 1976, which destroyed the FBI's ability to collect intelligence on foreign terrorist and subversive groups operating in this country. The Levi guidelines forbid the FBI from investigating a terrorist group unless it has solid evidence of a plan to commit a federal crime within 48 hours. The foolishness of those guidelines is illustrated by this fact: The plot carried out on September 11th took *years* to plan and carry out.

While it is proper for the FBI to *investigate* crimes, the Constitution specifies that law *enforcement* is almost exclusively a state and local responsibility. Over the past three decades, as federal funding and control over state and local police agencies have increased, their ability to collect intelligence on subversive and terrorist groups has been all but destroyed. This capacity must be restored immediately, if we are serious about preserving national security without creating a federally dominated garrison state.

As the Pentagon was burning, and with (fortunately inaccurate) reports of another hijacked plane en route, one Pentagon staffer cried out: "Where's our air cover?" Americans might well ask themselves a similar question: With all we spend on our military, why are we so defenseless? Why have we deployed troops to scores of nations around the world, when our homeland is vulnerable to attack? We must end our meddling in the affairs of other nations, bring our troops home, and build a military devoted exclusively to defending our nation. If we can identify the foreign enemy responsible for the attack, Congress should declare war and commit the necessary resources to defeating that enemy. But our first priority should be to defend our homeland.

Just days before our nation was attacked, UN Secretary-General Kofi Annan was communing with Arafat, Castro, and sundry other terrorists at the UN's "anti-racism" summit in Durban, South Africa. That event was a riotous festival of America-bashing led by regimes that almost certainly were connected to the attack on our country. This illustrates the compelling necessity to get our nation out of the UN, and to invite the world body to relocate to Durban, Damascus, or some similar haven of enlightenment.

There is obviously a compelling need to find and destroy the foreign enemies who attacked our nation. If we must make war, we should do so with strict fidelity to the Constitution, and unhindered by entangling alliances with multi-national bodies such as the UN and NATO. In prosecuting such a war we should make it clear to the world that America is willing to extend the hand of peace and honorable commerce to all nations who will reciprocate our goodwill—and that we are just as willing to punish without mercy those who make war upon us.

All of these steps would enhance our national security while preserving the constitutional framework of laws upon which our liberties depend. But it is obvious that for any of these steps to be taken, our government has to undergo some radical changes—not to its constitutional structure, but with regard to the people who are currently occupying positions of trust. We cannot expect sound leadership from the very officials who helped create this catastrophe. But new political leadership devoted to restoring our national security and preserving our independence will not emerge until the American public itself is educated in sound principles and mobilized to hold our leaders accountable.

As the human cost of the September 11th attack becomes clear, the temptation to set aside our laws in order to exact revenge will be almost irresistible. But resist we must, because if our laws fall silent, our freedom and independence will be destroyed—and terror will have its ultimate victory over liberty.

2005

Loving Big Brother

Birch Blog, July 26, 2005

The July 22 shooting death of Brazilian electrician Jean Charles de Menezes at the hands of plainclothes London police left Fox News commentator John Gibson swooning with admiration. "I love the way the Brits have 10 million cameras sticking up the nose of every citizen no matter where they are, except in the loo [bathroom]," exulted the host of the Fox program "The Big Story":

> What is also good is the Brit police tactics that we saw at work in the subway Friday morning. The tackle and kill team is incredible, if for no other reason than their bravery. Can you imagine the job of those cops? Tackle the guy wearing a vest bomb and hope your colleague is right behind with the gun to put five bullets in the noggin before he sets off the bomb.

The problem is, the Brazilian national didn't have a bomb, wasn't connected in any way to the terrorists responsible for recent attacks in London, was in the country legally, and hadn't been involved in any illegal activities of any kind. Much of this was known at the time Gibson wrote his mash note to the British cops just hours after the event. Still, he continued, one has to admire "the *cojones* of those Brit cops to go after him like that. . . . Five in the noggin is fine. Don't complain that sounds barbaric. We're fighting barbaric."

Gibson, like many other neo-"conservative" media figures, is a nebbishy pencil-neck whose pipe-cleaner arms would snap like dry twigs if he were forced to perform a push-up. It's tempting to say Gibson's essay, riddled with unconvincing tough-guy slang, represents what Dr. Thomas Fleming calls "vicarious masculinity." More serious than Gibson's man-crush on British counter-terrorism cops is his unbuttoned embrace of totalitarian police state tactics—a type of behavior becoming very common among Bush's conservative followers.

The lethal tactics extolled by Gibson ("five in the noggin" first, ask questions later) were taught to British counter-terrorism police by Israel's National Police (INP), and the Israeli Security Service, Shin Bet. Notes Canadian international affairs analyst Michel Chossudovsky: "The shoot to kill policy was undertaken under the auspices of 'Operation Kratos,' named after the mythical Spartan hero. It was carried out by the London Metropolitan's elite

SO19 firearms unit often referred to as the Blue Berets. . . . The training of the SO19 marksmen was patterned on that of Israel." According to The July 23 Scottish *Daily Record*, SO19 had been briefed "by officers who had been to Israel to meet their counterparts there and pick up tips gleaned from the experience of dealing with Hamas bombers."

Chossudovsky also points out that "Israel has also collaborated in the training of members of the FBI and the LAPD." A report in the July 15 *Houston Chronicle* documents that "the combat-garbed men patrolling light rail stations and bus transit centers" in Texas, individuals who "look like soldiers, but their uniforms say POLICE" have also received specialized training by Israeli counter-terrorism specialists.

In Houston, officers of the Special Operations Response Team (SORT) consists of "16 Metro police officers and two sergeants [who have] trained with 'experts from Israel' as well as from the FBI, Transportation Security Administration and several U.S. transit agencies," reported the *Chronicle*. The team "was formed shortly after the Sept. 11, 2001, terrorist attacks . . . but had not been deployed in public until the July 7 terrorist bombings of trains and a bus in London."

It's reasonable to suspect that SORT-style teams are being prepared in other major cities across the U.S., presumably trained in the same "five in the noggin" rules of engagement that made Gibson's heart beat ever so faster. And it's both interesting and unsettling to wonder what other surprises of this sort will be unveiled next time a terrorist attack occurs in London, New York, or elsewhere.

Incidentally, while Israeli counter-terrorist specialists have been training local police in Great Britain and the U.S. back in the 1990s, Washington was lavishing similar attention on the "security" forces of Yasser Arafat's regime. As *The New American* reported in 1997, the Bureau of Alcohol, Tobacco, and Firearms disclosed that fact during a counter-terrorism seminar in Chicago.

Complicating things even further is the fact that Hamas—the terrorist group whose murderous depredations justified the "shoot-to-kill" tactics employed by the Israelis, and taught to British and (most likely) U.S. police— was essentially a creation of Israeli intelligence. "Israel and Hamas may currently be locked in deadly combat, but, according to several current and former U.S. intelligence officials, beginning in the late 1970s, Tel Aviv gave direct and indirect financial aid to Hamas over a period of years," reported United Press International in 2002. "Israel 'aided Hamas directly—the Israelis wanted to use it as a counterbalance to the PLO [Palestinian Liberation Organization],' said Tony Cordesman, Middle East analyst for the Center for Strategic Studies."

It's an old story, one captured in Frederic Bastiat's despairing observation that governments increase their powers by creating the poison and the antidote in the same laboratory. The same governments supposedly protecting us from terrorism have long cultivated many of the same terrorists and terror organizations that now threaten us, leaving the public insecure and increasingly willing to surrender personal liberty in pursuit of safety.

And abetting this cynical power grab are purported journalists like John Gibson, who rather than confronting the corrupt exercise of power lecture the public about their duty to love Big Brother.

Do Armed Robbers have a Right to Self-Defense?

Birch Blog, December 1, 2005

An armed intruder breaks into a home. Suddenly he is confronted by the homeowner, who has brought a firearm of his own. With the homeowner preparing to fire, the intruder somehow beats him to the draw, killing him with a single shot.

There is no doubt that the robber confronted an immediate threat to his life. There is just as little doubt that his actions do not constitute self-defense. The intruder invaded another man's home with the intent of stealing his property. By arming himself the intruder also demonstrated his willingness to commit lethal violence, including murder, in order to accomplish his criminal ends. As the aggressor in this matter, the robber invalidated his right to self-defense; using force against the homeowner for any purpose—including self-preservation—is therefore an additional criminal act.

This principle is set forth in the Bible: "If a thief be found breaking up [i.e., breaking in] and be smitten that he die, there shall no blood be shed for him." (Exodus 22:2. KJV) This is to say that the killing of a robber who is caught in the act is not an act of murder, and should not be punished as such. This principle holds true even if the intruder in our example is an otherwise upstanding citizen, and the homeowner is the community wretch. And it holds true if the assailant is an agent of the government acting without a proper warrant. As John Locke pointed out, when an individual's rights are injured, "the injury and the crime is equal, whether committed by the crown or some petty villain."

Roughly a decade and a half ago, many conservatives became properly alarmed over the impunity enjoyed by government agents—both federal and state/local—in conducting unprovoked armed raids against American citizens. Among the most notorious examples were the 1993 federal raid against Waco's Branch Davidian sect, the 1992 federal armed assault on the family of Randy and Vicki Weaver, and the home invasion carried out in October of same year by several law enforcement agencies against business magnate Donald Scott in California.

In two of those cases—the Weaver and Scott slayings—subsequent investigations concluded that the government agents acted without legal

15

authority, which is to say that their conduct was not morally different from that of armed robbers.

In each of those episodes, government agents faced armed citizens who were not reluctant to shoot the unidentified armed intruders. Federal agents were killed at Ruby Ridge and Waco; Donald Scott, reacting to the terrified screams of his wife, confronted the invaders with a large caliber handgun, before he was gunned down himself.

Perhaps because these events became public scandals during the Clinton administration (although they all occurred, or were planned, during the first Bush administration), conservatives volubly condemned them as outrages against individual rights, and upheld the right of besieged citizens to use lethal force to defend themselves against unlawful assaults by federal agents. Of particular note was the exhortation by former FBI Special Agent (and convicted Watergate felon) G. Gordon Liddy that citizens on the receiving end of such an assault focus on taking "head shots," rather than targeting the body mass, since the feds are equipped with body armor.

Many, if not most, conservative commentators circa 1994 understood that if an armed federal party invaded a home without just cause or proper warrant, the homeowner was entirely justified to use whatever means were at hand to protect himself, his family, and his property until the situation was somehow brought under control. The arguments against using lethal force in such circumstances are prudential, not moral or legal.

Needless to say, those same commentators do not see how the Bush administration's aggressive war in Iraq is morally indistinguishable from the domestic federal raids they abhorred, or the actions of a band of armed robbers.

Republican slogan-spewers profess to be mortally offended by the use of the word "occupation," rather than "liberation," to describe our military presence in Iraq. However, our military was not invited into Iraq by its people, and the post-Saddam government has repeatedly expressed its desire to see our troops leave. The U.S. military entered Iraq, and maintains its presence there, through force. The attack and occupation of Iraq has been carried out without a congressional declaration of war. If Congress had issued a declaration, the war would have been constitutional—but it would not have been morally defensible, since Saddam's regime, loathsome as it was, never attacked our nation, nor did it pose any conceivable threat to us.

At this point defenders of the war would refer to the fact that Iraq frequently fired on U.S. and British warplanes enforcing the UN-inspired "No-fly zones" over Iraq between 1991 and 2003. But the salient fact is that those warplanes had no legal right to be patrolling that airspace—unless we assume that the UN represents a legitimate global legislative body that can authorize military missions of that variety, and whose mandates we must obey. Liberal defenders of the Iraq war may be comfortable with that position, but it's difficult to believe that many conservatives would be. This would leave them with the logical necessity of recognizing that patrolling the "No-fly zones" was illicit aggression. (The existence of those zones, as well, illustrated that Saddam was hardly a threat to the region, much less to a distant superpower, since he wasn't even firmly in control of his own nation's territory.)

"Well, all of that doesn't matter," the typical war proponent will insist. "It doesn't matter how or why the war began; now that we're in, we have to win."

This argument—if that word can be tortured into applying here—is the moral equivalent of the armed robber's claim that he shot the homeowner in self-defense: "It doesn't really matter how I got into the guy's home; once he pulled a gun on me, I had to shoot." If someone has invaded a home—or a homeland—by violence, without legal and moral authority, "*winning*" the conflict with the outraged residents is an even greater crime, not a victory.

To extend the armed robbery scenario just a bit further: What if the intruder claims that his intent was not to steal the homeowner's money, but rather to empty out his liquor cabinet, since the man of the house was a hopeless alcoholic who beat his wife, abused his kids, and made drunken threats against his neighbors? This wouldn't make any difference, since armed robbery and murder are crimes even if they are committed for supposedly humanitarian ends. The same is emphatically true of aggressive war conducted for the supposed purpose of promoting "democracy."

One of the largest tragedies of the Iraq war is the fact that it has placed our military personnel into an untenable position, both militarily and morally. Thousands have been killed, and several times as many maimed, in the course of a mission that is little better than armed robbery writ large—one utterly unworthy of such sacrifices. This is one of the most important reasons why George W. Bush, and his adult supervisor Dick Cheney, should be impeached and driven from office—and then placed in stocks in a public square and pelted with dead cats and rotten fruit.

Comply and Submit—Or Die

Birch Blog, December 9, 2005

"From what we know," lisped Bush administration spokesliar Scott McClellan after federal air marshals gunned down 44-year-old Rigoberto Alpizar in Miami, "the team of air marshals acted in a way that is consistent with the training they received. . . . It appears they followed the protocols and did what they were trained to do. . . . [W]e are very appreciative for all that the air marshals are doing to protect the American people."

Who's this "we," paleface?

Assuming that McClellan's assessment is correct, and the summary execution of Mr. Alpizar by the tax-fattened drones grandly styled "air marshals" was carried out according to federal "protocols," we no longer need to wonder whether terrorist sleeper cells continue to infest American commercial flights.

"Somebody came down the aisle and put a shotgun to the back of my head and said put your hands on the seat in front of you," recalled passenger John McAlhany in an interview with *Time*. Amid the confusion and tension that ensued when Alpizar bolted from the plane, McAlhany and the other passengers had been ordered by the flight crew to hit the deck. He was talking on his cellphone with his brother, looking through the seats to see what was coming and to take action if he saw an attack coming. His assailant approached him from behind and "karate-chopped" his cellphone away. "Then I realized it was an official," he explained. That is to say that those terrorizing the passengers worked for George W. Bush, not Osama bin Laden.

Make no mistake about it, this was a deadly terrorist incident. One man was killed, others were assaulted, and dozens were terrorized. "They [the air marshals] were pointing the guns directly at us instead of pointing them to the ground," McAlhany testifies. "One little girl was crying. There was a lady crying all the way to the hotel."

As if being terrorized at gunpoint weren't enough, the passengers were marched off the plane with their hands on their head and then repeatedly prompted by federal authorities to say that Alpizar claimed to have a bomb in his backpack. According to Daniel Adams of the Federal Air Marshal Service, prior to the shooting Alpizar had been running up and down the aisles of the plane shouting that he had a bomb in his possession—a claim not verified by any of the witnesses, and disputed by several of them.

In fact, the hapless Costa Rican immigrant, who became a naturalized U.S. citizen a few years ago, apparently suffered from a panic attack—which would understandably trigger alarm on the part of the flight crew and security officials, but is hardly a capital offense. Just before the Federales pumped several rounds into the panic-stricken American citizen, his wife—who had been trying to calm him down—frantically explained that her husband was "sick" and needed his medication. But before she could help Rigoberto, his life had been violently taken from him by the officials supposedly there to protect him.

Eyewitnesses described how Alpizar had been ordered by the marshals to fall flat on the ground, which he couldn't do because he was wearing a fanny pack. Some observers believed that Alpizar was attempting to adjust his fanny pack in order to comply with the demand when he was gunned down.

"Based on their training," asserted Adams, "[the air marshals] had to take appropriate action to defuse the situation to prevent a danger to themselves and also passengers in the terminal." Wouldn't it have been more sensible, if protecting the passengers was the objective, to find out what was actually happening before the lead began to fly?

Nope. Too risky. The only safe option was open gunplay.

The *Washington Times*, one of the Bush regime's most credulous and servile media shills, denounced those who engaged in "second-guessing" the actions of the air marshals. Embracing the unsubstantiated and self-serving account offered by the marshals service, the paper editorialized: "A marshal who hesitates to shoot someone behaving as Mr. Alpizar did is not doing his job. . . . Mr. Alpizar's death is a reminder of how seriously the marshals treat airline security. We should all take due notice."

In other words: Comply and submit, or die. If you happen to be the innocent victim of the mistaken application of federal "protocols," you'll be used as an object lesson, while your murderers (no other word fits) are extolled as brave defenders of the public.

The slaughter of Mr. Alpizar offers a perfect illustration of Paul Craig Roberts' warning that modern America is divided between those whom the law cannot restrain, and those it doesn't protect.

Oh, one other thing: In an age when the president and his cohorts claim the right to stage "preemptive" invasions of foreign countries, should we really be surprised when innocent American citizens are "preemptively" murdered by federal law enforcement officials?

Edmund Burke vs. the Busheviks

Birch Blog, December 21, 2005

In 1790, when our constitutional republic was in its infancy, the British statesman Edmund Burke published a prescient critique of Jacobin-led revolutionary upheaval in France. The revolution had its admirers on both sides of the Atlantic, who saw it as a triumph of democracy over despotism.

Burke, however, recognized the fundamentally lawless nature of the means used to bring about the revolution. Long before the true nature of the Revolution had been made obvious through terrorism at home and aggressive war abroad, Burke's *Reflections on the Revolution in France* anticipated the murderous consequences of emancipating power from accountability and the rule of law.

Some of Burke's most plangent warnings dealt with the practice of expediency in the name of "public benefit"—such as using criminal means for the supposed purpose of dealing with immediate threats, or uniquely intolerable circumstances.

The problem, Burke pointed out, is that:

> criminal means once tolerated are soon preferred. They present a shorter cut to the object than through the highway of the moral virtues. Justifying perfidy and murder for public benefit, public benefit would soon become the pretext, and perfidy and murder the end; until rapacity, malice, revenge, and fear more dreadful than revenge, could satiate their insatiable appetites. Such must be the consequences of losing, in the splendour of these triumphs of the rights of men, all natural sense of wrong and right.

Burke would have no difficulty recognizing the ideological kinship between the totalitarian Jacobins who ruled revolutionary France with blood and terror, and the modern Jacobins who infest the Bush regime. He would hear echoes of Jacobinism in Bush's promise—make that "threat"—to ignite a "fire in the minds of men" through aggressive wars to propagate global democracy. And he would see the foundations of a domestic terror state in the increasingly lawless conduct of President Bush.

Rousseau, the apostle of revolutionary violence and the progenitor of totalitarians from Robespierre to Lenin and Hitler, described the state as the agent of the "General Will." To that concept, Lenin added the detail of a "scientific dictatorship" exercising "power without limit, resting directly on force." Hitler's refinement to that concept defined the executive as the embodiment of the General Will, accountable only "to himself and the people."

The Bush administration's transliteration of these fundamentally anti-American concepts holds that the president possesses an unquantifiable and illimitable "Commander-in-Chief" power that justifies the use of lethal force, by the president or his duly authorized agents—whether in the form of military aggression, torture, imprisonment by decree, or even summary execution—against targets of the president's choosing, without limitation by law, congressional oversight, or judicial review.

Address the current furor over the administration's illegal use of domestic wiretaps—which, ironically, is in relative terms the most innocuous use of the powers claimed by Bush—Attorney General Alberto Gonzalez insists that "the president has the inherent authority under the Constitution, as commander in chief, to engage in this kind of activity."

Vice President Dick Cheney, who has both the demeanor and the soul of a Soviet Commissar, adverted to the concept of the executive as embodiment of the General Will in defending the regime's domestic surveillance program: "If there's a backlash pending, I think the backlash is going to be against those who are suggesting somehow we shouldn't have taken these steps in order to defend the country."

As Burke warned, and genuine patriots understand, it is impossible to defend our country using criminal means, since (to paraphrase Aldous Huxley) the means we employ are the ends in the making. Witness the murder, at the hands of federal air marshals supposedly in place to protect Americans, of U.S. Citizen Rigoberto Alpizar. The refusal of the Bush regime to conduct an inquiry into the actions of the marshals attests to the fact that those officials, like al Qaeda sleeper agents, can kill Americans with impunity.

In defending Bush's domestic surveillance program, the lackeys, liars, and lickspittles that compose the "conservative" media triumphantly note that Democrat presidents Carter and Clinton also "authorized" domestic spying without obtaining the required warrants. Leaving aside the fact that Mr. Bush publicly acknowledged that such warrants are required, violations of the law do not alter the law itself, or make obedience to that law merely optional.

Burke's critique of the French Revolution showed how the revolutionaries, rather than abolishing corrupt and unaccountable government, isolated and built upon precedents in official corruption set by French monarchs. A century and a half later, with the world set aflame by a global war waged by and among ideological descendants of the Jacobins in Soviet Russia, National Socialist Germany, Fascist Italy, and New Deal America, John T. Flynn made similar observations in his indispensable book *As We Go Marching.*

Flynn identified the foundations of Nazi and Fascist totalitarianism in the policies, practices, and constitutional frameworks devised by the democratic predecessors to those regimes. Upon being unified into nation-states, Flynn observed, both Italy and Germany fell under the rule of welfare states led by executives who enjoyed vast discretionary powers; in both countries, these relatively benign chief executives were forerunners to incredibly brutal and malignant dictatorships who had legal and constitutional license for their tyrannical rule.

In his recent book *The Coming of the Third Reich,* British historian Richard J. Evans recounts how Fredrich Ebert, the Social Democrat who served as the first president of Germany's Weimar Republic, pioneered the use of arbitrary executive power—particularly Article 48 of the constitution, which allowed the president to rule by decree—that was later used by Hitler to such murderous effect.

"The power to rule by decree was only intended for exceptional emergencies," recalls Evans. "But Ebert . . . made very extensive use of this power, employing it on no fewer than 136 separate occasions." This included orders dissolving elected governments in Saxony and Thuringia, and a 1920 order retroactively authorizing use of the death penalty for public disorder during a civil war in the Ruhr between Communist and proto-Nazi militias.

Upon assuming the office of chief executive, Field Marshal Paul von Hindenberg was "persuaded of the correctness of the use of Presidential emergency powers by the example of his predecessor," Evans continues. With the country in social and economic turmoil, Hindenberg "began to feel that a conservative dictatorship was the only way out of the crisis. . . ."

Hindenberg was, in the context of Weimar Germany, a conservative. His successor was not.

Article 48 of the Weimar Constitution did not specify how dictatorial executive power would be taken back; Article 25 even permitted the executive to dissolve the Reichstag. These provisions, coupled with the 1933 "Enabling

Act"—passed, amid public intimidation of the Reichstag by the Brownshirts, to deal with a terrorist crisis—gave Hitler's National Socialist regime the legal power to do—well, essentially what the Bush regime is doing now: Conduct surveillance of citizens, wage aggressive war abroad, use torture as a method of interrogation, imprison or execute citizens at will. . . .

While we have cause for relief in the fact that George W. Bush has not committed crimes of a magnitude comparable to those committed by the Nazi regime, we must also recognize that there is nothing to prevent him, or a successor, from doing so under the doctrine of executive power he and his handlers are urging upon us.

2006

Our Totalitarian State

Birch Blog, January 17, 2006

> [I]t is proper to take alarm at the first experiment on our
> liberties. We hold this prudent jealousy to be the first duty of
> Citizens, and one of the noblest characteristics of the late
> Revolution. The free men of America did not wait till usurped
> power had strengthened itself by exercise, and entangled the
> question in precedents. They saw all the consequences in the
> principle, and they avoided the consequences by denying the
> principle. We revere this lesson too much soon to forget it.
> —James Madison, June 20, 1785

Under what could be called Madison's precautionary principle of politics, Americans have a duty to recognize that the regime under which we presently live is totalitarian in nature, if only intermittently so in practice.

Totalitarianism exists when there are no effective restraints of the power of the state, and no effective protections for the individual rights of the subjects. The state, to borrow Lenin's axiom once again, exercises "power without limit, resting directly on force." The individual, by way of contrast, has no rights the state is bound to respect—to paraphrase just one of many pro-slavery rulings handed down by the Supreme Court.

The most recent illustration of the fundamentally totalitarian nature of our present regime is found in the case of Mohammed Yousry, a U.S. citizen of Egyptian birth who confronts a 20-year prison sentence for the supposed crime of acting as a court-appointed translator in the case of convicted terrorist Omar Abdel Rahman, the radical Muslim cleric whose religious exhortations inspired the first World Trade Center bombing in 1993.

On the basis of three years of detailed, invasive scrutiny of Yousry's life and private communications, FBI agents assigned to wiretap his phone, shadow his every movement, and pore over his computer files found not so much as a sub-atomic particle of evidence that the 50-year-old scholar had ever harmed anyone, much less broken any law.

"Yousry is not a practicing Muslim," admitted prosecutor Anthony Barkow in closing arguments before a federal district court in Manhattan. "He is not a fundamentalist. . . . Mohammed Yousry is not someone who supports or believes in the use of violence." In fact, Yousry, a Ph.D. candidate at New York

University, passed detailed and rigorous federal security checks before he was permitted to act as a translator on behalf of Rahman's defense team. An irreligious man married to an Evangelical Christian, whose daughter graduated from a Baptist college, Yousry finds Rahman's variety of Islam abhorrent, describing (accurately) the blind Egyptian Sheik as an exponent of "Muslim totalitarianism."

Nonetheless, Yousry was arrested at his home in Queens on April 9, 2002, by a platoon of FBI agents and helmeted police officers brandishing high-powered weaponry. There is nothing that brings out the warrior instincts of paramilitary police like the prospect of a full-force raid against unarmed, law-abiding, non-violent U.S. citizens. In this particular case, Yousry had been designated an enemy of the state for the newly minted crime of translating letters without federal permission.

Acting without legal training, and in the unsupportable belief that federal prosecutors are bound by constitutional standards of due process, Yousry translated a letter from Rahman "to Rahman's lawyer in Egypt," reports the *Washington Post*:

> In June 2000 [Rahman's defense attorney Lynne Stewart] released to a reporter a version of the letter, which discussed a cease-fire between Islamic militants and the Egyptian government. Prosecutors said that the lawyer and the translator, by these acts, conspired to use Rahman's words to incite others to carry out kidnappings and killings. No attack took place.

Ms. Stewart is a veteran Marxist revolutionary whose clients and affiliations include radical groups with terrorist connections. But as Paul Craig Roberts observes, in the Rahman case Stewart was "guilty" only of "represent[ing] her client in ways disapproved by prosecutors." Specifically, Stewart acted in defiance of "special administrative measures" denying Sheik Rahman access to mail, newspapers, and any visitors apart from his wife and legal counsel. The assumption was that Rahman's "words are weapons," and that anyone who helped him communicate with the outside world was effectively abetting terrorism.

Clark signed the document given to her by then-Attorney General Janet Reno; Yousry did not, acting only as he was instructed by Rahman's defense team. By translating a letter from Rahman, and reading to the Egyptian cleric letters written by radical supporters back home, Yousry "stuck his head in the sand and deliberately avoided knowing what should have been obvious," asserted federal prosecutor Robin Baker to the jury. "We don't have to prove why."

Indeed, the regime's prosecutors weren't interested in "proving" anything; instead, they focused on intimidating the jurors into "sending a message" by convicting Yousry. The trial took place just blocks from Ground Zero in Lower Manhattan. The prosecution repeatedly offered ritual invocations of 9/11 and Osama bin Laden, even though they weren't germane to the case.

One female juror, identified only as Juror 39, told the *Post* that Yousry's individual guilt or innocence didn't matter to her fellow jurors. "They [the other jurors] had an agenda. . . . People are so fearful that if you disagree with the government on one thing it makes you a terrorist." Despite her decent misgivings, Juror 39 voted to convict. "I have to plead guilty to being a coward," she conceded. "It doesn't feel good, but I punked out."

The *New York Sun*, the *Volkischer Beobachter* of the neo-"conservative" movement, will brook no second thoughts about Yousry's conviction.

"The war on terror involves going after the terrorists and those who help them," pronounced the *Sun's* editorial collective. "The Americans on the federal jury that convicted Yousry along with Stewart in . . . understood this. No doubt the interpreter conveys the impression of being a kindly scholar. But it is one of the facts in the kind of twilight war being levied against our country that not everyone is what they seem and danger comes in disguises."

The newsprint-defilers who publish the *Sun*, like others who believe that patriotism is displayed through bulimic regurgitation of the Bush regime's talking points, have no appetite for going after those in official positions who have helped terrorists, including Sheik Omar Abdel-Rahman. The same regime that prosecuted Yousry for translating messages to and from Rahman actively facilitated the terrorist conspiracy in which Sheik Omar played a critical role.

Sheik Omar was granted a one-year visa on May 10, 1990 from a CIA agent posing as an official at the U.S. consulate in Khartoum, Sudan; this permitted Rahman to avoid a State Department terrorism "watch list." He was received in New York by a network of Mujahideen who had received training and material assistance from the CIA and the U.S. military. In November 1990, Sheik Omar's visa was revoked, and the State Department advised the Immigration and Naturalization Service to be on the lookout for him. So attentive was the INS to this advisory that it issued a green card to Sheik Omar five months later. Not only did the federal government aid and abet Sheik Omar and his comrades, it acted as a passive accomplice to the first WTC bombing.

As I have written elsewhere, the FBI had abundant and detailed prior knowledge of the plot. Similar detailed warnings were offered to the FBI by an acquaintance of mine, a self-described former terrorist who was close to Rabbi Meir Kahane, the Jewish militant who had been murdered by Al-Sayyd Nosair, a participant in the first WTC bombing plot.

After Kahane was gunned down in cold blood by Nosair in November 1990, the FBI confiscated 49 boxes of documents from the murderer's New Jersey apartment. Among the detailed evidence found in that trove were bomb-making instructions, a hit list of public figures (including Kahane), paramilitary training materials, detailed pictures of famous buildings (including the World Trade Center), and sermons by Sheik Omar urging his followers to "destroy the edifices of capitalism."

All that was missing from that cache was an explicit note from the plotters stating, "We are going to bomb the World Trade Center," and a specific date and time for the attack. In fact, that information may very well have been provided to the Bureau by Emad Salem, the former Egyptian military intelligence officer who acted as Sheik Omar's bodyguard—while serving as an informant for the FBI. Salem recalled that the FBI's plan had been to replace the bomb meant for the WTC with a dud, and then arrest the plotters, but that the Bureau "messed up."

Forgive my skepticism, but not even the FBI is capable of incompetence of that magnitude. Stupidity can only explain so much.

Of the multitude of morbidly obese falsehoods fed to the public, this is by far the girthiest: The regime protects us from terrorism, rather than cultivating it, and exploiting it for its own purposes.

This perspective, of course, is usually dismissed as a "conspiracy theory"—which in common parlance refers to drawing impermissible anti-government conclusions from politically inconvenient facts. In the same sense, a "paranoid" is someone who notices things without government permission, and a "terrorist" is any individual—U.S. citizen or foreigner—whom the government summarily imprisons, or murders with extreme prejudice.

You're Fair Game

Birch Blog, January 18, 2006

If one can endure the mixture of pity and disgust provoked by the spectacle of Bush administration spokesliar Scott McClellan in action, White House press briefings can occasionally be useful. This isn't because McClellan would actually permit the truth to contaminate his ritualistic recitation of content-free talking points, but rather because the lies he tells, and the way in which he tells them, can help us understand, as if through a process of reverse engineering, what the Bush regime is actually doing.

Case in point: In his January 17 press briefing, McClellan was asked several questions about a lawsuit filed against the administration's by the ACLU and other activist groups protesting the use of warrantless wiretaps against U.S. citizens. Dismissing the lawsuit as "frivolous," McClellan performed the familiar liturgy of invoking 9/11 and praising our valiant Dear Leader (peace be upon him) for tirelessly working to protect "the safety and security of the American people" and doing "everything within his lawful power to protect Americans."

Truly, he is just and wise!

Then came a critical admission, threaded carefully into a familiar lie:

> If you're not talking to a known al Qaeda member or a member of an affiliated organization, you don't have to worry about this [practice of warrantless wiretapping]. The head of the NSA, or former head of the NSA talked about that in a briefing to reporters, about how limited this is and what it is aimed at. And that is the authorization that the President made after the attacks of September 11th.

This statement, like every other issued by a representative of the Leviathan State, should be read in terms of what the government claims the power to do, rather than the individual freedoms the state generously condescends to recognize.

Read in this fashion, here is what McClellan was actually saying: "If you are communicating with an individual that the administration can depict as somehow connected to someone in the orbit of al Qaeda, then you're fair game."

Not one American in 10,000,000 is aware of the fact that the Bush regime—in formal arguments before a federal judge—has claimed the right not only to keep under surveillance, but also to arrest and indefinitely detain as "enemy combatants," people who have any connection to terrorist suspects, no matter how innocuous that connection may be. The regime also contends that it does not have the legal obligation to establish *mens rea*—that is, criminal intent—on the part of those it chooses to detain.

The people under discussion here, incidentally, aren't savagely bearded Jihadis or Mullahs, wild-eyed anarchists, or beady-eyed neo-Nazis. The specific examples discussed by Bush regime attorneys were charitable elderly ladies and English tutors.

In December 2004, a hearing before U.S. District Judge Joyce Hens Green dealt with the legal status of detainees held in Guantanamo Bay. Judge Green inquired of Deputy Associate Attorney General Brian Boyle if a "little old lady in Switzerland" who sent a check to an orphanage in Afghanistan could be seized and held as an "enemy combatant" if some of that money—unbeknownst to her—wound up in the hands of al Qaeda.

"She could," replied comrade Boyle. "Someone's intention is clearly not a factor that would disable detention."

Note well the curious use of the term "disable"; this suggests that for Boyle, who spoke on behalf of the regime, the default setting would lead to the exercise of police state powers, absent a presidential determination to the contrary.

Judge Green asked about another scenario in which a hypothetical resident of England was found to be tutoring the child of an al Qaeda leader in English; could that tutor be scooped up and imprisoned at Gitmo, or "rendered" into the hands of a brutal ally (such as Egypt or Uzbekistan)? Yes, answered Commissar Boyle, since "al Qaeda could be trying to learn English to stage attacks [in England]," and offering English instruction under such circumstances would be akin to "shipping bullets to the front." And according to Boyle, the power to carry out such detentions applies to everyone, since "the conflict with al Qaeda has a global reach."

Let us consider just a few of the myriad potential permutations of these claims:

> Did you innocently provide plumbing services to someone accused of acting on behalf of al Qaeda? You may unknowingly

be teaching the enemy how to sabotage city water systems! Away to Gitmo with you!

Have you ignorantly rented a home or a business to people accused of acting on behalf of al Qaeda? That's just the same as being a quartermaster for the enemy in time of war! Oh, sure, your renters did nothing to provoke your suspicion, but this doesn't extenuate your guilt (call this the Mary Surratt principle). Away to Gitmo with you!

Do you run an ISP that has—unknown to you—facilitated communications among suspected Jihadis? Traitor! In The Global War on Terrorism, Extremism, and Other Evil Things To Be Named Later™, words are weapons! You might as well be planting roadside bombs with your own perfidious hands! AWAY TO GITMO WITH YOU!

Judge Green wasn't particularly impressed with Boyle's arguments, ruling against the regime's claim that those detained at Gitmo have no right to contest their imprisonment through the courts. But as George W. Bush has demonstrated on many occasions, he and the oligarchy he represents do not consider themselves bound by laws, or subject to the checks and balances exercised by Congress or the courts.

Long story short: In the era of Il Duce Busholini, the "lawful powers" of the president include the power to do anything he wants to anyone, anywhere, anytime, for any reason he chooses. If the regime claims the power to send you to Gitmo because you once gave a generous tip to a waiter whose other customers included al Qaeda suspects (why, it's just like giving field rations to enemy troops!), it's a near certainty that Bush and Company consider you fair game for surveillance, as well.

Patriots, Rebels, and Terrorists

Birch Blog, January 20, 2006

In a Pentagon press conference late last November, Chief Commissar for Aggression and Occupation Donald Rumsfeld shared what he called an "epiphany" regarding the armed resistance to Washington's benevolent errand in Iraq.

"This is a group of people who don't merit the word 'insurgency,' I think," Rumsfeld insisted. "I think that you can have a legitimate insurgency in a country that has popular support and has a cohesiveness and has a legitimate gripe. These people don't have a legitimate gripe."

If the term "insurgents" is not to be used in describing "these people," what should we call them? In comments made shortly after leaving to become head of the World Bank, Rumsfeld's former deputy Paul Wolfowitz used the orthodox Marxist expression "forces of reaction" to describe those who had taken up arms against the glorious forces of democratic liberation.

In fact, Wolfowitz—who, like the other chief architects of the Iraq war, has never been in so much as a fistfight, let alone a firefight—slapped down Gen. John Abizaid, the head of Central Command, during an August 2003 Baghdad press conference for referring to Iraqi guerrillas as a "coordinated resistance." "It's not a resistance," pontificated Comrade Wolfowitz. "They are forces of reaction."

Translated into Russian, the comments by Rumsfeld and Wolfowitz could easily have been made by Soviet officials dealing with the "bandits" and "reactionaries" who attacked Red Army units during the glorious liberation of Afghanistan.

As veteran foreign affairs analyst Eric Margolis points out, the Soviet occupation of Afghanistan brought about democratic elections, the emancipation of women, efforts to develop and modernize the nation's infrastructure, an end to fundamentalist Islamic rule, and other benefits—at the price of domination by an ideologically hostile foreign power that killed millions of people. Curiously, this transaction wasn't seen as a bargain by most of the Afghans themselves—but why should their opinion count? They're reactionaries, remember?

True, in Soviet-dominated Afghanistan, just as in U.S.-occupied Iraq, armed resistance has included many nasty individuals—both home-grown as well as imported Jihadis—who are terrorists by any rational definition. The

33

opportunism of Washington's neo-Trotskyites, who seek to turn Iraq into a staging area in their "global democratic revolution," has been matched by that of Islamo-Leninists who view occupied Iraq as a recruiting and training ground for their global jihad.

But rebellion is the normal, predictable, and quite commendable human reaction (if you'll forgive the use of that term) to foreign occupation. It is rooted in patriotism, the love of a particular place, people, and culture. It is recognized and respected by true patriots of all nations, which is why it is unintelligible to the likes of Rumsfeld and Wolfowitz.

"I can't really blame these people for not wanting us to be here," states Pfc. Thomas Turner of the 82nd Airborne deployed to Fallujah. "I wouldn't want some other country to just come in and take over our country, and drive through our streets. . . . I've gotta admit, we're pretty intimidating when we roll in. . . . I guess they have to fight back."

Turner is among the U.S. soldiers profiled in "Occupation: Dreamland," a riveting documentary shot in Fallujah in early 2004—shortly before several civilian security contractors were killed and mutilated there, and months before the town was all but wiped out in a major U.S. operation. (The assault on Fallujah included the use of chemical weapons against the city's inhabitants.) The film captures the pride, frustration, and anxieties of U.S. fighting men. Most of them genuinely want to help the Iraqis; some of them begin to resent the sullen, suspicious stares that follow them as they patrol the streets of Fallujah—even if they can understand the sentiments behind those stares.

In one remarkable scene, a middle-aged Fallujah resident gets right into the face of a soldier leading a local patrol to express what can only be called patriotic outrage.

"We don't accept colonialism," the Iraqi man declared through a translator. "America can go to the moon, and make nuclear rockets, and make weapons, but it can't make people. It can't make the people—we make the people. And most of them are innocent. And why do you take the women? Where is the civilization that Bush talks about? Is it in the [Abu Ghraib] prison?"

Forgive me, Commissar Rumsfeld, but it sounds to me like this fellow has "a legitimate gripe"—or several dozen. The same is true of the soldiers Rumsfeld and his comrades dispatched to Iraq.

"I want some answers—some clarification," Pfc. Turner muses at one point in the film. "I guess somebody smarter than me knows what's going on."

That "somebody" certainly isn't Rumsfeld, nor the president he serves; those guys clearly can't tell Fedayeen from fettucine.

Cowboys and Poseurs

Birch Blog, February 2, 2006

"How cool would it be to give a State of the Union address in a Porter Wagoner outfit?" pandered the president in his recent address at the Grand Old Opry. Given Little George's insatiable appetite for playing dress-up—he's been through enough faux-macho costumes to qualify as an honorary member of the Village People—I wouldn't be surprised to see him decked out in Rhinestone Cowboy garb for the next SOTU.

Press accounts of the Opry speech mentioned the presence of "several country music stars, including Barbara Mandrell, Larry Gatlin, Lee Greenwood, Lorrie Morgan and the Oak Ridge Boys." Conspicuous by his absence was Merle Haggard, the King of Country Music by acclamation and the genre's patriot nonpareil.

It was Haggard who penned "The Fighting Side of Me" ("If you're running down my country, man you're walkin' on the fighting side of me") and "Okie From Muskogee," an unabashed celebration of attachment to a particular community. Haggard's "Okie" could be considered an isolationist, and would probably feel no grief over being tagged with the label. Thus he wouldn't have shared Bush's concern that "people . . . [would] decide to adopt isolationist policies" as a result of disenchantment with the Iraq war.

Haggard, in fact, has vehemently condemned the Iraq war. His 2003 song "In The News" offered a perceptive—and prescient—critique of the Iraq War:

"Suddenly the cost of war is somethin' out of sight. Lost a lotta heroes in the fight. Politicians do all the talkin': soldiers pay the dues. Suddenly the war is over, that's the news."

Haggard wrote those words at about the same time the strutting little fool in the White House issued his now-infamous taunt to the Iraqi insurgency: "Bring it on." Politicians do all the talkin'; soldiers pay the dues. . . .

His latest disc, "Chicago Wind," includes two undisguised shots at the Bush regime: "America First," and "Where's All the Freedom?" The former gives full-throated voice to the bone-bred patriotism that Bush and his scriptwriters dismiss as "isolationism":

"Why don't we liberate these United States,
We're the ones that need it worst.

36

Let the rest of the world help us for a change,
And let's rebuild America first."

Note that Haggard correctly refers to "these" United States, recognizing the fact that our republic is supposed to be a union of sovereign states with the central government confined to a few very modest functions. Our present imperial system inverts these priorities. As Robert E. Lee prophesied, the conquest of the states by Washington in the Civil War set the stage for imperialism abroad, a process that began with the utterly unjustified 1898 war against Spain and continues to this day.

"Where's All the Freedom?" is an even more pointed indictment of the Bush junta, and its war on what remains of our liberties and prosperity:

"Where's all the freedom that we're fightin' for?
Is it still our creed from shore to shore?
Every soldier fights: should we read him his new rights?
There's not that many to read any more.
Where's all the freedom that we're fightin' for?. . . .

How long do we cower down? Is this really still our ground?
Our country's like a prisoner of war.
Where's all the freedom that we're fightin' for?"

Haggard is a close friend of Toby Keith (who is hardly the cartoonish jingoist some perceive him to be). He was also close to Ronald Reagan. Yet he gallantly rode to the defense of the Dixie Chicks when the Bu'ushists declared them enemies of the state for profaning the name of the Dear Leader (peace be upon him). Like the late (and *very* badly missed) Johnny Cash, who also opposed the war in Iraq, Haggard is an authentic man who has made his share of mistakes, and has done his best to surmount them. He seeks to live honorably and to promote honor through his art.

Haggard is utterly alien to the contemporary Country Music industry, which extrudes a homogenized product that resembles real Cowboy music (or Bluegrass, or any other authentic strain of American roots music) about as much as "pasteurized processed cheese food product" resembles aged Swiss. Or about as much as George W. Bush resembles an authentic patriot, let alone a cowboy.

How Common is Torture?

Birch Blog, February 13, 2006

"I can't believe what I just saw," exclaimed my lovely wife Korrin, concern etched into her alabaster brow. She had just returned from visiting a friend who runs a day care center. Among that friend's charges was a 3-year-old boy who supposedly suffers from either Attention Deficit Disorder, Attention Deficit Hyperactivity Disorder, or some more exotic variation on that spurious diagnosis.

Like most other children thus classified, this rambunctious youngster displays all of the symptoms of being a normal, healthy, energetic young male, a condition increasingly treated through some combination of chemical castration and/or torture.

I do not exaggerate.

This little kid is on some toxic cocktail of psychotropic drugs. When he acts up—which is going to happen, naturally—he is punished through the use of what have come to be known as "stress positions."

"The doctor told the parents that when this little kid acts up, he has to stick his arms straight out and hold them that way for a long time," Korrin told me. The day care provider was told to administer the same punishment. "I can't believe how long he was forced to stand that way," Korrin continued. "He would have this hateful and angry look in his eyes. And if he dropped his arms too soon, he had to start over again. It was like torture."

"No, honey, it wasn't 'just like' torture," I commented, "it *was* torture."

Once again I'm compelled to review Alfred McCoy's sobering and indispensable book, *A Question of Torture*. Chapter 2, which deals with the CIA's MK-Ultra drug and behavior experiments, also refers to the origins of what are now called "stress positions." In the mid-1950s, CIA-connected researchers examined "nonviolent" interrogation methods employed by the KGB and their Chinese counterparts that included such apparently innocuous routines as forcing people to stand still for 18–24 hours.

Those forced to stand still for hours on end suffer excruciating pain—ankles doubling in size, the eruption of blisters on their feet, racing heart rates, kidney failure, and so on. (This KGB torture method is also described in the book *The Long Walk* by Slavomir Rawicz.) The whole point of such treatment is not merely to inflict pain—any nitwit equipped with a club or brass knuckles can accomplish that—but rather to break the will of the subject by forcing him to inflict pain on himself.

The CIA, writes McCoy, updated its own interrogation methods by adapting "many of the KGB's distinctive techniques," placing "self-inflicted pain" at the center of its 1963 "Kubark Counterintelligence Manual"—a basic reference used to train interrogators throughout the Third World. One CIA trademark was interrogation in which victims were made to assume "'stress positions' without any external mechanism."

As the KGB had demonstrated, it was possible to inflict terrifying pain on a subject, and break his will to resist, without necessarily touching him—simply by compelling him, under threat of direct physical assault, to maintain a stress position for a protracted time. Interrogators may force a subject to stand, crouch, hold one's arms overhead or at the sides for long periods; they may involve force him to do endless deep knee bends, as was required of some detainees at Abu Ghraib.

"The frog," a variation of this last method, was used by Romanian Communists to break down the resistance of young Christian rebels sent to re-education camps.

In his memoir *The Anti-Humans*, Romanian anti-Communist Dumitru Bacu (a pseudonym) writes of how "the frog" was used in the "cycle of tortures" employed against those deemed to be "fanatics" in their resistance to the new regime.

"One of the tests for the fanatical students was forced gymnastics, especially the semi-squat or 'frog,'" writes Bacu. "To touch the heels with the buttocks was not permitted, and the hands had to be held laterally the whole time, stretched out, or raised high above the head. During this semi-squat posture, the student had to raise and lower himself in time to a rhythm set by the re-educator by hitting on wood with a stick hours on end, uninterruptedly."

"Normally and without any coercion," he continues, "a man in good physical condition can do up to fifty flexions of this kind, after which his legs begin to stiffen. The student A.D. from the Faculty of Letters in Bucharest, arrested in 1948 and sentenced to ten years, did in a single night, above the portable toilet, over one thousand."

Donald Rumsfeld once snarkily dismissed the description of stress positions as torture by claiming that he stands up for most of the working day (which isn't true, of course). Various forms of Yoga and isometric exercise involve what could be called stress positions. Special Forces operators and some intelligence agents undergo "waterboarding"—simulated drowning—as part of their training. And practically anybody who wants to become a professional wrestler will be required, as a basic qualifying test, to perform at least 500 consecutive deep knee bends. (I'm not in anything resembling competitive shape, and I can do more than 2,000 deep knee bends without stopping.) So what's the big deal?

The central issue here is the use of coercion to make a person inflict pain on himself, for extended periods, long past the limits of his endurance, as a way of breaking his will and making him submit to the state. This approach doesn't always work, of course—and when it doesn't, other methods can always be tried.

Of the student forced to do one thousand squats in the Romanian re-education camp, Bacu writes:

> When he stepped down he still had the strength to continue; it was the fatigue of the rhythm-beater which stopped the performance. To what mysterious force can be attributed this physical resistance on the part of a man exhausted by malnutrition, sleepless nights, and the obligatory positions [that is, stress positions] imposed on him in the days preceding this test? For this case is but one from among the hundreds of victims who managed to pass the one thousand-mark of such flexions without breaking down. Only strength of will, a manifestation of spirit, could thus temporarily overcome the body's fatigue and successfully control it.

Ulpian, a prominent jurist in imperial Rome, pointed out that torture avails little, since the strong will resist and the weak will say or do anything to avoid or end the pain. Elaborating on that point, Alfred McCoy observes that the only way to compensate for torture's unreliability as an interrogation method is to commit to widespread and indiscriminate torture as a general policy. This will yield two undesirable outcomes: First, it will leave the society thus "protected" with a brutal and brutalized government habituated to sadistic violence; second, it will leave the targeted insurgency stronger and more efficient, as the less disciplined and strong-willed members are culled from the ranks.

Which brings me back to that hapless little child who was tortured by his own mother, and by a very kind-hearted and decent day care provider, as supposed treatment for a mythical disorder. My wife saw hatred, frustration, and defiance radiating from that 3-year-old's tormented eyes.

There are probably hundreds of thousands of little boys receiving exactly the same treatment. Some of them will surmount this experience. Others will become criminals. At least a portion will go on to become law enforcement officers, soldiers, or—God help us, although we hardly deserve it—politicians.

A War About Nothing

Birch Blog, February 22, 2006

"I cannot support a mission that leads to corruption, human rights abuse and liars," protested Col. Ted Westhusing in a letter he wrote last June. "I am sullied. I came to serve honorably and feel dishonored. Death before being dishonored any more."

Shortly after committing those words to paper, Col. Westhusing, a 44-year-old husband and father, devout Catholic, West Point graduate, and Special Forces veteran who volunteered to serve in Iraq, killed himself with a single shot to the head from his service pistol. His lifeless body was found in his office in Baghdad's "Green Zone." The day before his apparent suicide, Col. Westhusing had been commended on the work he had done training Iraqi police. He had less than a month remaining before his return to the U.S.

A few weeks before his death, reported the *Los Angeles Times*, Col. Westhusing received an anonymous four-page letter accusing USIS, the Virginia-based military contractor for whom he worked, of serious crimes, ranging from embezzlement to the murder of innocent Iraqis. As a man devoted to honor, Westhusing felt himself deeply implicated in the alleged crimes. His mood and disposition changed immediately. In letters, emails, and telephone conversations, the once confident and optimistic man displayed fear, frustration, and disillusionment.

An Army psychologist who reviewed Westhusing's emails following his suicide determined that the Colonel "had placed too much pressure on himself to succeed and that he was unusually rigid in his thinking," recounts the *Times*. A fellow military officer concurred, telling the newspaper that Westhusing "had trouble reconciling his ideals with Iraq's reality. Iraq 'isn't a black-and-white place,' the officer said. 'There's a lot of gray.'"

That assessment is impossible to harmonize with the strident language of "moral clarity" spoken by the war's Chickenhawk cheering section. For such invertebrates, "moral clarity" refers to a commitment to adhere to their Dear Leader, no matter how morally unsupportable or self-contradictory his directives may be.

Col. Westhusing, by way of contrast, was wholeheartedly committed to West Point's moral code: "A cadet will not lie, cheat, or steal—or tolerate those who do." In one of his emails home, Westhusing "seemed especially upset by

42

one conclusion he had reached: that traditional military values such as duty, honor and country had been replaced by profit motives in Iraq, where the U.S. had come to rely heavily on contractors for jobs once done by the military." (Some of Colonel Westhusing's friends and family suspect that people associated with those contractors may have murdered him.)

There is absolutely nothing dishonorable about honest profit. But there can be no honest profit in an enterprise that boils down to armed robbery on a massive scale. This is why Col. Westhusing, a serious and accomplished scholar of ethics and a Christian patriot, came to believe that his soul had been "sullied."

Separated from his family by thousands of miles, living in a moral universe he couldn't understand, Col. Westhusing took his own life. He held the gun, but it was the Bush regime, acting on behalf of the amoral Power Elite that it serves, that pulled the trigger. And the regime's enablers (yes that includes you, Hannity) served as accessories in the death of Col. Westhusing.

Westhusing's was just one out of tens of thousands of irreplaceable human lives consumed by the crime against humanity and Christian decency that is the war in Iraq.

A recent dispatch from Samarra published by Knight-Ridder describes, in unbearable detail, the loss of another husband and father near Patrol Base Uvanni, which was established by U.S. soldiers in an abandoned schoolhouse. Named in honor of National Guard Sergeant Michael Uvanni of Rome, New York, who was killed in Samarra in October 2004, the post is also called "The Alamo" by the soldiers of the Second Platoon, Bravo Company of the 101st Airborne's Rakkasan Brigade, who man it.

"American units in Iraq usually fire warning shots," notes the wire service account. "The Rakkasans don't. . . . A warning shot in the vernacular of the Rakkasans . . . was a bullet that hit one Iraqi man while others could see."

"That's how you warn his buddy, is to pop him in the face with a kill shot?" asked an incredulous 1st Lt. Dennis Call as he investigated the shooting of an Iraqi civilian. "But what about when his buddy comes back with another guy . . . that and the other 15 guys in his family who you've made terrorists?"

As Call asked that question, an Iraqi man laid at his feet, his internal organs hanging from his side after taking several rounds from a .50 caliber machine gun.

The National Guard medic, Specialist Patrick McCreery (a 35-year-old foundry worker from Michigan), couldn't answer. Apparently the man was gunned down without warning because he had wandered into a 100-yard "kill zone" near the base. "The Army had forced the residents of the block to leave [their] houses last year to create the security perimeter," explains the Knight-Ridder account.

The unnamed man, his life quickly bleeding into the street as a call to prayer resounded from a nearby mosque, gestured to Specialist McCreery and pointed a trembling finger toward a nearby house. "This my house," he whispered huskily to McCreery in English.

Dropping to a knee, the medic did what little he could to minister to the dying civilian, who was praying: "Ya Allah, Ya Allah" ("Oh, God, Oh God").

"He's fading!" McCreery shouted, hoping an ambulance would arrive. "He's fading!" He bent down to look into the man's eyes, hoping at least to provide some human companionship as his life expired.

"Haji, Haji, look at me," McCreery whispered urgently, using that honorific—which has been used by some as a dehumanizing slur—in its proper sense.

"Why?" asked the Iraqi as his eyes began to close. "Why?"

"Haji, I don't know," McCreery replied, tears beginning to join the sweat pouring from his face.

His name was Wissam Abbas. The 31-year-old man was gunned down within feet of his home by a foreign army that had invaded and occupied his city in obedience to a lying ruler devoid of honor or conscience.

A few days after Wissam was killed, orders were issued to photograph the entrails left in the wake of the shooting in order to document that Wissam was inside the kill zone when he was shot. This wasn't possible, since dogs had already eaten what had remained behind.

Sgt. Michael Pena, the soldier who had shot Wissam, "didn't say a word about the man he'd killed," reports Knight-Ridder. "As he stared at a patch of earth in front of him, at Samarra and its wreckage, he couldn't contain his frustration."

"No one told me why I'm putting my life on the line in Samarra, and you know why they don't?" commented Sgt. Pena. "Because there is no f*****g reason."

In that incident, one life was ended, and at least two others were irreparably damaged. For *nothing*.

The invasion of Iraq was rooted in lies, and it has blossomed into a monumental crime. The only reason our troops remain in Iraq is to forestall the inevitable loss of prestige that our government will suffer once they leave, as they eventually will. And until that time, more lives will be lost and ruined, and more enemies will be made—needlessly.

I recognize that in the fallen world we live in, there are times (very few, as it turns out) when it is necessary to kill and die to defend our country. Our country is worth that price. "Our" government is not.

"Children Rawly Left"

Birch Blog, March 2, 2006

Last Sunday night, Robyn Schornak of Franklin, Kentucky received an urgent call from her mother.

When her husband Chris was deployed to Iraq with the 101st Airborne a few years ago, Robyn—six months pregnant when her husband was deployed to Iraq as part of the Idiot King's useless war—had moved in with her mother. Since then, her son Tristan had been born; Chris had come home, briefly found employment with a heavy equipment company in Alabama, re-enlisted, and was sent back to Iraq. Amid all of these changes, the Pentagon had not received an updated home address for the Schornak family.

Accordingly, when the notification team sought out Robyn, it was sent to her mother's address.

"Her mom did not say why Robyn must come quickly," recounted the *Tennessean*:

> On the 10-minute drive, she prayed there wouldn't be a car with government tags in the driveway. When she saw the government car, she prayed the men inside would be wearing their camouflage "battle dress" uniforms, the Army's version of everyday wear, instead of their "Class A" dress uniforms, buttons gleaming, shoes shining. BDUs would mean Chris was wounded. Class A's would mean he was gone.

The notification team was wearing Class A's.

Robyn had last spoken with her husband on Saturday night. He was killed the following night (which would have been early Sunday in the U.S.) during a routine patrol, slain by "a slanting shot that entered his chest high, near the shoulder, an area not covered by the body armor."

Just that quickly, Robyn's husband, Tristan's father, was stolen from them. The thief was an Iraqi sniper. The chief accomplice was the granite-headed criminal infesting the White House.

Tristan was born on April 1, 2003. His literal birthday is the symbolic birthday of everyone who clings to the notion that the war in Iraq has anything to do with protecting our nation or promoting freedom. Tristan "is too young to comprehend the tragedy that has befallen him and his mother, a widow at 24," writes Leon Alligood of the *Tennessean*, who has written 50 obituaries of servicemen killed in Iraq. Alligood got to know Sergeant Christopher Schornak in February 2004, while covering the war.

As they stood in line "at a Pizza Hut concession" (yes, the people running this war divvy out corporate concessions, as if it were a sporting event), Alligood and Schornak "talked of many things, of the horrors and fears of war, of his pride in his men, and, as he reached into his wallet to retrieve a baby's photo, of a son he wanted to get to know."

Roughly a week before Robyn was left a widow and Tristan lost his father, 38-year-old Staff Sgt. Gregson Glenn Gourley, a native of Midvale, Utah, was killed near Hawijah, Iraq, when a roadside bomb was detonated next to his Humvee. Like Sgt. Schornak, Staff Sgt. Gourley was a member of the 101st. Like Schornak, Gourley was on his second tour in that utterly unnecessary war.

And like Schornak, Gourley was a father, and his widow resides in Kentucky. Notes the *Deseret Morning News*: "Greg Gourley leaves behind a wife, Collette, three sons younger than 11 and a newborn daughter, all of whom live in Hopkinsville, Ky, where the family had recently purchased a new home." Gourley's widow is left with four small children and a mortgage, and no source of income.

In a battle's eve discussion with his disguised Commander-in-Chief, "Michael Williams," an English soldier from Shakespeare's *Henry V*, warned that Kings who make war needlessly will eventually be held accountable by God:

> If the cause be not good, the King himself hath a heavy reckoning to make when all those legs and arms and heads, chopp'd off in a battle, shall join together at the latter day and cry all "We died at such a place"—some swearing, some crying for a surgeon, some upon their wives left poor behind them, some upon the debts they owe, some upon their children rawly left. I am afeard there are few die well that die in a battle; for how can they charitably dispose of anything when blood is their argument? Now, if these men do not die well, it will be a black matter for the King that led them to it.

As Prince Harry, the man who would later be King Henry V (per Shakespeare's depiction) was a shallow, spoiled party animal. Summoned to his father's deathbed, Harry received the famous admonition: "Therefore, my Harry, be it that course to busy giddy minds with foreign quarrels, that action, hence borne may waste the memory of the former days."

Which is to say: You're a silly little boy devoid of gravitas, and the only way to acquire it is to raid the treasury and imbrue the countryside with the blood of husbands and fathers. If you're going to be a king, don't just stand there—start killing people!

As Harry becomes King Henry V, the first thing he does is publicly denounce his erstwhile drinking buddy John Falstaff—"The tutor and feeder of my riots." The second thing he does is to call Parliament into session. Prince John of Lancaster, seeing these developments, knows what they portend: "I will lay odds that, ere this year expire, we bear our civil swords and native fire as far as France. . . ."

All that was missing was a pretext, which the Archbishop of Canterbury was happy to supply—a convoluted reading of abstruse ancient statutes and pedigrees that gave Henry a diaphanous claim to the throne of France. But just before the Archbishop disgorged this confabulated *casus belli*, Henry decants an elegantly self-justifying speech:

> God doth know how many man, now in health, shall drop their
> blood in approbation of what your reverence shall incite us to;
> therefore take heed how you impawn our person, how you
> awake the sleeping sword of war; we charge you, in the name
> of God, take heed; for never two such kingdoms did contend
> without much fall of blood; whose guiltless drops are every one
> a woe, a sore complaint 'gainst him whose wrongs give edge
> unto the swords that make such waste in brief mortality.

The same Henry who professed such agonized reluctance to resort to arms would later threaten to unleash an orgy of rape and child-killing against the French village of Harfleur:

> The blind and bloody soldier with foul hand [shall] defile the
> locks of your shrill-shrieking daughters; your fathers [will be]
> taken by the silver beards, and their most reverend heads [be]

dash'd to the walls; your naked infants [will be] spitted on pikes, whiles the mad mothers with their howls confused do break the clouds, as did the wives of Jewry at Herod's bloody-hunting slaughtermen.

For the supposed crime of defending themselves against the English onslaught.

Harfleur, Henry insisted, was "guilty in defense." *They* were "illegal combatants," nay, terrorists, for daring to fight back against the alien army that had invaded their country and killed their neighbors. Later during the Battle of St. Crispin's Day, Henry—the "mirror of Christian kings"—orders his men to slaughter their helpless prisoners. And when informed that the English were victorious, Henry piously exclaims: "Praised be God, and not our strength for it!"

On the strength of Shakespeare's ironic rendering of the story, it is not difficult to imagine The Almighty replying: "Don't be so modest, Harry—you did it all by yourself."

Whatever one thinks of Henry V, this much should be said for him: Unlike our incumbent Dimwit-in-Chief, Henry led from the front. He was in the thick of battle. When he wore military garb, it was with the authority of one who had seen battle; he didn't prance and swan about in soldier drag after exploiting his political connections to avoid combat.

It's hard to imagine the victorious Henry V making a heavily guarded peek-a-boo visit to conquered France, like the fleeting visit Bush the Dumber just paid to "liberated" Afghanistan. But it's impossible to believe that Bush would entertain even the transient, trivial misgivings about sending husbands and fathers to die that Henry was made to express.

Thoughts on being "Anti-Government"

Birch Blog, March 5, 2006

Like others who chronicle the criminal behavior of the degenerate people who presume to rule us, I am occasionally accused of being "anti-government." More often than not I'm tempted to reply: "And your point would be. . .?" No particular disrepute attaches to those opposed to cancer, or earthquakes, or hurricanes, and government has proven to be immeasurably more murderous and destructive than any of those plagues or natural calamities.

Actually, since government seems to be an ineradicable reality of the fallen human condition, I vastly prefer to see as many of them as possible. One government ruling the world would be an unmitigated disaster, which is why (I believe) God disrupted the Babel project, thereby creating separate nations and languages—and, most importantly, governments.

Peoples may mingle, and the language barrier can be overcome, but blending governments together leads to murderous impunity on the part of rulers (see Genesis 11:6). So the governments were divided at Babel. What God has made separate, let no man join together.

A world divided into dozens of national governments is infinitely preferable to one ruled by a single centralized regime. In similar fashion, a federated constitutional republic in which power is limited by law and divided among numerous contending governments is more desirable than what our Founders called a "unitary" government. Unfortunately, the regime under which we live today is a unitary state ruled by a Unitary Executive—in much the same way that Rome under Augustus retained the trappings and rhetorical habits of its noble republican heritage, even as it mutated into a tyrannical empire.

The Framers of our Constitution well understood that the tendency of every government is to enlarge itself beyond its legal limits, absorbing social functions over which it has no proper jurisdiction and emerging as the most lethal threat to the lives, liberties, and properties of the governed. This is because fallen human beings act in that fashion, and government is (in Madison's words) the greatest of all reflections on human nature. Governments are composed of men. To paraphrase John Locke, those who think that men are purged of their faults and failings when they are invested with public authority are whack. (Like I said, that's a paraphrase.)

Idolatry is the besetting sin of the human condition, and the most prevalent variety of idolatry is the worship of the state. Most people who worship the state do so unconsciously, by way of cultivated reflex rather than conscious devotion. That reflex is on display anytime people behave as if the state somehow enjoys an exception from any of the moral laws governing individuals.

As I understand it—and I am aware that there are serious and sober people who take a slightly different view—God created Man and the family. The state, by way of contrast, is a human artifact. God gave man laws to govern his affairs, but the basic divine framework—the Ten Commandments, and the Two Great Commandments—do *not* envision a necessary role for a secular government.

Yes, a properly constituted government can play a role in enforcing the divine law against murder, theft, and fraud, but that's really the limit of the state's role. Paul's famous and much-misused admonition from Romans 13 that Christians "submit to the governing authorities" specifies only one function of government for which Christians are liable to pay taxes—that of wielding the sword of justice against those who threaten persons and property. That is the limit of government's authority—which means, of necessity, that governments involved in other matters have no legitimate claim on the obedience of Christian believers. Indeed, such governments are by definition among the "evildoers" against which, as Paul wrote, governments are supposed to protect the governed.

When citizens' rights are threatened by government, how can they rely on government for protection? The Americanist answer is that this can be done through the separation of powers among several contending governments, each of which is limited by law. Christian subjects of the Roman Emperor or other monarchs had the misfortune of living under a regime in which Caesar or the king claimed to be the law, and were required to pray for that monarch in the hope that God would use him for righteous ends. In the American republic, however, "the law is king," as Thomas Paine put it (a statement falling into the category of "Things that are true even if Thomas Paine said them").

Monarchy, as far as the Israelites were concerned, wasn't instituted *by* God, but *in defiance of Him.*

As recounted in I Samuel 8, the Israelites had grown weary of the corruption of the Priests and the indifference of the judges. Opportunistic and power-craving men exploited that weariness in order to create a monarchy as the focal point of what we would now call the welfare-warfare state, and this process was consummated in perfectly democratic fashion. God permitted this to happen, but as He did so He explicitly said that Israel had rejected Him (I Samuel

8:7). The selling point, for those who embraced that apostasy, would be a king who would lead Israel into battle; God's people would reject their distinctive blessings, and become like all other nations (I Samuel 8:19).

The lesson here is that God did not institute a government to rule over man; man did that to himself, and God permitted it. Granted, even in that circumstance, God did not abandon His people to the whims of the sinful men who would become king; instead, he had Samuel compose a scroll containing the "regulations of the kingship," which included God's detailed warnings of the abuses of power (beginning, interestingly enough, with conscription); this meant, in effect, that the government God suffered His people to create was a constitutional monarchy (see 10:25, and 8:10–18).

My view of this matter is strongly influenced by *Vindiciae Contra Tyrannos*, the 1579 Calvinist tract that John Adams considered to be among the most influential works in the American colonies on the eve of our War for Independence. The gravamen of the essay is that since God exercises unqualified sovereignty over men, all men are His subjects, and equal before Him. This means that those appointed to kings, rulers, or leaders have one duty, as the heroic John Knox instructed Queen Mary—that of creating conditions that permit the people to obey God's law.

In addressing the creation of kingship, *Vindiciae* summarizes the process as one in which the Lord effectively said: "according to your desires Saul is given you for your king, to lead you in the wars, but with this condition annexed, that he follow the law of God." The same condition attaches to the reign of any other ruler. When rulers violate the terms and conditions of their delegated authority, it is not only appropriate but necessary to remove them. Kings must "always remember that it is from God, but *by the people*, and for the people's sake that they do reign, and that in their glory they say not (as is their custom) they hold their kingdom only of God and their sword, but withal add that it was *it was the people who first gift them with that sword*."

As *Vindiciae* documents, the fact that kings exercised contingent and derivative power (as the "gift" of the people) was once commonly understood. While history is replete with kings and other rulers who became tyrants, it wasn't until the emergence of modern democracy that the State became an omnivorous idol, emancipated from any limit on its powers and presumed to be divine.

Government of some sort is inevitable. When it is limited by law, divided against itself, and shrunk to a size that makes it manageable (which means, to be blunt, vulnerable to the armed resistance of the people, should it become a menace to their liberties), government can even be modestly beneficial. But there is nothing to commend the lawless State in any of its murderous and loathsome varieties, and I honestly can't see how any decent person could say otherwise.

Assassins, Public and Private (or, Why the Feds are Worse than the Mob)

Birch Blog, March 16, 2006

"He came walking out of his house with his daughter, a little girl, like seven years old or so," writes former Mob hitman Kevin Weeks of an intended victim. "They were headed towards a silver Volvo, he had her by the hand."

Weeks's target was *Boston Herald* columnist Howie Carr, who had become an intolerable irritant to Boston's Irish Mob boss James "Whitey" Bulger. As Weeks describes the event in his memoir, *Brutal*, "I couldn't take a chance of the bullet fragmenting and ricocheting or hitting her or just killing her father in front of her."

Bear in mind, we're discussing the self-serving memoir of a Mob assassin—Whitey Bulger's most trusted confidante for decades, prior to turning against the mobster six years ago. Bulger, who has fled the country, has been charged with committing 20 murders, and is suspected of at least 20 more. For nearly a quarter-century, Bulger was a prized asset of the FBI, which protected him as an informant even as he carried out a lucrative—and murderous—racketeering business. Interestingly, Bulger's relationship with the Feds began while, as an inmate at Alcatraz, he consented to being a subject in CIA-connected LSD experiments in exchange for time off his sentence.

This arrangement was mutually beneficial for Bulger and his FBI handler, John J. Connolly, each of whom rapidly ascended through the ranks of his organization. In 1999, Weeks turned federal informant, eventually offering the testimony that led to Connolly's conviction: In addition to turning a blind eye on Bulger's crimes (which included the sexual exploitation of teenage girls), the FBI agent served as a lookout on a Mob hit. Weeks claims Bulger "had six [agents] he could call on anytime and they would willingly hop in the car with him with the machine gun."

Although Connolly has described the entente with Bulger as a brilliant "business" strategy—protecting one Mob chieftain to take down scores of others—he acknowledges that Bulger and his other "business" partners were killers, albeit of a selective kind: "I don't think they ever killed anyone who wasn't trying to kill them or wasn't going to rat them out," Connolly insists. "They would only kill people who were a threat to them."

Connolly's observation tends to enhance Weeks's plausibility, at least where the hitman describes his reluctance to imperil a young girl the Mob considered a non-combatant. And it italicizes a useful distinction between the criminal syndicate that we call the federal government and its private sector competition, such as the Irish Mob: Private mafias tend to discriminate between combatants and non-combatants, and have some scruples about collateral damage. The Feds labor beneath no similar burdens.

Roughly eighteen years after Connolly and Bulger created an alliance between the FBI and the Mob, the FBI annihilated scores of civilians during the assault on the Branch Davidians outside Waco. Among the victims were seventeen small children. During the 51-day siege that led to the final assault, FBI followed a strategy denounced by one former federal official as "torturing the children to make their parents surrender"; this included cutting off the water supply, barraging the domicile with lights and loud noises in order to prevent sleep, and various other forms of intimidation and threats. This protracted ordeal began with a needless (and illegal) ATF assault that left several Davidians and federal agents dead; it ended with an attack with poison gas and incendiary rounds, resulting in a holocaust that wiped out nearly the entire religious community.

Just days ago, U.S. occupation forces in Iraq conducted a raid on a home near Balad that was suspected of concealing a suspected "insurgent." Under fire, the troops called for reinforcements, both from aircraft and armor. The home was demolished, killing several civilians—including four or five children, including 6-month-old child.

While the troops obviously didn't target the children, it is to be expected that children will be harmed anytime the military attacks a home. But the people running the regime that rules us, unlike Kevin Weeks and other Mob hitmen, have no scruples about killing children.

A few months prior to the Waco Holocaust, FBI sniper Lon Horiuchi made the shot that Kevin Weeks simply couldn't take.

The FBI's Hostage Rescue Team had surrounded the "compound" of the Randy Weaver home near Ruby Ridge, Idaho. ("Compound" is the term used to describe any dwelling that has come under lethal assault by the Feds; the building could be a tarpaper shack barely able to withstand a light breeze, and its occupants could be bedridden geriatrics armed with spitballs, but once a federal attack takes place the event will inevitably be described as a raid on an "armed compound.")

Horiuchi fixed his sights on Vicki Weaver, an unarmed mother holding an infant. An FBI psych profile had identified Vicki as the family's dominant personality; "neutralizing" her would be the key to ending the stand-off, which had grown out of Randy Weaver's refusal to act as an informant within the Aryan Nation white supremacist group. Weaver, a Special Forces veteran with no criminal record, wasn't interested in the Aryan Nation's dogmas, and even less interested in working for the Feds. So another undercover informant lured the cash-strapped Weaver into an "illegal" gun deal.

While Weaver, an honest citizen possessed of some eccentric political ideas, was first entrapped and then assaulted by the Feds, Whitey Bulger—a murderer, racketeer, and sexual predator—was literally wined, dined, and protected by the FBI.

And where Kevin Weeks couldn't carry out his sniper assignment for fear of harming an innocent non-combatant, Lon Horiuchi (who, like Bulger, is in hiding, albeit with federal protection) squeezed the trigger without a second thought.

In the difference that separates Mob assassin Kevin Weeks from federal assassin Lon Horiuchi we can find the exact meaning of the phrase, "good enough for government work."

The Differences between Boys and Girls

Birch Blog, March 30, 2006

After enrolling in a local wrestling club, my oldest sons, William Wallace (8) and Isaiah Athanasius (6) developed a taste for a conditioning drill called "Bulldog"—or, at least, that's what it's called around here.

In the exercise, a small number of competitors are placed in the center of the wrestling room on their hands and knees, and are told to tackle the other kids as they sprint past them. Those who are taken down then become "bulldogs," and join in the hunt until all of the remaining participants have been captured. "Bulldog" combines sprinting, tests of agility, skill development (in this case, take-downs), and wholesome violence.

The kids love "Bulldog" so much they don't realize that they're being run ragged, although their grateful parents recognize the benefits when their boys come home and go right to bed, their anarchic energies temporarily depleted.

The club's enrollment includes kids from five years of age to about fifteen. Among that number are several young girls, who are there primarily for the conditioning benefits. One of them, a lovely little ten-year-old Latina, is an instinctive grappler who will do very well in Judo someday. She has a knack for unbalancing her opponents, and more than holds her own against boys her age in the live take-down competitions—due, at least in part, to the inhibited way the boys behave when they are required to place hands on a girl and throw her to the mat. That sort of thing doesn't come naturally to 8-to-10-year-old boys, particularly after they've absorbed several years of admonitions about not picking on girls.

During one round of "Bulldog," that talented and athletic 10-year-old girl received a rude reality check in the form of a full-speed collision with my 8-year-old son, who was looking the other way and had no opportunity to avoid the girl or mitigate the blow. The results were predictable, and momentarily worrisome. She was bruised and had the wind knocked out of her, but otherwise unharmed—to my great relief, as well as that of her mother, since a concussion had been a very good possibility.

Another favorite drill is the "Human Tug-of-War," in which participants are told to push, pull, or drag each other across No Man's Land.

"You ought to see what it's like when we get the High School wrestlers out doing this," chuckled the coach amid the mayhem. "Elbows, shoulder-blocks, punches—those kids let it all fly."

I mentioned to him a similar conditioning drill-*cum*-gangfight called "Shepherd Ball" or "Black-Bottom," which was devised by our High School wrestling coach in Rexburg, Idaho. Participants were taken into the padded wrestling room and divided into numerically identical teams of approximately the same aggregate weight. A "ball" was fashioned from a towel that had been wrapped in duct tape. Goals consisted of a duct-taped square on opposing walls, placed just above eye-level.

"Okay," Coach Karges told us. "The objective is for each team to get the 'ball' into the box, in any way this can be accomplished. The other team can do anything it wants to stop them. Have fun."

Then he'd blow a whistle, and testosterone-fueled trench warfare would ensue. Imagine Rugby minus the rules and the delicacy for which that sport is renowned. Very quickly the field would be thinned down as the smaller and less pathologically competitive participants were culled out. Sometimes we were dimly aware of the coach's indulgent—nay, sadistic—laughter as he watched the spectacle unfold. Occasionally he would leave the room—and the *real* fun would begin.

The first couple of times we played "Shepherd Ball," my younger brother Jeff (we're adopted "Irish Twins," born within a year of each other) and I were assigned to the same team. Despite the fact that we are not blood-related, we had roughly the same build, and a nearly identical taste for combat sports. Each of us took turns using the other as a battering ram. So Coach Karges pretty soon made a point of splitting us up.

How I **loved** that game. Needless to say, co-ed "Shepherd Ball" didn't exist.

As the comedian and philosopher Sinbad would put it, "Women be different than men." Where contact sports (let alone collision sports, like Football, and combat sports, like wrestling) are concerned, those differences achieve salience at around age ten or eleven, if not sooner. There is the occasional anomaly, a virago who punches over her weight, as it were. But a brutal, non-negotiable fact of nature is that the half of humanity equipped with dangling anatomy has a functional monopoly on those roles involving violent physical conflict between humans.

It has become *de rigeur* for television programs to depict women in combat roles, as police officers, security personnel, or soldiers. The recent versions of *Star Trek*, for example, seemed to operate under a studio directive to the effect that every depiction of a security team would include at least one female, preferably in a leadership role.

The film *Starship Troopers*—*not*, I emphasize, the novel on which it was based—depicted women as combat ground-pounders, taking fire with the male grunts and indifferently showering alongside them. Early in that film, Dizzy Flores, a beautiful, small-boned female, is shown playing quarterback for her school's football team; at one point she dispatches a blitzing defender by lowering her shoulder and bowling him over.

Yeah, right.

Spectacles of that sort might be expected in science fiction. But the "Xena, Warrior Princess" conceit is increasingly at work in public policy circles as well. *I Am A Soldier, Too*, plaintively insists the title of Jessica Lynch's autobiography. The appropriate response is: No, you're not; you're a pretty, fragile blond girl from West Virginia who enlisted in the Army for reasons of indigence and had no business being within a continent of a combat zone.

The March 28 issue of *Thrive Weekly*, a Boise community newspaper, praises the "toughness" and "tenacity" of the "Women of the Boise Police Department." Yes, the Sistahs are doin' it for themselves, insists writer Erin Ryan, who seems to think that police work is a vehicle for self-actualization.

"The next time you get in a bar brawl downtown," writes Ryan, "thank whatever god you pray to that Sgt. Danielle Young is no longer on that beat. She may be 5 feet 1 inch tall and only 120 pounds, but she knows how to throw a punch."

"I'm tiny," says Young, "but any of the guys who have been in fights with me know better. . . . You have to have a Jack Russell Terrier mentality, like 'I weigh 120 pounds, but I think I weigh 300 pounds.' It's all about how you carry yourself. You have to have a commanding presence."

Awwwww, isn't that cute?

No, it isn't. It's delusional.

I find myself offering a prayer of gratitude that Sgt. Young's place on bar patrol has been taken by someone more qualified. A soprano voice issuing from a tiny blond woman doesn't translate into "a commanding presence," but rather into an incitement. And a Jack Russell Terrier shouldn't be playing "Bulldog" with Rottweilers.

The legendary Sheriff Buford Pusser could often break up a bar fight simply by walking into the room. Bo Dietl, who worked as a police detective in a particularly grungy section of New York City, never once had to pull his gun. This isn't just because they were formidable physical specimens—Pusser a former pro wrestler who once "fought" a bear, Dietl an accomplished amateur power-lifter. It was because they coupled their naturally commanding physical presence with a talent for de-escalating dangerous situations.

The only way that a small, blond woman can assert "command" in a bar brawl is through the implicit threat of lethal violence from the large armed men who necessarily have her back.

De-escalation under those circumstances is much less likely—which is just fine for those who believe that the police should be in the business of making the public submit to "reality" as the state seeks to reconstruct it.

Perverts with Power

Birch Blog, April 5, 2006

One otherwise pleasant afternoon last February, the agreeable torpor of the Little Falls Library in Bethesda, Maryland was dispelled by the arrival of two stern-faced men wearing uniforms topped by baseball caps bearing the legend "Homeland Security."

The jacked-up martinets loudly informed library patrons that the "viewing of Internet pornography was forbidden," reported the *Washington Post*. They then pounced on some schmo at a local Internet computer and demanded that he step outside. A librarian jumped into the fray, and the two heroic defenders of the *Vaterland* eventually had to leave without their prey.

This feat of spectacular ineptitude required the skill-set found in a particular kind of bully—a human type that is well-represented in government, particularly in the homeland security apparatus. Private sector thugs wouldn't target bookworms for intimidation, and probably wouldn't leave with their tails between their legs after getting called out by a librarian. The Montgomery County affiliate of the *Abteilung der Vaterlandsicherheit* doesn't have jurisdiction over obscenity laws, but it has to do *something* to justify its $3.6 million budget, and a public library is a soft target.

It's likely that at the exact moment the poor schlub in Bethesda was being harassed by Homeland Security goons for his taste in websites, Silver Spring resident Brian Doyle was in a chatroom trying to arrange a sexual liaison with an underage girl. Doyle, the fourth highest-ranking official in the propaganda directorate for the federal Homeland Security Department, was arrested last night (Tuesday, April 4) and charged with "trying to 'seduce' a 14-year-old Polk County [Florida] girl over the Internet," reports *The Ledger* of Lakeland. Doyle "didn't know he was communicating with an undercover Polk County Sheriff's detective."

Doyle began his sexual overtures on March 12 after reading the profile of the nonexistent young girl on an Internet site. He did nothing to disguise his identity; apparently, he even used his position at Homeland Security as a come-on. Arrested at his home in Silver Spring, Doyle was booked into Montgomery County jail and prepped for extradition to Florida. I wonder if he will have the chance to chat with the County Homeland Security department's intrepid cyber-porn police.

61

When news of this story broke last night I was irresistibly reminded of the opening scenes of *"V" for Vendetta*, which is set in the quasi-totalitarian England of a few years hence. After breaking curfew en route to a late-night assignation, the heroine, Evey, is surrounded by three leering, malodorous predators who identify themselves as "Fingermen"—agents of the secret police hired to enforce the curfew. They are empowered to do whatever they please to women who break the curfew, and are prepared to rape and otherwise molest Evey when she is rescued by the masked terrorist who gives the movie its name.

Later in the film, Evey reluctantly goes undercover to entrap the corrupt Archbishop of Canterbury, a servant of the regime (rather than God) with a penchant for underage girls. Evey, a winsome girl in her early 20s, is considered a bit long in the tooth for the Archbishop's taste, but she compensates by donning an infantilizing costume. The concupiscent cleric—whose previous career included a stint participating in bio-warfare experiments using innocent people as test subjects—is so intent on sating his illicit lust that he ignores Evey's warnings that V is about to kill him.

As is attested by the existence of kitschy smut films of the *Ilsa, She-Wolf of the SS* variety, the nexus between totalitarian police organs and sexual depravity is well-known, if only dimly understood. The contrast between the puritanical public face of German National Socialism and the unfathomable private depravity of its leadership caste, appeals to the prurient interests of people who regard the Nazi regime as a lurid anomaly, rather than a particularly forceful expression of every government's latent capacity for mass murder and wanton destruction.

One need not be Freudian to perceive a connection between the *libido sexualis* and the *libido dominandi*—the lust to rule over others. Emancipating the latter will usually involve releasing any restraints on the former. Many who find themselves at the top of the totalitarian pyramid aren't all that interested in indulging their sexual whims (although some are—Mao, for example). But the appeal of such indulgences is attractive to the personality type found manning the regime's instruments of repression. And it's all that much better if the regime can garb its amorality in the radiant rhetoric of liberation.

"We reject the old systems of morality," declared the first issue of *Krasnyi Mech* (The Red Sword), a newspaper published by the Cheka, the ancestor of the Soviet KGB:

No Quarter

> Our morality has no precedent, and our humanity is absolute because it rests on a new ideal. Our aim is to destroy all forms of oppression and violence. To us, everything is permitted, for we are the first to raise the sword not to oppress races and reduce them to slavery, but to liberate humanity from its shackles. . . . Blood? Let blood flow like water, for only through the death of the old world can we liberate ourselves. . . .

No, gentle reader, those sentiments weren't expressed in a speech by George W. Bush extolling the Glorious Global Democratic Revolution, or in a fawning editorial published by a lickspittle courtier scribbler in *National Review* heaping servile praise on the Dear Leader for his bold vision—although I can see where reasonable people might make such a mistake.

Impunity plus sanctimony generally equals mass depravity. Accordingly, it's not surprising that the ranks of the Cheka—the chief instrument of Soviet terror—were quickly filled by the most degenerate elements of society. "This organization is rotten to the core," observed Bolshevik official Serafina Gopner in a March 22, 1919 letter to Lenin. Those who enlisted to be the "sword and shield" of the revolution were, almost without exception, "common criminals and the dregs of society, men armed to the teeth who simply execute anyone they don't like. They steal, loot, rape . . . practice extortion and blackmail, and will let anyone go in exchange for huge sums of money."

"The Cheka are looting and arresting everyone indiscriminately," reported a Bolshevik regional secretary in Yaroslavl on September 26th of the same year. "Safe in the knowledge that they cannot be punished, they have transformed the Cheka headquarters into a huge brothel where they take all the bourgeois women. Drunkenness is rife. Cocaine is being used quite widely among the supervisors."

(Incidentally, these quotations are drawn from *The Black Book of Communism*, an indispensable study published in 1997.)

Accused pedophile/predator Brian Doyle, we will be assured, is an anomaly, just like the handful of "bad apples" at Abu Ghraib, the relatively few Transportation Security Administration drones who pilfer property from air travelers or abuse wheelchair-bound elderly women, the random protected FBI informant—or Special Agent on the take to the Mob—who commits murder while on the federal payroll. . . .

2006

I grant that we're not yet living in Amerika or the United Soviet States of America. But the trend-line is obvious, and the gradient of our descent into totalitarianism is increasingly steep.

Perverts with Power, Part II: The Plot Sickens

Birch Blog, April 5, 2006

The wheels of the blogosphere grind coarsely, but exceedingly fast.

The heroic Jim Bovard, author of numerous valuable forensic studies of the myriad crimes committed by our rulers, adds some critical background regarding Homeland Security honcho—and accused cyber-pederast—Brian Doyle.

"After [Transportation Security Administration] air marshals gunned down Rigoberto Alpizar outside of a plane in Miami last December, Doyle justified the killing to the media: 'He threatened that he had a bomb in his backpack,'" Bovard recalls. "Other TSA spokesmen claimed that Alpizar had shouted that he had a bomb as he ran up and down the plane aisle. None of the passengers on the plane heard Alpizar say anything about a bomb." Of course, Bovard wryly comments, "false statements by federal spokesmen are a public service, not a federal crime."

Doyle used his position at the Department of Homeland Security as a come-on in what he believed was a cyber-chat with an underage girl. I grant that it's hard to believe that any self-respecting pedophile would admit to working for the Bush administration, but there it is.

"What has this nation come to if bragging about being a spokesman for a federal agency can supposedly help a guy get laid?" asks Bovard. As it happens, this wasn't actually an effective pickup line, since the recipient was actually a police detective posing as a 14-year-old girl. While there have been "gross abuses in some previous online porn stings," Bovard notes, there is reason to believe that "Mr. Doyle could be on the other end of the wand for a long time."

Doyle may find himself in the company of at least two other disgraced agents of the *Heimatsicherheitsdienst* (formerly referred to in this space as the *Abteilung der Vaterlandsicherheit*; reader Gene Berkman of Riverside, California's Renaissance Books kindly suggested the punchier translation).

Frank Figueroa, the former head of a federal anti-molester initiative called "Operation Predator," was arrested at an Orlando shopping mall last October 25. He was charged with exposing himself to a 16-year-old girl and, ah, engaging in the practice made famous in Philip Roth's most notable novel.

Confronted by mall security as he tried to flee the scene, Figueroa whipped out something else he was unduly proud of: The badge identifying him as the special agent in charge of the Tampa office of the Department of Immigration and Customs enforcement—one of the main appendages, as it were, of the DHS.

Other bloggers have keyed on a fleeting but important disclosure found in the transcript of the February 3 installment of *Dateline NBC*. The news magazine chronicled a sting operation for sexual cyber-predators conducted by the program in conjunction with California's Riverside County Sheriff's Department and an activist group bearing the unfortunate name Perverted Justice.

Various men ranging in age from 19 to the mid-60s had conducted sexually explicit online conversations with what they believed to be boys or girls 12 or 13 years of age. They agreed to a rendezvous at a house in Southern California, where a Dateline correspondent and camera crew awaited them—as well as a contingent from the Sheriff's Department.

Among those snagged was an officer of the Department of Homeland Security named Michael Burks.

"My father was a police officer," whines Burks as he is interrogated by detectives. "I was a police officer. I work for the Department of Homeland Security. I understand you guys have a job to do and I'm not trying to tell anything else other than that. I swear to God, as God is my witness, I'm wearing a St. Michael's medal right now, okay? I was not going to do anything with her."

Decades ago, F.A. Hayek observed (I'm paraphrasing liberally) that in politics, it is the scum, rather than the cream, that rises to the top. The DHS perverts we're dealing with here are mid-level functionaries. One wonders what we would find if we had a candid look at the behavior of those who've climbed to the top of the slippery pole.

Perverts with Power, Part III: Bad Touches from the TSA

Birch Blog, April 14, 2006

This is just getting sick:

> A Ketchum [Idaho] resident employed by the federal Transportation Security Administration was arrested Tuesday on one count of second-degree kidnapping.

A 49-year-old man identified as Robert Joe Harrison Jr. was arrested by the local police on April 11 after he had brought home a 10-year-old boy whom he had enticed into his pickup truck. The boy left and described the incident to his mother, who called the police. The suspect is employed by the *Heimatsicherheitsdienst* (or HSD, the name of the Department of Homeland Security in the original German) as a "screener"—you know, those pleasant people who loiter around in airports, where they perform such vital functions as fondling nubile females, as well as the occasional pregnant young mother, while helping themselves to whatever swag they can pilfer from passenger luggage.

It defies belief that a suspected child kidnapper could be found lurking in the talent pool from which such sterling public servants are drawn. (For the benefit of Sean Hannity and other cerebrally deficient people: I'm being sarcastic.)

Mr. "Harrison" insisted to police that he had never seen the youngster. However, as a follow-up report from MSNBC relates, the police "found four additional Social Security numbers and documents showing four other dates of birth" during a search of the apartment. So the HSD doesn't even know the real identity of this guy.

"Harrison"—who bears an uncanny resemblance to Jim Bonnick, a small-time con-man from the TV series "Magnum, PI"—is the *fourth* potential pederast discovered in the ranks of the HSD in the last week. It makes me wonder how many HSD officials belong to the department's "Aqualung Club."[1]

When they're not preying on kids, the gallant agents of the HSD have been terrorizing them by abusing innocent teachers in front of them. On April 4,

Leander Pickett, a teacher's assistant at Englewood Elementary school in Jacksonville, Florida, was bracketed by a pair of the HSD's finest, slammed against a car, handcuffed, and held for 30 minutes—for no reason at all.

While directing bus traffic in front of the school, Pickett noticed a couple of disreputable-looking men in a car blocking the loading zone.

"I walked up to [the driver] and said, 'Sir, you need to move,'" recalls Pickett. "That's when he said 'I'm a police officer. I'm with Homeland Security. . . I'll move when I want to.' That's when he started grabbing me on my arm."

Ah, yes: We're with the Government, and we can do what we want—the eternal refrain of the tax-feeding parasite class. Pickett was assaulted by those chair-moisteners for making a reasonable request—although once he learned that they were with the HSD, Pickett was probably understandably concerned for the safety of the schoolchildren.

"Mr. Pickett asked the guy blocking the bus loading zone to move, and the guy told him he would move his car when he got ready to move it," confirmed eyewitness Alton Jackson, a coach at the school. A second eyewitness, school employee Terri Dreisonstok, added: "At that point I intervened, and I went up to the gentleman and said, 'Mr. Pickett is an employee here,' and they said it didn't matter."

School principal Gail Brinson, who also witnessed the unprovoked assault, recalled: "'We're with Homeland Security,' and on and on they went, and pretty soon, before you know it, [Pickett] is handcuffed and slammed against a car. . . . All the children are watching, they're all upset."

Pickett was released without being charged and—of course—without receiving an apology. Being a Fed means *never* having to say you're sorry.

"You know you hear these stories every day and say, 'This will never happen to me,' but . . . it happened to me," comments Pickett. "If this is Homeland Security, I think we ought to be a little afraid."

Not to put too fine a point on the matter, Pickett isn't exaggerating. Since 9/11, Homeland Security agents—TSA screeners, Air Marshals, and various other functionaries—have harassed, intimidated, terrorized, and (in the case of Rigoberto Alpizar) murdered American citizens, while al Qaeda has injured nobody within our shores during the same period. That contrast is instructive, to those whose minds have not been clotted with partisan cant about the regime's efforts to protect us from the Evil-Doers.

[1] For those insufficiently familiar with 1970s-era rock—and you should be ashamed of yourselves!—"Aqualung" refers not to the self-contained underwater breathing apparatus, but rather the track of that title by the British group Jethro Tull. The central figure of that song is pictured "Sitting on a park bench, eyeing little girls with bad intent. . . ."

Henceforth, "Aqualung" will be the unofficial anthem of the *Heimatsicherheitsdienst*, in memory (not in "honor," of course) of J. Brian Doyle, Robert Figueroa, Michael Burks, and now "Robert Joe Harrison Jr."—the distilled, evil essence of the HSD.

April 19, 1993

Birch Blog, April 19, 2006

When the smoke cleared on February 28, 1993 following the shootout at Mt. Carmel near Waco, Texas, six members of the Branch Davidian sect were dead, along with four agents of the Bureau of Alcohol, Tobacco, and Firearms.

The ATF's attack, code-named "Showtime," was intended as an exercise in spin control: By taking down an armed, eccentric religious community headed by a suspected polygamist whose alleged seraglio was said to include teenage girls, the ATF would banish from the headlines a recent sexual harassment scandal at the agency. It was supposed to be a simple smash-and-grab raid—a "cakewalk," to use the now familiar term.

With air support from helicopters, ATF paramilitaries would swarm the Davidian "compound" (as any dwelling under federal assault is inevitably described), kick in the doors, drag the group's leader David Koresh away in irons, display the community's "arsenal" (as any collection of weapons seized by the Feds is inevitably described) as trophies, and wrap things up in time to enjoy rhapsodic media coverage over brewskis during a victory party at the local bar.

The Davidians, however, didn't follow the script.

For months in advance of the raid, Koresh had attempted to clear up the ATF's contrived concerns about his "arsenal." Hours before the raid began, Koresh confronted Richard Rodriguez, the ATF informant inside the Mt. Carmel community, in an attempt to prevent the attack. After the raiders arrived, but before they opened fire, Koresh emerged from the sanctuary and pleaded—without avail—for the Feds not to attack.

The ATF had expected to conduct an armed publicity stunt. It quickly found itself in a hell-for-leather firefight—and it got its ass kicked good and hard, as it richly deserved to.

Yes, it is a tragedy that ten human beings died in that needless exchange of gunfire. It's a shame that the ATF administrative pukes who planned the attack weren't the first off the flatbed trucks and into the line of fire that morning. The ATF agents, having committed an act of lawless aggression, were forced to withdraw; the Davidians, in command of the battlefield, held their fire as the attackers gathered their dead and wounded.

A criminal assault on a peaceful community had been repelled through righteous, lawful force. This was a victory for liberty, albeit one achieved at a terrible cost.

The Feds, of course, had to even the score—and then some. The result was the holocaust that claimed scores of innocent lives thirteen years ago today, an atrocity that resulted from a chemical warfare attack staged by the FBI with hands-on support from Delta Force commandos.

The most charitable assessment of the Feds' actions on April 19 would lead to the conclusion that those who planned and carried out the gas attack were guilty of mass murder through depraved indifference.

But the forensic evidence leads to the unavoidable conclusion that something much worse than indifference was at work.

Forward-looking infrared footage of the final assault offers incontestable evidence that automatic weapons fire was directed into the burning sanctuary, ensuring that there would be no survivors. Those seeking to flee the fire would be cut down; meanwhile, the FBI kept firefighting and emergency vehicles miles away.

Obviously, the Feds were determined to annihilate the Davidians. The Waco Holocaust was an act of undisguised state terrorism and mass murder. The raid out of which that crime grew was planned during the administration of George Bush the Elder, but consummated in the early days of Bill Clinton's reign.

I have previously made the point that the government under which we suffer is immeasurably worse than even the most depraved criminal syndicate. An illustration of that principle can be found in an anecdote related by Howie Carr in his new book *The Brothers Bulger*, which recounts the history of the FBI's relationship with James "Whitey" Bulger, the head of Boston's Irish Mob.

In May 1965, Raymond Patriarca, the head of the Italian Mob in Boston, was having problems with a hitman named Joe Barboza, who wanted permission to whack an unidentified hoodlum on whom Patriarca had a contract.

"He lives in a three-story house," Barboza told Patriarca in a conversation recorded by an FBI informant. "So what I'm gonna do is, I'm gonna break into the basement and pour gasoline all around and torch the place, after which I either get him with the smoke inhalation or I pick him off when he's climbing out the window."

"Barboza had worked out a plan for every contingency," relates Carr. "He would bring three shooters with him, to watch each side of the house. They

71

would cut the telephone lines to the houses, so that the victim couldn't call the fire department. And just in case one of the neighbors called, before setting the house on fire Barboza planned to phone in false alarms across the city to tie up every fire company."

This proposed Mob hit anticipated the FBI's plan for April 19 in uncanny detail: The use of fire to kill the targeted victim(s), either through immolation or asphyxiation; the use of snipers to pick off anybody who flees; cutting off communications into and out of the targeted home; interdiction of fire and emergency crews. Of course, the Patriarca Family didn't have the luxury of tanks and other armored vehicles equipped with poison gas, as the Feds did on April 19, 1993. Still, it makes one wonder if the plan used by the FBI wasn't in some way inspired by Barboza's proposed hit.

Here's the kicker: ***Patriarca turned down Barboza's plan because it was disproportionate.***

"Patriarca asked Barboza if anyone else lived in [the target's] house, and Barboza mentioned the victim's mother," narrates Carr.

"You're gonna kill his mother too?" Patriarca asked.

"It ain't my fault she lives there," snorted the hitman.

"Patriarca canceled the contract," concludes Carr.

The FBI displayed no similar capacity for mercy in its treatment of the Branch Davidians.

Oh, by the way: Barboza, a deranged mass murderer, was recruited by the FBI to serve as a protected informant. A few years later, the Bureau recruited another Boston thug named Steve Flemmi—another psychotic killer who was also an incorrigible pedophile—to be a "top echelon" informant. Flemmi was part of a package deal with James Bulger, another murderer and pederast.

During the quarter century they were able to murder, extort, and rape with impunity as FBI assets, Flemmi and Bulger managed to kill perhaps half as many people as the Feds annihilated on April 19, 1993.

Mongols and Feds

Birch Blog, April 20, 2006

As a teenager in Rexburg, Idaho, I lived with my family across the street from one of that community's few bars, an establishment bearing the unappealing name "POD's Place" (the acronym, I was told, stood for "Poor Old Don," the owner). One Saturday each year, in either July or August, the bar's parking lot would be filled with hundreds of motorcycles as the Hells Angels would stop for a beer or two hundred en route to Yellowstone National Park.

For reasons obvious to anyone whose cerebral output is sufficient to cause an EEG needle to twitch—and perhaps even to Sean Hannity, for that matter—everybody gave the Angels a wide berth while they were in Rexburg. The few individual gang members I saw from across the street didn't seem to be *all that*, but even as a testosterone-intoxicated teenager I knew better than to test that perception by doing something rash, like crossing the street and chatting them up. Or even letting them catch me looking their direction.

During the subsequent quarter-century, I served several stints in various bar bands, playing some mixture of Country and Classic Rock. In that line of work I played in more than a few biker bars, and met my share of biker gang members, many of whom defied the relevant stereotypes. Some of them were exceptionally nice people. Since I neither drink nor have any interest in controlled substances, those contacts didn't involve illicit transactions of any sort. I found that many of them shared my appreciation for Thin Lizzy (no, that's not an anorexic model, for those of you shamefully ignorant of history's finest rock band and the staggering genius of its frontman/lyricist, the immortal Philip Lynott).

There was nothing appealing to me about the biker gang milieu, and a great deal about it I found repulsive. But it was a world that I could easily avoid, and as long as I didn't actively seek to borrow trouble, as it were, I was okay.

William Queen, an undercover agent for the Bureau of Alcohol, Tobacco, and Firearms, borrowed a ton of trouble during a two-and-a-half-year assignment to infiltrate the Mongols Motorcycle Club. After a long and very dangerous probationary period, during which he was subjected by the Mongols to a background screening more rigorous than the one administered to applicants for the Department of Homeland Security (I exaggerate not one whit), Queen, under the cover name Billy St. John, was "patched in" as a Mongol. (The expression refers to the gang insignia worn on motorcycle jackets.)

The Mongols are less than minuscule in membership, boasting some 350 members across the U.S. and Mexico. But they are considered to be fiercer and more formidable than the supposed gold standard for Outlaw Motorcycle Gangs (OMGs), the Hells Angels. Queen recounts a confrontation in Laughlin, Nevada during which he "stood shoulder-to-shoulder with the Mongols against the notorious Hells Angels. We . . . backed them down. Right in their own yard, in front of God and every other eyewitness."

Owing to the brief and superficial contacts I had with the world of OMGs, I admire Queen's intrepidity. However, after reading his memoir *Under and Alone* (the film rights to which have been bought by Mel Gibson, who wants to play the role of Queen/St. John), I find myself wondering what exactly was the point of the whole exercise—apart from enhancing the power and prestige of the even more dangerous gang Queen worked for full-time.

After Queen's undercover assignment ended in May 2000, a nationwide raid by ATF Special Response Teams and various law enforcement agencies against Mongol members across the country "netted some seventy illegal firearms, including handguns, machine guns, and assault rifles, as well as explosives; seventeen stolen motorcycles; two kilograms of cocaine; significant quantities of marijuana and methamphetamine; and tens of thousands of dollars in cash."

That's *it*?

Queen's exceptionally perilous undercover assignment alienated his children and his ex-wife, who learned what he had been doing only after they were seized by the Feds in California, taken into the Witness Protection Program, and re-settled a continent away in Florida. Perhaps this would have been worthwhile if he had uncovered a terrorist cell bent on killing dozens, scores, or hundreds of people. But all he could show for his efforts was the seizure of seventy "illegal" firearms. The rest of the haul (which was actually pretty pitiful) had nothing to do with the ATF's area of responsibility. And since the ATF has no constitutional reason to exist, the gun seizure is a pretty slender reed on which to rest this whole undertaking.

Indeed, for those (like myself) who regard the War on Drugs to be a murderous and unnecessary farce, the only worthwhile result of this operation was the recovery of the stolen motorcycles, which almost certainly could have been accomplished without federal intervention. The same is true of the other violent crimes against persons and property (including murder) committed by members of the Mongol gang, as described in Queen's book.

Almost as if to compensate for the operation's trivial achievements, Queen spends a great deal of time ruminating on the Mongol gang's capacity for mayhem. He infiltrated the gang as part of the FedGov's effort "to curb a growing problem of organized violence in the United States." Worthy as that objective is, I'm constrained to point out that the Federal Government is by far the greatest practitioner of organized violence not only in our country, but in the world.

Reflecting on the physical and sexual abuse inflicted on wives and girlfriends of Mongols, Queen describes the impunity enjoyed by those who belong to the gang: "While they are wearing that patch, they are untouchable to the world at large. No one can make trouble for them without bringing down the fury of the whole Mongol Nation."

The same can be said of the tax-enriched gang-bangers who proudly wear the insignia of the Federal Government. Daunting as it may be to contemplate the wrath of the Mongol Nation, that "nation" doesn't have an army, air force, or nuclear weapons. The Branch Davidians discovered that resisting an illegal assault by Queen's gang, the ATF, brought down the fury of the entire apparatus of federal repression.

"Living full-time as an outlaw gave me a perspective few law-enforcement officers ever get to experience," writes Queen. "I was often more at risk from my supposed brothers in blue than from my adopted brothers in the gang. Just as there were some decent qualities—loyalty, love, respect—among the outlaw bikers, there were some law-enforcement officers who were little more than outlaws with badges."

To which many law-abiding citizens, suffering under the heel of an increasingly federalized, centralized, and militarized garrison state leviathan would react: "Gee, ya *think*?"

I don't mean to minimize the seriousness of the crimes committed by Mongols and other outlaw bikers. But the dangers posed by the Mongols and other OMGs are eminently avoidable. This isn't true of the depredations committed by the criminal syndicate called the federal government. While the Mongols have done many terrible and bloody things, they—unlike the gang that provided William Queen's paycheck—never shot up a church.

The Robber State

Birch Blog, April 27, 2006

Thieves for their robbery have authority when judges steal themselves.

—Shakespeare, *Measure for Measure*

In cities and counties across our fair land, cops are turning into robbers:

Cleveland, Ohio: A newly enacted "emergency ordinance" permits the confiscation of automobiles from citizens who "are associated with four or more of any combination of unpaid parking infraction judgments and/or notices of liability" for such things as "red light or speeding violations."

Under the proposed ordinance, observes the invaluable online journal *TheNewspaper.com*, "the guilt or innocence of the owner to the original charge is irrelevant. . . . [S]eized vehicles will only be released if the owner admits guilt and pays towing, storage, impound and administration fees on top of the cost of the original tickets. . . ." Those who receive four tickets in the mail as a result of camera enforcement—a process that is not reviewed for accuracy—must plead guilty in order to have their automobiles returned. "The city plans to make $4 million a year from camera tickets," continues the report, which also notes that "the cash-strapped city" will plow some of the proceeds into hiring bounty hunters "to collect on unpaid tickets."

Peoria, Illinois: Another "emergency ordinance" enacted in that fine city will permit police—acting on their own subjective and definitive assessment—to confiscate vehicles with excessively loud stereos. "The city will collect $105 in fees for the first offense, and $355 on subsequent offenses without first offering the accused a defense in a proper court of law," summarizes *The Newspaper.com*.

I yield to no one in my abhorrence of what pours forth from too many car stereos, particularly that aural pestilence called "Rap" (as I've said before, music is to Rap as food is to that which food becomes). I would much rather deal with peripatetic nitwits assailing me from all sides with the simian outpourings of 50 Cent and his ilk than with a police department empowered to seize property at whim.

God help us if this variety of totalitarianism plays in Peoria.

Et tu, Delaware?: "Delaware Insurance Commissioner Matt Denn held an event . . . touting the state's use of agents who confiscate license plates belonging to anyone the commission's database says is uninsured," reports *The Newspaper*. "Last June, lawmakers enacted a provision granting insurance commission agents the authority to mail a letter to the registered owner of any vehicle the computer database believes is uninsured. Seven days later, if the owner has not proved his innocence, the agents will attempt to locate the vehicle and take its license plates. Each time, the state will collect substantial fines for the retrieval of the plates."

Houston, we have a problem—namely, a police force addicted to DUI revenue: "Police officers in Houston, Texas are earning massive salaries by arresting individuals for drunk driving." Members of a Driving While Intoxicated Task Force, which receives federal subsidies (natch) for overtime, are making more than City Mayor Bill White. The average salary of the eight task force members is $103,000.

"Poor but honest cops"? Yeah, *right*.

Federal Land Grab underway in Utah: Needless to say, the criminal syndicate called the Federal Government is deeply involved in this variety of plunder. This is hardly surprising, since Washington subsidizes much, if not most, of the thuggish behavior described above, and has abetted the corruption of state and local police by encouraging the practice of "asset forfeiture"—in which property and money suspected of being connected to narcotics trafficking can be seized without Due Process.

The 1992 murder of California millionaire Donald Scott by a narcotics enforcement SWAT team had its origins in a scheme to "forfeit" his property. Police purportedly spotted, from the air, a small quantity of marijuana (by some counts, a single plant) growing on Scott's property. A single marijuana plant provided a slender reed on which to rest the case for a late-night home invasion of Scott's dwelling, during which he was gunned down for confronting the armed intruders with a gun in his hand.

From the *Salt Lake City Weekly* comes news of a similar scheme underway in Spanish Fork Canyon. Last August, Trudy Childs and her family leased their Canyon property for use in an "electronic music concert." The Childs got all of the proper permits, hired EMTs, and otherwise cross all of the myriad T's and dotted all the requisite I's.

In a development surprising to nobody with a scintilla of knowledge about popular music culture, some concert-goers *may have* consumed psychoactive substances.

In a development that was predictable to students of the emerging garrison state, the concert was subjected to a paramilitary SWAT raid on the pretext that it was an illegal "rave."

Nothing brings out the raw, hairy-chested courage of a Jackbooted Thug like the prospect of doing battle with a group of unarmed, skinny white kids. (I make that observation as a large, brown, gun-owning male who looks a bit like Cobra Bubbles—'cept with hair.)

The Childs had planned to hold a benefit concert later this summer. Trudy Childs recently received a snotty letter from Stephen Sorenson, the gelded hack who serves as acting U.S. attorney for Utah, the relevant portion of which states:

> The United States has received information that you are again considering leasing your property for an outdoor music concert. . . . If you choose to lease your land again for another similar event, we can assure you that there will be drug trafficking on your property. You property can be civilly forfeited to the United States if it is merely used for or facilitates the distribution of narcotics.

Remember when Washington invaded Iraq because, supposedly, at some point Saddam *may* have been able to make unconventional weapons—while the obvious objective was to assume control over Iraq's oil reserves?

Same deal, different context.

"The Childs think Sorenson's sudden interest in their concert plans stems from the federal government wanting to get its hands on their land," reports *Salt Lake Weekly*. "Just one day before the U.S. attorney sent the latter . . . Sorenson had telephoned the Childs' attorney to make an offer on their land on behalf of two federal agencies." The Feds have coveted that property since 1990.

"If they don't want to sell the land, all they have to do is say so," simpers Sorenson. "If they want to avoid the risk of criminal or civil liability, all they need to do is not allow the rave on their property."

The Childs aren't planning a "rave," but rather a benefit concert for Parkinson's disease research. As Childs points out, politically favored figures aren't put through the same wringer she's been fed into: "I attended the Rolling Stones and U2 concerts last year at the Delta Center [in Salt Lake City], and my guess is there were probably drugs being used and probably people under the influence of drugs at both those concerts. Why don't [the Feds] send a letter to Larry Miller [who owns the Delta Center and the Utah Jazz]?"

The obvious answer is that Miller doesn't have what the Feds—of whom the epicene fascist Stephen Sorenson is a perfect specimen—are interested in stealing, at least right now.

How Whitey Bulger Bought Boston

The American Conservative magazine, May 2006

Peggy Westcoat was a woman of small skills and modest ambitions. Just before Christmas in 1980, two men broke into the single-family home Peggy shared with a live-in boyfriend in southwest Dade County. The intruders threw a rope around the boyfriend's neck and hanged him near the front door. They then grabbed Peggy, shoved her against the kitchen sink, draped a noose around her neck, and began feeding the other end of the rope into a garbage disposal.

With the rope tight enough to terrify the victim without rendering her unconscious, the assailants turned off the grinder and began asking the terrified woman about her work as a cashier at the Miami "fronton" (or arena) of World Jai Alai, an exotic Iberian sport that had been controlled by Bostonians since the 1920s. A few months earlier, World Jai Alai had been sold to a new owner, and Boston's Winter Hill mob—led by James "Whitey" Bulger—wanted to know if the new owners had discovered the mob's skimming operation. Satisfied by Peggy's panicked answers, the invaders flipped the switch on the disposal.

"When the cops found the two bodies the next day," notes *Boston Herald* columnist Howie Carr in *The Brothers Bulger*, "they chalked it up as another Miami drug deal gone bad." In fact, it was just one of scores of murders committed by a Boston crime combine that wedded the Irish mob to the FBI. That marriage eventually broke up in 1996, when Bulger—tipped off by his FBI handler, John Connolly—fled the United States one step ahead of several murder indictments. He is presently number two on the FBI's Most Wanted list, below another one-time asset of the federal government named Osama bin Laden.

Connolly, convicted of various racketeering charges, is in prison until at least 2010. He also faces first-degree murder charges in Florida for allegedly providing information that led to the murder of Peggy Westcoat's one-time boss, World Jai Alai president John Callahan.

At the time of Peggy Westcoat's murder, the head of security for World Jai Alai was retired FBI Special Agent H. Paul Rico. Rico had taken note of Whitey Bulger in the early 1950s, when the future head of the Irish mob was a small-caliber hoodlum working as a homosexual prostitute. Rico, writes Carr, "could justify his sojourns to the Bay Village gay clubs as reaching out to new 'sources.'"

From the very beginning of his career as a South Boston thug, Bulger was an informant. Gangsters planning to hijack a truck "might mention something about a future score to Whitey, just in passing, and sure enough, when they showed up to grab the truck, the FBI or the local cops would be there waiting," Carr recounts. "H. Paul Rico's personnel file soon included commendations from the director, J. Edgar Hoover. At the same time, no one suspected Whitey— it was inconceivable that one of Southie's own would become a rat."

Sent to prison in Atlanta for bank robbery in 1956, Whitey volunteered to serve as a test subject in LSD experiments in exchange for time off his 20-year sentence. "We were recruited by deception," Bulger later complained, recalling that he was supposedly helping find "a cure for schizophrenia." Dr. Jules Pfeiffer, who supervised the experiments, was working off a grant provided by the CIA, which probably wasn't interested in humanitarian applications of the drug.

Whitey returned to Southie in 1965, just in time to benefit from three critical developments.

First, the FBI—in keeping with Robert Kennedy's priorities—had decided to tear into La Cosa Nostra (better known as the Mafia). Special Agent Rico thus began to cultivate informants and allies within the Winter Hill mob, the Mafia's deadly rival.

Second, just days before Whitey's return, one of Rico's informants, Jimmy "The Bear" Flemmi, murdered an undistinguished thug named Edward Deegan. In order to protect their informant, the Boston FBI office conducted a cover-up, sending four admittedly unsavory men to prison for Deegan's murder, which they didn't commit. By collaborating in that murder and cover-up, the Boston FBI office effectively "made its bones" as a full-fledged ally of the Irish mob.

But for Whitey Bulger the most propitious development was the emergence of his younger brother Billy as a rising political star in Bay State politics, which Carr describes as seamlessly integrated with the underworld.

In 1961, when the Kennedy family entered the White House and Billy Bulger made his debut as a state legislator, the informal rules of conduct on Beacon Hill "boiled down to three points: Nothing on the level; everything is a deal; no deal [is] too small," writes Carr. Massachusetts novelist Edwin O'Connor describes state politics as "a special kind of tainted, small-time fellowship" through which "even the sleaziest poolroom bookie managed, in some way, however obscure, to be in touch with the mayor's office or the governor's chair."

Billy Bulger would eventually become president of the state Senate, a post that allowed him to dispense patronage as he saw fit. Boston-born FBI agents like Paul Rico, who confronted mandatory retirement at 50, were eager to cultivate Billy Bulger's favor. By racking up arrests of Italian mobsters, the G-men could earn promotions and plaudits. By taking care of the Bulger family, they could supplement their federal paychecks and maybe arrange cushy post-retirement sinecures at Boston Edison or some other hack habitat.

Before leaving Boston for Miami in 1970, Rico recruited Steve Flemmi, a close associate of Whitey Bulger who was also tied in with the Italian mob, as a "top echelon informant." Five years later, Whitey—who had by then established himself as a secure but unremarkable racketeer—was also granted "top echelon" status. Flemmi would scrape up intelligence on the Italians, and Whitey would pass it along to the feds. As Flemmi later described it, this relationship produced a perverse alchemy: "Me and Whitey gave [the Feds] sh-t, and they gave us gold."

Why was Whitey included in this package deal, when Flemmi was the one with the mob contacts? As Carr points out, the Boston FBI office "didn't need Whitey nearly as much as they needed his brother Billy"—and the favors that Billy could dispense on those who took care of his interests, including Whitey.

By 1980, Whitey, Stevie, and the FBI "were partners," notes Carr. "And from the beginning, it was a one-sided deal. Each side would do 'favors' for the other, but the FBI's were a lot more valuable than the cash and gifts that Whitey and Stevie would pass on to their agents." Whitey and his handler, Special Agent Connolly, had grown up a few blocks apart from each other. They both wanted to take down Boston's Italian mob—Connolly because doing so was the key to promotion within the bureau and Bulger because he wanted to clear the field of any rivals.

Connolly, who has tried unsuccessfully to sell a screenplay lionizing himself as the man who took down the Boston branch of the Mafia, has described his entente with Bulger as a brilliant "business" strategy—protecting one mob chieftain to take down scores of others. But that business arrangement was nothing less than a license for Bulger and his cronies to murder, extort, and rape with impunity. They also seized control over the local narcotics trade even as Bulger was heralded in the *Boston Globe* as a kind-hearted Robin Hood who was "keeping drugs out of Southie."

In his own memoir, *Brutal*, one-time Bulger henchman Kevin Weeks observed of Whitey that while "nothing seemed to relax him or feel quite so good as a murder," he was "calculating" and disciplined in killing. Flemmi, on the other hand, "would kill someone, anywhere, anytime." Bulger and Flemmi were also incorrigible pederasts, the latter indulging a taste for underage girls, the former preying on children of both sexes.

Weeks also claims that Connolly and his corrupt fellow agents did more than merely look the other way. He asserts that Bulger "had six [agents] he could call on anytime and they would willingly hop in the car with him with the machine gun." Being on the take was quite profitable for Connolly. A former secretary testifies that she once saw no fewer than ten uncashed federal paychecks in Connolly's desk—a potent illustration of the contempt he felt for the substantial if unspectacular wages paid to an honest G-man.

While Connolly and his ilk were living large, honest Southies were living in terror. Carr and Weeks both describe the plight of Steve "Stippo" Rakes, a Southie who in 1983 scraped together enough money to buy a small piece of commercial property that he turned into a liquor store—the only one on Old Colony Avenue with convenient parking. As Rakes's store began to prosper, anonymous death threats came spilling from his telephone. He soon fell prey to a Bulger protection racket and was forced to sell his business on concessionary terms. Renamed the South Boston Liquor Mart, the pilfered business soon became a favored hang-out of Bulger's political allies.

During the 1987 Christmas season, relates Carr, "agents of the Boston FBI office bought the booze for the annual holiday party at the South Boston Liquor Mart. For the FBI the price was always right." At John Connolly's retirement party three years later, after the corrupted agent had heaped praise on Billy Bulger for getting him his job at the bureau and arranging his post-retirement gig at Boston Edison, he was handed a bottle of wine he was told came "courtesy of South Boston Liquors." "No finer liquor store in the commonwealth," replied Connolly with a knowing smirk.

What of Steve Rakes, who had that liquor store stolen from him by the FBI's "top echelon informant"? Summoned to testify before two grand juries, Rakes—who had a wife and two daughters to protect—refused to talk. He was eventually convicted of perjury and sentenced to probation. Facing destitution, Rakes sought out a hack job with the Massachusetts Bay Transportation Authority. A friendly politician arranged one for him—in exchange for a $3,000 bribe.

"Absent justice," wrote Augustine in *The City of God*, "what are kingdoms but vast robberies?" The unfathomably corrupt union of the criminal underworld and political "overworld" described by Carr offers a compelling illustration of what Augustine had in mind.

Helot on Wheels

Birch Blog, May 12, 2006

Helot *(n.)—A slave in ancient Sparta who could be killed by the agents of the state with impunity; see* **Krypteia**.

"The basic rule of driver safety, is to avoid recklessness," explained the retired police chief teaching the "Traffic Safety School" I'd been sentenced to attend for the supposed crime of not wearing a seatbelt. "'Recklessness' refers to deviating from the standard a normal person would use."

That's a very sound standard, one in harmony with the Golden Rule, I thought. *So why are volumes of recondite traffic regulations necessary, unless the purpose is to provide stress-free employment for the parasite class?*

Since all of us in the classroom wanted to get out of there as soon as possible, I didn't express that thought aloud.

That uncharacteristic restraint failed me, however, when the instructor turned to the subject of "probable cause."

"A police officer cannot stop your vehicle without probable cause," he explained, "which can take the form of any suspicious driver behavior, or anything suspicious about the vehicle itself." Specific examples cited by the instructor included such things as driving too slowly, glancing nervously at the officer or in the rear-view mirror, reaching toward the floor of the car or into the back seat . . . in brief, just about anything a driver could do, or not do.

My hand shot skyward irresistibly.

"Doesn't that standard of probable cause conflict with the 'normal person' standard you just mentioned?" I asked. "It seems to me unlikely that a normal person would see anything suspicious in any of the behaviors you describe."

The instructor—a genial and very decent man—didn't like the question, but he answered it.

"The defining factor is officer safety," he admitted. "That's something the police officer takes into account, and he will judge your actions on the basis of what threat you may pose to him."

Ah, I see, I thought once again. *Then shouldn't the course be entitled "Officer Safety," rather than "Driver Safety"?*

This conversation took place in the first five minutes of what was scheduled to be a five-hour class, and since I didn't want to steal any more time from my classmates (perhaps "cellmates" would be a better expression), I demurred from further comment.

But the critical disclosure had been made: The key purpose of this exercise was to impress on the student-detainees the fact that they were subordinate to the State and its agents, and those acting on behalf of the State are simply more important than the common run of humanity.

That point was reinforced by a dramatization presented to the class of a woman who is stopped in Ontario, Oregon, and cannot find her driver's license. Because the officer cannot identify her in his computer database, she is arrested and jailed until someone can identify her, and she is cleared of wants and warrants. "You WILL BE HANDCUFFED," the PowerPoint screen admonished the class. "You WILL BE DETAINED."

And this is necessary, we were told, because of the possibility that you would present a danger to the community or, more shockingly, to the incomparably valuable people who represent the Almighty State.

"These laws are made for our safety's sake," explained the co-instructor, a very nice lady about my age. "But there are so many of them the officers can't remember them all."

How reassuring, I thought, *that even those paid to enforce those laws don't know what they are.*

The female instructor described the restrictions placed on young drivers in Oregon by that state's "provisional driver's license," which severely limits how and when they can drive for a year. "There's a big push on to move up he driving age to 17, and then have provisional restrictions apply until age 19," she pointed out. "They do kind of rule you there for a little while, but it's for your own good," she soothingly assured the younger detainees.

That's quite interesting, I mused. *What this means is that you could be of draft age—18 years old—and not qualified to operate a motor vehicle without restrictions. Hmmm. . . what are the odds that this might be used as a way of forcing kids to register for the draft when it's brought back? I'd round them up to, oh, about one hundred percent.*

Nothing is more innately American than owning and driving a car. And in no other activity are most Americans as likely to find themselves on the business end of our proto-totalitarian police state.

The operational assumption of traffic law enforcement, as the instructor so kindly pointed out to me, is that any officer can stop any driver at any time for any reason the officer deems suitable. This includes mis-application of the myriad laws the officer can enforce but doesn't need to know—although where drivers are concerned, "ignorance of the law is no excuse."

Drivers aren't free citizens. We're helots on wheels, as it were.

Through grants issued on the pretext of fighting drunk driving and seatbelt laws, the federal government (or, to be blunt, The Enemy) has effectively taken control of both the legislative and enforcement policies of the states regarding traffic safety. The Enemy's intention, of course, is to absorb all state and local police into a centralized Leviathan Law Enforcement Body.

The grim fact we must confront is that—with the exception of a relative handful of very small police and Sheriff's departments—we no longer have *local* police. We have local franchises of a nationalized police state.

This isn't irreversible. And it's also quite true that most police officers still think of themselves as agents of their particular communities, rather than representatives of the Homeland Security Leviathan—at least, most of the time. But things are getting much worse, in a hurry.

The most important reason why police should be locally controlled and locally accountable is to protect the rights of law-abiding local citizens from potentially lethal mis-applications of the police power.

Police are individuals who volunteer to serve communities by protecting them from criminal violence, and to the extent they carry out that function they are entitled to support, respect, and gratitude.

But as armed agents of the most lethal human agency, the State, police themselves are a potential threat, and must be kept on a short leash by the community.

The Enemy is now holding that leash, and a culture of murderous impunity has taken hold of what used to be local police agencies.

The murder of 43-year-old Michael Kreca by San Diego police offers an instructive case in point.

Kreca, a harmless tech writer of a libertarian bent, was walking in Sorrento Mesa when he was accosted by two police officers who said they had heard gunshots. He told the officers he had not been shooting and hadn't heard gunshots. He consented to a body search that turned up a 9mm pistol in the waistband of his baggy clothes.

The officer, Samantha Fleming, told Kreca that she was going to handcuff him "for her safety," according to an official report. "No, you're not going to do that," replied Kreca. "Let me go; I want to leave." As he tried to leave, the other officer—Sergeant Elmer Edwards—heroically placed his gun against Kreca's chest and fired twice, killing him.

Predictably, an official inquiry found that Sgt. Edwards "acted within the law," since California statutes permit police "to use deadly force to protect themselves and members of the public from serious injury or death. . . ."

Let's see: There were two armed police officers (well, one and a half, since one of them was a she-police), and one pedestrian. After the police murdered Kreca they found that his gun wasn't loaded—which means that he couldn't shoot them even if he had wanted to. The police eventually "determined" that he had been shooting earlier, which most likely means that they settled on that story as a way of disposing of the matter.

And let's not forget that the kill-shots were executed with the *gun in the victim's chest*, not by an officer diving for cover.

Michael Kreca's only "crime" was failing to display the docility required of helots by permitting himself to be handcuffed and arrested for no damn reason. In the proto-totalitarian order we are now living under, such trivial acts of resistance are capital offenses.

Oh—and if you resist characterizing this crime as "murder," ask yourself this question: How would that incident have been treated if an armed citizen, fearing lethal violence from the police, had shot and killed two officers under similar circumstances?

Here Come the "Behavior Police"

Birch Blog, May 17, 2006

"Well, *that's* not something you see every day," I mused to myself as roughly a half-dozen police cars materialized on the street in front of our house. In short order what seemed like a platoon of policemen had gathered, and several teenage boys found themselves splayed—hands out, feet spread apart—on the hood of one of the police cruisers.

About fifteen minutes later, a solitary suspect—who looked to me like a badly undernourished fifteen-year-old—was handcuffed and taken away in a police car.

Since I was writing on deadline, and the arrest didn't seem relevant to the story, I wasn't able to find out what had happened until the crowd had dispersed.

"So—did they just take down an al Qaeda sleeper cell?" I asked our sardonic next-door neighbor, a wonderful guy who looks like Stonewall Jackson and acts like a character from a Patrick McManus novel.

"Well, it looks like the boy the cops hauled away just beat the tar out of another kid out in the field behind the block," he replied, a faint hint of puzzled disapproval coloring his words.

"So we just had half the Payette police force out here to take down the winner of an adolescent fist-fight?" I asked, not bothering to disguise my incredulity.

"That's about the size of it," my neighbor replied. His teenage son had recently been rousted for the same supposed offense roughly two weeks ago. Two police cars and several officers had visited their home to arrest the young man—who didn't resist or defy the police in any way.

"He's got one year juvenile probation," my neighbor explained, "and we had to pay a fine of nearly six hundred dollars. Back when I was his age, when kids got into a fist-fight at school, they'd be handed the boxing gloves and told to finish it outside."

"I vaguely remember that same era," I commented. "It was a time when boys were expected to have a tussle or two, and people didn't treat that kind of thing as a harbinger of apocalyptic violence."

Of course, that was long before the advent of the "Zero Tolerance" hysteria that has prompted school officials to confiscate minuscule pocketknives and even items such as compasses and rulers as potential "weapons."

My neighbor and I both have 40 solar circuits in the rear-view, but it's not as if the society we remember can only be studied through examinations of cave paintings or crumbling stele. I grant that some of our customs would strike modern teenagers as odd, such as our practice of listening to music that was distributed on vinyl, *just as God intended it to be.*

Teenage boys today are growing up in a culture that elevates both effeminacy—the cringing fear of unruly adolescent masculinity—and state-approved vulgar machismo—in the form of the stormtroopers on whom the state has come to rely.

The most recent incident offered a timely illustration of a law enforcement trend I'd read about in the local daily, the *Argus Observer*, just two days earlier:

> The [Ontario, Oregon police] department showed an eight percent increase in arrests for 2005, according to the department's annual report. . . . The report shows a decline in property and person crimes—the fourth straight year those numbers declined. . . . The majority of major property crimes in Ontario, including burglaries, thefts from vehicles, and structure vandalism are all down from a year ago. . . . Person-to-person crimes in Ontario also continue to fall.

This is *wonderful* news: Crimes against persons and property—the *only* kinds that the state and its agents are authorized to investigate, prosecute, and deter—are declining!

So why are arrests *increasing*?

The answer: Because "behavior" crimes are on the rise. That category includes (to quote the *Argus*) "prostitution, drug laws, weapons laws, gambling, crimes against family, DUI, disorderly conduct, curfew and runaways."

I would assume that "disorderly conduct" includes such things as teenage fist-fights.

There are some sober and responsible people who believe that the list of behaviors quoted above, with the possible exception of crimes against the family, are victimless and thus not properly the business of the state. Whatever the merits of that view, the fact that the local police force in a town like Ontario, Oregon (population about 12,000) is spending so much time, effort, and resources dealing with "behavior" crimes is an ominous illustration of the extent to which our society has embraced totalitarian premises.

Government's role in a free society is *only* to protect the individual against force and fraud. Totalitarian states, on the other hand, are entirely devoted to controlling and modifying the behavior of their subjects to bring them into conformity with an ideological model.

Another symptom of incipient totalitarianism is an inclination on behalf of the ruling class and its agents toward a paranoid view of its subjects. A little more than a decade ago, law enforcement consultant Tony Cooper, an instructor in terrorism negotiation skills at the University of Texas-Dallas, diagnosed that tendency in our increasingly federalized law enforcement community: "I see the formation of a curious crusading mentality among certain law enforcement agencies to stamp out what they see as a threat to government generally. It's an exaggerated concern that they are facing a nationwide conspiracy and that somehow this will get out of control unless it is stamped out at a very early stage."

Cooper was referring specifically to the impulses that helped fuel atrocities at Waco and Ruby Ridge. But there is ample evidence that the Feds, through subsidy and indoctrination, have managed to infect practically every police department in the country with the same authoritarian tendencies.

I should point out that the Payette PD, which was very helpful and kind when our son Jefferson went missing, is staffed with genuinely decent and professional people who are exceptionally community-minded. This is why, as I contemplated the bizarre melodrama that unfolded outside our living room window yesterday afternoon, I mused to myself: If it's this bad in the green wood, what's it like in the dry?

"Privatizing" the Police State

Birch Blog, June 21, 2006

Federal and local police agencies nationwide "have been gathering Americans' phone records from private data brokers without subpoenas or warrants," reports the AP. The wire service does not exaggerate in its observation that this privatized subversion of the Fourth Amendment "raises civil liberties questions."

Indeed.

The question that occurs to me is this: If the federal Homeland Security apparatus, or its local affiliates (what were once independent, local police agencies) can circumvent constitutional restrictions by contracting with private agencies to do the dirty work, do we retain any civil liberties at all?

The AP story points out that at least $30 million was paid last year by the Feds to various information vendors, but that this figure is probably much too low because "brokers said they rarely charge law enforcement agencies."

Yes, I'm sure vendors are more than willing to comp a few jobs for the police, since many of them are engaged in unethical or illegal activities themselves.

Witness the fact that executives from firms acting as data brokers are planning to take the Fifth when they're summoned to testify before Congress about their activities.

Hey, here's an idea.

If Congress really wants to get to the bottom of what these guys are up to, why doesn't it contract with a private interrogation firm—one that's not bound by the Fifth Amendment—to question the data brokers?

I'd be willing to perform any hands-on questioning for a very reasonable fee. If the interrogation involves the people responsible for selling my phone number to the pestilential phone solicitors who continue to plague my household, I'd be willing to offer my services in exchange for . . . let's say a Thai dinner and full legal immunity.

In defense of the criminal means used by private data brokers to collect personal information, James Bearden, an attorney for several of those firms, deploys what I call the "Measure for Measure Defense." That name is taken from a key line in my favorite offering by the Bard: "Thieves for their robbery have authority when judges steal themselves."

92

Bearden, reported the AP, "likened the [data broker] companies' activities to the National Security Agency, which reportedly compiles the phone records of ordinary Americans." "The government is doing exactly what these people are accused of doing," whines Braden. "These people are being demonized. These are people who are partners with law enforcement on a regular basis."

Right on, bro! Equal rights for private-sector police state thugs! Why should the Feds alone enjoy the privilege of spying on ordinary citizens, rummaging through their personal business without a warrant, or even detaining, torturing, or killing them when the Great Decider deems it necessary?

Of course, in "liberated" Iraq, private contractors already free to do all of those things. Why should America's Homeland Security apparatus and its private appendages be denied similar privileges?

After the long-percolating NSA illegal surveillance scandal finally bubbled to the surface last December, many of Bush administration's defenders insisted that Americans really shouldn't be alarmed, their privacy is routinely violated by private data brokers anyway. Now private info brokers insist that what they're doing *must* be legal, since the government's doing the same thing.

Here we see a perfect circle of mutually beneficial, self-justifying corruption.

Imagine the victim of a gang rape being told that he or she has no legal recourse, because police officers were among the assailants: Since the rape was going to happen *anyway*, the police were entitled to join in, and participation by the police conferred legitimacy on the actions of the private sector rapists.

Prior to being appointed CIA director, Colonel Klink lookalike General Michael Hayden presided over the illegal surveillance program as deputy director of the NSA.

When confronted about the program by reporter Jonathan Landay of the Knight Ridder news service, Gen. Hayden blithely rewrote the Fourth Amendment to omit the need for search warrants issued on the basis of "probable cause."

"My understanding," stated Landay, "is that you must have probable cause to be able to do a search that does not violate an America's right against unlawful searches and seizures."

"No, actually the Fourth Amendment actually protects us all against unreasonable search and seizure," replied Klink-Hayden. "That's what it says."

This is a bit like claiming the Seventh Commandment says, "Thou shalt . . . commit adultery"—which it certainly does, if we're willing to excise one troublesome word, to wit, "not."

Similarly, the Fourth Amendment specifies that the right to protection against unreasonable search and seizure is "violated" unless the government first obtains a warrant issued "upon probable cause, supported by oath or affirmation and particularly describing the place to be searched and the persons or things to be seized."

"Believe me," insisted Klink-Hayden, "if there is any amendment to the Constitution that employees of the National Security Agency are familiar with, it's the Fourth. . . ."

This is true in exactly the same sense that bank robbers are intimately acquainted with laws against robbing banks.

Criminals are generally quite familiar with the laws they break.

But according to Klink-Hayden, the NSA was given a plenary indulgence to violate the Constitution: "I am responding to a legal order, alright? The Attorney General has averred to the lawfulness of the order. . . . I am convinced that what we're doing is lawful, because what it is we're doing is reasonable."

As long as a high-ranking spokesman for the regime avers that something is legal, it must be legal. That fits pretty nicely with Saddam Hussein's ruling doctrine: "Law consists of two lines above my signature."

Saddam's ruling philosophy was cognate with the Bush administration's doctrine of the "unitary executive," under which whatever George W. Bush decrees is law—and anything done by his authorized representatives is legal. Through the process of privatization, that same immunity is extended to corporate contractors as well as government employees.

And it's not just a handful of grubby snoops or low-caliber thugs we're talking about, either.

For example: Since 2002, the NSA has apparently been using a major St. Louis AT&T facility to spy on internet traffic. Former AT&T employees described to *Salon* a secret room at the facility to which only Spooked-up government drones were admitted:

> . . . only government officials or AT&T employees with top-secret security clearance are admitted to the room, located inside AT&T's facility in Bridgeton. The room's tight security includes a biometric "mantrap" or highly sophisticated double

door, secured with retinal and fingerprint scanners. The former workers say company supervisors told them that employees working inside the room were "monitoring network traffic" and that the room was being used by "a government agency."

Most likely our dear friends at NSA. This cyber-spy facility went online in 2002, under Gen. Hayden's supervision.

It's worth remembering that the fusion of corporate interests and an all-powerful central government under a lawless executive is called "Fascism."

From the files of Police Squad!

Birch Blog, June 26, 2006

"When I see five weirdos in togas stabbing a man in plain view of a hundred people," explained the earnest but maladroit Detective Lieutenant Frank Drebin, "I shoot the b*****ds, that's my policy."

"That was a Shakespeare in the Park production of *Julius Caesar*, you moron!" replied Mayor Barker. "You killed five actors! *Good ones!*"

A news item in the *Greeley Tribune* suggests that either that community's SWAT team has collectively gotten in touch with its inner Frank Drebin, or that they're moonlighting as preemptive film critics:

> In a bizarre twist of events, what should have been a routine film shoot turned into a real-life thriller. Members of a film crew got the shock of their lives Saturday when a Larimer County SWAT team surrounded the crew and ordered everyone on their knees, hands behind their heads.

A Denver-based independent film company was shooting a Roger Corman-caliber thriller called "Different Kinds" in a campground near Loveland when our paramilitary heroes showed up, locked and loaded and ready to throw down.

Chris Borden, playing the central role of the story's heavy, was holding a character hostage and pistol-whipping a Good Samaritan when the SWAT team arrived, apparently tipped off to the apparent crime by a pedestrian.

Notes the *Tribune*:

> The crew had a park permit and had been shooting the movie for several hours when the SWAT team moved in. . . . The entire crew was ordered to drop to their knees with M-16 rifles pointed at their backs and then were forced to lay on the ground for 15 to 20 minutes. Several crew members tried to explain that they were just filming a movie, but were ordered by the SWAT team to shut up.

"They told me they were going to send rounds my way," recalls an incredulous Borden.

Great googlymoogly, who *talks* that way? You just know the guys who hurled that line at Borden had spent hours rehearsing their tough-guy patter in front of a mirror, and the results aren't exactly worthy of David Mamet.

I'd urge them not to quit their day jobs . . . but since that job makes them a menace to himself and innocent law-abiding people, I think the community would be better off if they were to go into acting, or professional wrestling, or some other line of work that could feed their very hungry egos without endangering the public.

The cast and film crew were held at gunpoint and interrogated for a half-hour before being released without an explanation or an apology—and both Borden and director Eileen Agosta were issued citations, for disorderly conduct and being an accessory thereto, respectively.

So let's see: A group of law-abiding people engaged in a peaceful business venture in a public park, after obtaining the proper permits, is assaulted by a group of government thugs and effectively kidnapped at gunpoint for a half-hour—and the *victims* of this outrage are the ones who are up on criminal charges.

It's amazing how a criminal assault becomes a matter of public indifference when the assailants are wearing state-issued costume jewelry.

"Just think," reflects a melancholy Frank Drebin after he is (temporarily) relieved of his badge, "the next time I shoot someone, I could go to jail."

This isn't the only recent incident involving an armed take-down of an innocent performed by over-eager armed government goons.

In April, a University of Georgia student bearing the unlikely name Jeremiah Ransom was returning from a "Pirate vs. Ninja" theme party when he suddenly found himself face-down in the dirt, a boot on the back of his neck, staring into the barrels of government-issued firearms in the hands of ATF agents:

> "It was surreal," Ransom said. "I was jogging from Wesley to Snelling [cafeteria] when I heard someone yell 'freeze.'" But the feds soon found that Ransom wasn't a masked man hell-bent on mayhem—he was just a regular, law-abiding ninja who'd been hanging with some pirates at a campus event. Ransom told the student newspaper he was on his way back from a Wesley Foundation pirate vs. ninja shindig when he was

nabbed by gun-bearing agents, but was released soon after he was found to have violated no laws.

Of course, as those of us who remember Waco know all too well, harmless, law-abiding people are the ATF's favorite quarry.

It's Happening Here

Birch Blog, June 30, 2006

We will not recognize it as it rises. It will wear no black shirts here. It will probably have no marching songs. It will rise out of a congealing of a group of elements that exist here and that are the essential components of Fascism. . . .

It will be at first decorous, humane, glowing with homely American sentiment. But a dictatorship cannot remain benevolent. To continue, it must become ruthless. When this stage is reached we shall see that appeal by radio, movies, and government-controlled newspapers to all the worst instincts and emotions of our people. The rough, the violent, the lawless men will come to the surface and into power. This is the terrifying prospect as we move along our present course.

—John T. Flynn, *American Mercury*, February 1941

For decades, beginning with the 1950 publication of Theodor Adorno's study *The Authoritarian Personality*, the conservative movement was regularly described as a form of incipient fascism. Cultural Marxists of the Frankfurt School, Adorno and his comrades denounced as innately "fascist" any organized effort to preserve traditional culture, institutions, and values from state-abetted subversion.

Adorno and his cohorts pulled off a neat little inversion of reality, given that Fascism—as instituted by Mussolini (who drew his inspiration from Lenin) was an effort to make all institutions subordinate to the state. Furthermore, from the time *The Authoritarian Personality* made its debut, until roughly the mid-1960s, the dominant strains in conservative thought were anti-interventionist, anti-militarist, as well as opposed to the growth of state power domestically—in short, very much the exact opposite of the Fascist program.

However, while Adorno and his ilk were spreading the bovine residue from which a thousand dishonest "academic" exposés of the Right would sprout, the seeds of an authentically fascist "conservatism" were being planted elsewhere.

In 1952, the individual who would become the Johnny Appleseed of American neo-Fascism, William F. Buckley, adumbrated that vision in an essay published by *Commonweal*. Owing to the threat posed by the Soviet Union, Buckley asserted,

> we have to accept Big Government for the duration—for neither an offensive nor defensive war can be waged given our present government skills, except through the instrument of a totalitarian bureaucracy within our shores. . . [Thus we] will have to support large armies and air forces, atomic energy, central intelligence, war production boards, and the attendant of centralization of power in Washington. . . .

Buckley never deigned to explain how home-grown totalitarianism would be preferable to the version exported by the Soviets, or how distant, impoverished Soviet Russia—even armed with atomic weapons it developed with the aid of its allies in the FDR regime—could pose a more credible threat to our freedoms than the government headquartered in Washington, D.C.

But these questions were of no moment to Buckley; his objective was to cure conservatism of its suspicions about Big Government and its tendency to seek the preservation of freedom. One of the first things he did was to reject for publication in *National Review* an essay written by the well-respected John T. Flynn warning that the real enemy of our freedoms was in Washington, rather than Moscow or Peking.

He then proceeded to conduct a purge—using methods infinitely milder than those employed by the Soviets, but following very similar priorities—of conservative elements deemed unsuitable, including the John Birch Society, followers of Ayn Rand and other libertarians, and sundry unsavory and insignificant figures whose worldview was entirely defined by racial or religious prejudices.

By the mid-1960s, the general outline of Buckley-style conservatism was well-established: It would countenance occasional complaints about tax rates or business regulation, as well as wistful efforts to defend traditional mores (as long as those efforts posed no serious threat to the cultural "consensus")—but the Warfare State was utterly sacrosanct.

Preservation of the Warfare State eventually requires redefinition of the State's domestic role, and inevitably this leads to efforts to redefine dissent as sedition.

By 1969, with the cultural conflict over Vietnam raging and other social conflicts feeding urban violence, *National Review* published an essay bearing the melodramatic title "Shall We Let America Die?" Harking back to Buckley's 1952 "murder-suicide" formula for "winning" the Cold War, the later essay seemed to argue that rather than *letting* America (a nation defined by liberty under law) die, we should *put it to death* through a program the author described as "expediential fascism."

"The very nature of the situation creates competing codes and doctrines extreme in content and alien to the balancing compromises of liberal polity," wrote NR contributor Donald Atwell Zoll, whose gifts obviously did not include clarity of expression:

> The stringent demands of such a rudimentary struggle of power and ideas invites political approaches that are totalitarian in nature; not quite in the original fascist sense that puts all aspects of life under the aegis of political authority, at least in the general sense that political theory can no longer restrict itself to general conditions and procedural rules, but must offer a comprehensive, authoritative resolution of a number of specific political and social questions.

Take the basic thought expressed in that paragraph, denude it of the academic vocabulary, dumb it down to the point of infantilization, and you have the standard-issue harangue delivered five days a week, three hours a day, by Sean Hannity: The liberals are only interested in power, they'll do *anything* to get it back, and so we have to be willing to do *anything* to keep it.

One of the fundamental conceits of the totalitarian mind-set is that reality itself must yield to the demands of the Party's ideology—and that mind-set is well-represented in the GOP-aligned Right. From there it's but a few goose-steps to the conclusion that those who persist on interpreting reality without the supposed benefit of the official ideology really should be killed.

And the Bu'ushists are already there.

Witness the comments from Ann Coulter that Rep. John Murtha, a decorated 37-year Marine combat veteran, should be "fragged" for his public (and highly qualified) opposition to the Great Decider's war in Iraq.

Witness as well the diseased musings of Ann Coulter wannabe Melanie Morgan (a radio talk show host and occasional guest on cable television) about putting various journalists to death for the supposed crime of publicizing the Bush regime's misdeeds:

> [T]he best solution that I can think of to deal with any newspaper editor, whether it's from the NY Times, LAT, WaPo, or the Wall Street Journal who is responsible for leaking national security classified information, is to be locked in a steel cage with the family members of slain troop members who would happily deliver the ultimate punishment of death.

By "national security classified information," Comrade Morgan means concealed official misconduct. She also obviously employs some kind of reverse sliding scale in handing out death sentences, given that she hasn't issued a similar malediction against the Bush regime for its misuse of classified information to punish whistle-blowers.

(And if Morgan were serious about allowing survivors of "slain troop members" to have a crack at those Americans responsible for their deaths, the suggestion she would have to make would earn her a visit from the Secret Service.)

The ever-vigilant Lew Rockwell points to another illustration of this proto-fascist mindset, which comes in the form of a prefabricated "patriotic" spam email, the likes of which we've come to know altogether too well.

Written in the form of a religious homily, the email describes the same question asked by anguished mothers whose sons have died in foreign wars, from Iraq backwards to the War for Independence. In each instance the mother asks a sound and penetrating question of the president: Why did my son have to die on a battlefield?

"Then long, long ago," concludes the author of this little exercise in blasphemous State-worship, "a mother asked, 'Heavenly Father, why did my Son have to die on a cross outside of Jerusalem?' The answers to all these are similar—'So that others may have life and dwell in peace, happiness and freedom.'"

This exemplifies a third element of the totalitarian worldview—the deification of the State as the collective expression of a sanctified people.

Not content to cast the U.S. President in the role of God the Father, and the president's victims in a role akin to that of God the Son, the email concludes with that most Christian of expressions, the vulgar death threat:

"IF YOU DON'T STAND BEHIND OUR TROOPS, PLEASE, FEEL FREE TO STAND IN FRONT OF THEM."

A half-century ago, describing conservatism as a species of incipient fascism was a vile and despicable canard. As for what is advertised as "conservatism" today, however. . . .

A Shakedown from Sea to Shining Sea

Birch Blog, July 3, 2006

Anyone who has taken in his share of mob movies has probably seen a confrontation between the mob Boss and a footsoldier who isn't bringing in enough loot. The Boss warns his wayward subordinate that he needs to squeeze more out of his protection racket—or an "adjustment" will have to be made.

Bert Reeves, the Boss Hogg avatar serving as mayor of Cottageville, South Carolina—described by the *Charleston Post and Courier* as a "well-known Lowcountry speed trap"—was captured on tape playing out that classic Mafia scene in meeting with Officer Jeremy Shomber. The conversation was taped by Shomber using the same wireless microphone he triggers during traffic stops, and the tape was provided to the local media by an anonymous source.

"If you're not writing tickets, you're not paying for yourself, you need to hit the road," said Reeves during a November 22, 2004 meeting with Officer Shomber and Police Chief Ray Taylor. "The main priority of your job—and I don't like it—is to generate revenue. . . . That's in order to pay for your position. Yours is the lowest position. I'm just being point-blank."

Rewind the tape, Officer Shomber: "The *main priority* of your job . . . is to generate revenue."

So I guess the whole "serve and protect" business is just pious eyewash, right?

Seeking further clarification during the brief period when Mayor Reeves was called away, Officer Shomber asked Chief Roscoe P. Coltrane—er, that is, Chief Taylor (and I don't mean Andy Taylor) if he should pull the Mayor over next time he catches him speeding.

"That probably wouldn't be a good idea," Chief Taylor told the young officer.

So obviously the chief business of Cottageville's Finest was something other than law enforcement.

Otherwise one of their first priorities would be to rein in the Mayor, who (according to the *Post and Courier*) was recently "clocked going 71 mph in a 55 mph zone just outside town limits" and has "an extensive list of violations, including a habitual offender conviction and a conviction for driving under suspension."

Because the small town doesn't have much of a tax base, Chief Taylor told Shomber in their 2004 conversation, the younger officer should concentrate on writing at least one ticket an hour. "The tickets are there to write," the Chief suggested helpfully. "Whether you want to call it making up numbers, yes, some tickets are bad tickets, but the majority of tickets that come through are good tickets." Shomber's job, his Chief told him, was to do what was necessary "in order to keep the department the size we are."

This is a pretty good summation of the statist's view of society: A community is nothing more than a support system for the government that regiments it, and parasitically draws life from it.

Shomber had been hauled on the carpet for posting a photo of himself in uniform on MySpace.com, which is certainly a more serious infraction than committing armed robbery under the color of government authority, which is what a police officer does when he knowingly writes bad tickets.

Like a Mob underboss trying to motivate a poorly performing footsoldier, Chief Taylor chided Shomber and emphasized what a sweet arrangement he'd lucked into:

> If you're not writing tickets, you're not paying for yourself. You got a chip on your shoulder. As far as I'm concerned you'd be fired now. I want someone to play on my team. . . . If you got canned today, and you had to go out looking, you'd come back in a couple months and say you know what, I had it made.

The young officer eventually had a surfeit of that sweet deal: After a year and a half of working for the Cottageville police, Shomber decided to go straight.

This kind of thing is happening throughout the United States as revenue streams constrict.

Robert Militzer of Berkley, Michigan learned how deadly earnest the forces of law and order can be when it comes to mulcting residents for the purpose of keeping the local government well-fed.

Last May 29, Militzer, a 38-year-old computer programmer, received a $10 ticket for leaving his car parked overnight in front of a friend's house.

"He said he had not parked in the street in prior visits due to clearly posted signs that prohibit parking on city streets from 2 AM to 6 AM," reported the *Detroit News*. "But the day Militzer arrived at his friend's house, the signs were gone from the street. . . ." "They had come down . . . and a day or two prior a friend had left a car in [the] street overnight without any problem so my friend said, 'leave it,'" Militzer recalled.

Seeing the ticket on his windshield left him understandably frustrated and angry: "I thought they were gaming me, collecting fines without giving people a fair chance to avoid it," he observed.

Now—why on *earth* would he think such a thing?

In any case, Militzer paid dutifully paid his ticket, writing in the memo space of his check a clear and obvious explanation of the expenditure: "BULLS**T MONEY GRAB."

A couple of weeks later, two of Allen Park's Finest materialized on his doorstep to serve a summons—which is to say, give notice of a supplementary money grab: He was ordered to appear before a municipal judge to face a criminal contempt charge, with a penalty of up to 30 days in jail and a $250 fine. "They said, 'If you don't [appear], we will have to come back and get you and bring you in.'"

That's another variation on a familiar Mob Movie trope: "We know where you live, and it would be a real shame for something to happen to you. . . ."

This comparison is utterly unfair. Mafiosi don't punish people for expressing opinions, after all, particularly if—like Militzer—they make their protection payments on time. Militzer eventually paid the fine a second time with an expurgated check.

In other communities, authorities are getting to be rather creative in devising ways of using the police as revenue streams:

> In Milwaukee, local authorities are seeking the power to let "police seize cars by declaring them a 'nuisance,'" reports the *Journal-Sentinel*. The program, which would employ citizen "spotters"—that is, informants—is advertised as a way to deal with traffic jams occasioned by "cruising" (a useless and expensive activity, yes, but nowhere near as pointless or profligate as 99 percent of what every government does). "We will arrest people, we will tow cars, we will do whatever is necessary," insists Milwaukee Police Chief Nannette Hegerty, another she-police promoted well above her Peter Principle limit. Once the "crisis" is passed, Milwaukee residents can expect the measure to remain in place as a source of revenue.

No Quarter

In Elk Grove, California, a new ban on street racing would not
only impose a $1,500 fine, a year-long driver's license
suspension, and a 60-day vehicle impoundment, but would also
impose $1,000 fine on passengers and spectators of such events
as well. Does any reasonable person doubt that the measure
would be interpreted broadly enough to justify ticketing people
who just happen to be passing through the neighborhood when
a couple of motorized morons decide to rumble?

The New Jersey Mob—no, not the Sopranos, the government—permits
local police to charge storage and impound fees from families of drivers who die
in auto accidents. The family of 18-year-old Daniel Mackay was charged
$694.90 for storage of Daniel's 1992 Honda, in which the young man died
during a June 4 single-vehicle accident. State Assemblyman John Burzichelli,
who has apparently not been in politics long enough to lose his decency, is
proposing a measure that would grant a 30-day moratorium on towing, storage,
and service fees for families of such fatal accidents.

At least some cities are probably finding ways to transmute revenue from
tickets, impoundments, and other fees into federal subsidies.

The July 2 *New York Times* reports: "Cities and towns . . . across the
country are increasingly . . . putting lobbyists on retainer to leverage their local
tax dollars into federal tax dollars." Under the reign of the Republicans, the use
of budget earmarks for special expenditures has increased dramatically, and
municipal governments are increasingly turning to lobbyists to bring home the
boodle. "We're all in competition for the same dollars, and you want all the
advantages you can have," explained John Litton, city manager for the small
town of Lake Mary, Florida.

How can cash-strapped towns afford to keep their own junior-league Jack
Abramoffs on retainer?

Does anyone want to bet against the idea that this process often involves
speed traps, parking traps, and other ploys by police to carry out their "main
priority"—collecting revenue?

I didn't think so.

Da Gangstas of Dallas County

Birch Blog, July 14, 2006

Last November, when my family relocated from Wisconsin to Idaho, we decided to take a northern route through Minnesota, North Dakota, and Montana, rather than taking I-80 through Iowa.

For reasons I'll describe shortly, I'm wondering if that decision may have saved us from virtual impoverishment at the hands of what may be one of the most insidious criminal gangs in the Midwest.

After discarding everything from which we could stand to part, including a few items that were borderline indispensable (such as my uber-sweet Ibanez RG electric and my Takamine single cutaway amplified acoustic), we loaded up our van like the Beverly Hillbillies and hit the road. Stashed away in various inaccessible places in our vehicle were several thousand dollars in cash and precious metals, as well as assorted firearms.

If we had taken I-80 and passed through Iowa's Dallas County, chances are pretty good that we would have been stopped by the heroic paladins of public order who work under Sheriff Brian Gilbert.

The Grigg family, which had no home address at the time (that's right—we were homeless!), would have been traveling through the county in an SUV with out-of-state license plates, driven by a large Latino male who looks either black or Arab, depending on one's aesthetic sensibilities. (Life can be interesting when you're a racial Rorschach Test.)[1]

Had we passed through Dallas County, it's likely—thanks to the official corruption abetted by the federal "war on drugs"—that we would have had a very unpleasant run-in with the Sheriff's Department.

According to the *Des Moines Register*, "Sheriff Brian Gilbert and his deputies seized $1.75 million in cash and vehicles over the past four years, much of it from black and Latino drivers who were stopped for traffic violations in vehicles with out-of-state plates."

As I have mentioned previously, a law enforcement officer can find "probable cause" for a traffic stop practically any time he wishes. Perhaps a motorist is driving a bit *too* carefully; isn't that suspicious? Maybe something sets off the officer's Spidey Sense, or he feels a disturbance in the Force—whatever. Where there is money to be made, traffic violations or suspicions of the same will always materialize.

And the heroes of Dallas County excelled at extracting "probable cause" to stop motorists who seemed to fit a certain profile. And through the miracle of "forfeiture," through which police departments can seize property found "guilty" of involvement in criminal activity, Da Boyz in Blue were able to take in quite a haul.

Notes the *Register*:

> Law enforcement agencies have taken in $2.4 million in cash and property from accused criminals in Dallas County over the past four years. Nearly 90 percent came from a 24-mile stretch of I-80. The total, which also includes seizures by the Iowa State Patrol and eight local police departments, might be higher, since many documents and details don't become public until the final stages of court proceedings.

And of course, "no one tracks the amount of cash police are handed by suspects who just want to get away."

The Gangstas among those who proudly wear the colors of the Dallas County Sheriff's Department made off with three-quarters of the documented take, and I'll bet they've got da bling to prove it.

At least some of the motorists stopped in Dallas County were probably involved in some illicit activity, such as ferrying money on behalf of drug dealers. Is this a more serious offense than armed robbery committed under the color of government authority?

Attorney F. Montgomery Brown, who has represented both sides of the drug war in Dallas County, refers to highway seizures as "the dirty little secret of the war on drugs."

Actually, the "secret" here is the symbiotic relationship between drug dealers—whose profit margin is radically enhanced by prohibition—and corrupted law enforcement agencies, who likewise profit handsomely from the arrangement.

The use of such seizures "allows us, we believe, to take ill-gotten proceeds off the street and put our small dent in the illegal drug trade," insists Gilbert. The instrument has yet to be invented that could detect the sub-microscopic "dent" in the drug trade Gilbert professes to see. Much more obvious damage is done to the rule of law, civil liberties, and the integrity of local law enforcement through this type of legalized highway robbery. And obviously Gilbert and his comrades wouldn't want to put *too* big a "dent" in the trade, seeing how it's been so profitable to them.

And when the trap is sprung on someone who is completely innocent? Ah, well . . . such are the vicissitudes of war, even metaphorical ones. We can't have a decent war without some collateral damage, after all.

It's tempting to conclude that Sheriff Gilbert and his associates aren't so much Peace Officers (a noble and worthy calling) than descendants of India's late, unlamented Thugee cult, preying on unsuspecting travelers in the guise of offering them protection.

Sheriff Gilbert's department has its routine down cold. Although court approval is required before police can take ownership of seized property or money, Gilbert's department often induces motorists to sign waivers treating the vehicles or cash as abandoned property. A public notice is then published in the local paper asking interested parties to come forward within a month to claim the "abandoned" property.

And here's a neat catch: Even if no criminal charges are filed, the police get to keep what they've seized. Take the case of Hoscar Castillo-Rodriguez of Los Angeles, who had cached more than $40,000 in his 1999 Ford Expedition. "Charges against Castillo . . . were dropped due to a lack of evidence," notes the *Register*. "But Dallas County kept the cash and the SUV."

I can think of many reasons why someone would carry and conceal large amounts of cash while driving across the country. Had we been stopped during our move last fall, it's entirely likely that we would have found ourselves in a very nasty mess—not because of anything I had done or was likely to do, but because of what the murderous, fraudulent exercise called the "war on drugs" permits outfits like the Dallas County Sheriff's Department to get away with.

In recent weeks, Sheriff Gilbert has been on vacation as "state agents and auditors searched his home and pored over the department's evidence records," investigating the disappearance of money seized from motorist Jesus Quinonez-Jimenez. Mr. Quinonez, who has not been charged with a crime, a waiver forfeiting his 2000 Audi and $781,000 in cash separated into 27 bundles, only 26 of which are accounted for.

The problem, according to Iowa authorities and opinion molders, is insufficient "oversight" of the Dallas County seizure program. So perhaps the solution, from their perspective, is to set a thief to watch the thieves—rather than putting an end to the whole corrupt business altogether.

[1] Since writing that essay, I've met my birth mother, who informed me—much to my astonishment—that my dark complexion doesn't reflect a Latino heritage, but rather a Polynesian/Cherokee/Irish/Basque heritage.

When Johnny Comes Marching Home from Iraq. . .

Birch Blog, July 18, 2006

. . . will he be able to make an honest living, or will he have to continue working for the government?

Kevin Mauga of Tampa is 23, engaged, broke, unemployed, and drowning in debt. "He has half a tank of gas in his Chevy Impala, less than $50 in the bank and a stack of resumes few employers seem to want," reports the *St. Petersburg Times*.

His old employer, the U.S. Army, wants Kevin back. With overdue bills accumulating and no other prospects, Kevin may have to re-up—not an inviting prospect for a young man who spent his tours in Iraq driving a 5,000-ton fuel truck between Ramadi and Habbaniya.

Back in Iraq, Kevin's commander had urged him to re-enlist, citing the dismal employment prospects awaiting him back home. "I told him, 'I'll take my chances,'" Kevin told the *Times*. More recently, he's told his fiancee that if he can't find a job soon "I may have to go back in."

There in one more stop on the job search circuit before Kevin seriously considers going back to the Army: "First, he's going to check out a career in law enforcement. The Tampa Police Department seemed interested at [a recent] job fair. Maybe they'll pay as well as the Army. Or maybe, he thinks, he'll call the Florida Highway Patrol. Maybe they're hiring."

If Kevin gets a law enforcement job, I hope he's treated better than Officer Scott Rhodes, a Marine veteran of the first Iraq war, and Officer Markus Bristol, an Army veteran who likewise served in the Gulf War's first installment. Both Rhodes and Bristol, ten-year veterans of the Falls Church, Virginia police department, have been punished by the department after blowing the whistle on its traffic ticket quota system. Rhodes, head of the city's police union, was fired; Bristol, the union's vice president, has been suspended.

Back in 2004, Rhodes and Bristol revealed that "Falls Church officers were being evaluated based partially on high quotas for writing traffic tickets," notes the July 17 *Washington Post*. "They said officers were writing multiple tickets in one traffic stop rather than pursuing more time-consuming matters such as drunk drivers."

"It's not unusual for patrol officers in the city of Falls Church to hand a motorist two, three or even four tickets during one traffic stop," reported a *Post* story from August 2004. "I answer the citizens honestly," Rhodes told the paper. "Did I write them [the tickets] because of a quota? Yes, sir, I did."

Continued the *Post*:

> Falls Church police require patrol officers to write an average of three tickets, or make three arrests, every 12-hour shift, and to accumulate a minimum total of 400 tickets and arrests per year. In terms of quotas, writing a ticket for a broken taillight carries the same weight as an arrest for armed robbery. Failure to meet quotas results in an automatic 90-day probationary period with no pay raise and a possible demotion or dismissal if ticket or arrest numbers aren't immediately raised to acceptable levels.

After Rhodes and Bristol spoke out, the ticket quota was quietly dispensed with—but the department, apparently, is seeking its pound of flesh.

And this is hardly the only police department that is slapping down police officers who rebel against being used as revenue farmers for corrupt governments (please forgive the redundancy—to say the latter is to acknowledge the former) in various municipalities.

Five police in Monroe, Louisiana were "banned from working off-duty jobs for one month because they didn't perform their jobs adequately," reported the *News Star*. The specific inadequacy, claim several of the police officers, was their failure to write a sufficient number of traffic tickets while on duty: The officers were falling short on what they describe as a ticket quota.

Police Chief Ron Schleuter insisted that the officers were punished for deficiencies in keeping record of their time on duty, and that "there is not a quota on tickets." But with the city reaping over a half-million dollars annually from fines, Chief Schleuter's admitted fixation on ticket-writing performance certainly has the appearance and odor of a "quota."

A similar situation has developed in Ogden, Utah, reports the *Salt Lake Tribune*:

> Some rank-and-file Ogden police officers suspect the focus of their jobs could soon shift—from fighting crime to writing

113

tickets. And they believe that shift is spurred by the city's new justice court that [opened on July 3].

"We see a direct link between the two," maintained Sgt. Troy Arrowsmith, head of the Ogden Police Benefits Association. "Our sliding performance scale means we write more citations, which means the justice court brings in more revenues to fund itself and other things in the city. . . . It turns us into revenue generators. We had a hard time with that quota before, and now they want us to write more." And the new performance scale takes away officer discretion, Arrowsmith points out: "In cases where you normally just issue a warning, now this will force us to give citations."

Police Chief Jon Grenier, who dismisses the complaint as posturing by work-aversive police officers (now, *there's* a motivational leader!), sniffily insists that there is no "quota" for tickets—just "standards."

Asked by the *Tribune* if officers could "camp out at ticket-rich 'fishing holes' to fill their quotas, or meet that standard," Chief Grenier, interestingly, offered a non-denial: "You can call them fishing holes. The area in front of Mount Ogden Park generates tickets all day long."

"To Protect and Serve"? Many, probably most, of those who volunteer to become police earnestly desire to live by that credo. The people who go into politics see the police function in radically different terms, however—more along the lines of "To Prey upon, and shake down."

Think again of Kevin Mauga, a young Iraq veteran with few if any employment prospects outside of law enforcement. As the war grinds on, tens of thousands of young men just like him will return, looking for work. Many of them will be absorbed by our growing (and increasingly centralized) law enforcement system.

From dodging IEDs and small arms fire in Baghdad, to shaking down motorists at the behest of degenerate, cash-hungry municipal governments in Butte, Boise, or Boston: that's not a very attractive career track.

Informants, Patsies, and Provocateurs

Birch Blog, July 19, 2006

About twenty years ago, Randy Weaver, a wiry ex-Green Beret living in northern Idaho, met a corpulent undercover ATF agent named Kenneth Fadeley at the annual World Aryan Congress in Hayden Lake. Weaver was a self-described white separatist in loose orbit around the neo-Nazi Aryan Nation group; Fadeley was posing as an outlaw biker named Gus Masigono.

Fadeley concluded that Weaver, despite his eccentric and in some ways repellent beliefs, was relatively harmless and vulnerable to being "pitched." But like the other professional bullies kept on salary by the Feds, Fadeley wanted some insurance. Accordingly, a few years after he the first meeting, Fadeley suborned Weaver—whose family was barely keeping body and soul together—into selling him a quantity of rifles whose stocks had been sawed off to Fadeley's specifications. The ATF agent had specifically instructed Weaver to cut the stocks three-eighths of an inch shorter than the legally required overall length of twenty-eight inches.

Armed with evidence of Weaver's supposed crime, the ATF confronted him in July 1990 and demanded that he act as a federal informant within the Aryan Nation. Displaying considerable strength of character, Weaver refused. Thus began a stand-off between Weaver and the Feds that would lead to the 1992 shootout and siege at Ruby Ridge, which resulted in the murder of Weaver's son Sammy and wife Vicky by federal agents, and the death of U.S. Marshal William Deagan—either by federal "friendly fire" or by a round fired by the Weavers in self-defense.

(The terms "murder" and "self-defense" are entirely justified, since the ATF created the circumstances leading to the shootout; a jury of his peers accepted Weaver's claim of self-defense in acquitting him of the murder charge in his 1993 trial; and the Feds eventually paid a $3.1 million settlement to the Weaver family in acknowledgment of the wrongful death of Vicky Weaver. This is a pretty decent summary of the whole infuriating story.)

I don't know what happened to Keith Fadeley, the predatory, opportunistic ATF agent whose attempt to extort Weaver's cooperation as an informant led directly to the deaths at Ruby Ridge. What is clear, however, is that the Soviet-style methods he used to entrap Weaver are alive and well in the contemporary *Heimatsicherheitsdienst*.

In November of last year, 24-year-old Yassine Ouassif, a legal U.S. resident who was born in Morocco, was offered a version of the same deal presented to Randy Weaver: Become a federal informant (and, quite possibly, an *agent provocateur*—about which more anon) within his Muslim community in San Francisco, or else.

FBI counter-terrorism agent Daniel Fliflet told Ouassif that if the young Moroccan refused to become an informant, "I will work hard to deport you to Morocco as soon as possible."

"I want to tell you something important," continued Special Agent Fliflet. "America is just like a bus, and you have a choice to make: Either you board the bus or you leave."

Ouassif won a green card in a State Department lottery in 2001. Last September he flew back to Morocco to visit family. For no reason apart from the FBI's desire to blackmail him into becoming an informant, Ouassif's name was put on a "no-fly list." As a result, an airliner he boarded in Paris was turned around in mid-flight so that he could be detained and interrogated by authorities, including Moroccan officials who told him he may "never see the light of day again."

Eventually the young man was released and allowed to fly to Montreal. He tried to enter the U.S. by bus, but was intercepted at the border, handcuffed, and held in a cell for several hours. His green card was seized, and he was told that once he returned to the Bay Area he should look up Special Agent Fliflet. On meeting the FBI agent, Ouassif was accused of having "jihadi" beliefs and presented with the ultimatum that could have sent him back to Morocco, to face imprisonment—or worse.

Ouassif was treated this way despite the fact that he had broken no laws, had no history of criminal or radical behavior, and threatened no one. The gallant defenders of the *Vaterland* simply believed that they could browbeat this innocent man into becoming an informant.

In a way, Ouassif could consider himself fortunate. He could have been detained indefinitely as an "enemy combatant," like Jose Padilla—a U.S. citizen from a less than reputable background whom the feds likewise wanted to blackmail into serving as an informant.

In recent testimony offered before U.S. Magistrate Stephen Brown in Miami, FBI Special Agent Russell Fincher said of Padilla: "I didn't want to arrest him. I needed his cooperation" when the former gang member was detained at Chicago's O'Hare airport four years ago. The idea, explains a UPI account of Fincher's testimony, was "to recruit him as an inside informant" to "provide information about an al-Qaida plot to detonate a so-called 'dirty bomb' on U.S. soil."

Without being advised of his constitutional rights, Padilla described his upbringing in Chicago, his time in prison, and his conversion to Islam. At that point, Fincher related, Padilla demanded a lawyer, whereupon the Special Agent arrested him.

Padilla had nothing to do with a "dirty bomb" plot. This was known at the time of his arrest. Yet John Ashcroft, the deranged individual who was Bush's Attorney General at the time, used a press conference in—appropriately— Moscow to announce the arrest as a masterstroke in the war on terror. And Padilla remained imprisoned by presidential decree, without legal recourse of any kind, for three and a half years—until the prospect of a Supreme Court challenge the Bush regime knew it couldn't win prompted the "Justice" Department to file a criminal indictment.

I mentioned earlier my suspicion that the Feds might have wanted to induce Yassine Ouassif to be an *agent provocateur*; I have similar suspicions about the case of Jose Padilla, as well. Think back to the original World Trade Center bombing of 1993, which was carried out by a terror cell nurtured by the Pentagon and the CIA, and included an Egyptian fellow named Emad Salem.

Months before the January 1993 bombing, Salem had infiltrated the plot and had been assured by his FBI handler that the agency's plan called for "building the bomb with a phony powder" and "grabbing the people involved" in the plot before it came to fruition. Of course, the plot was carried out, much to Salem's distress: In a recorded conversation with his handler after the bombing, Salem rebuked the Special Agent for "watching the bomb go off" when the Feds are "paid . . . to prevent problems like this from happening."

Fast-forward now to the recent arrests in Miami of the so-called "Liberty Seven," a group of religious eccentrics who have been described as an al Qaeda cell supposedly plotting to blow up Chicago's Sears Tower.

The "Seas of David" religious sect appeared to be entirely non-violent and apolitical—until they were, in the words of an ABC News account, "infiltrated by a government informant who allegedly led them to believe he was an Islamic radical. . . ."

The informant, who worked for the South Florida Joint Anti-Terrorism Task Force, claims to have recruited the cultists (at least some of whom have an

IQ just south of 70, or roughly twenty points higher than Sean Hannity's) into an al Qaeda cell, complete with an oath of loyalty to Osama bin Laden.

The Feds who brought us this made-for-television event proudly call the Liberty Seven bust an act of preemption. Given their track record, I suspect it's a case of the Feds making business for themselves. What's really scary is the fact that—in the Weaver, Ouassif, and Padilla episodes—the Feds have displayed a willingness to imprison or even kill those who refuse to play along in their schemes.

The Gitmo Archipelago

Birch Blog, August 8, 2006

In *Against All Hope*, the prison memoir of Cuban dissident Armando Valladares, we find the story of a pre-Castro Cuban ruler who had built a ridiculously huge prison complex—one far exceeding any imaginable demand. Asked why he would build such a prison when much of it would remain unused, the dictator smirked and replied: "Don't worry—someone will come along who will fill it up."

That someone, of course, was Fidel Castro.

That story came to mind while I was reading *Grand Theft Pentagon*, a collection of essays by investigative reporter Jeffrey St. Clair describing the ongoing transmutation of our once-free republic into a corporatist Reich. In his dissection of the multifaceted, metastasizing evil that is the Halliburton conglomerate, St. Clair describes how Bill Clinton laid the groundwork for the Gitmo detention camps that play such an iconic role in the Bush regime's "war on terror."

"The Clinton years were very good to Halliburton right to the final days," notes St. Clair:

> In the fall of 2000, Halliburton won a $300 million contract to build a massive prison at Guantanamo Bay in Cuba. That prison, which serves as the torture and interrogation center for Bush's wars, was originally designed to hold Haitians and, according to some sources, Cubans, in the event of the collapse of the Castro government. Two years later, Halliburton would land the contract to build the other big torture center at Bagram Air Base in Afghanistan.

And earlier this year, Halliburton subsidiary KBR received a $385 million contract from the *Heimatsicherheitsdienst* (that's "Department of Homeland Security" in the original German) to provide "temporary detention and processing facilities" for use within the United States.

Those facilities would be available to deal with social turmoil resulting from "an emergency influx of immigrants, or to support the rapid development of new programs" should another crisis arise, such as "a natural disaster" or, of course, another 9/11-style terrorist strike.

Now, tell me if you've heard *this* one before:

> "A spokeswoman for Immigration and Customs Enforcement, Jamie Zuieback, [told the *New York Times* that] KBR would build the centers only in an emergency like the one when thousands of Cubans floated on rafts to the United States. She emphasized that the centers might never be built if such an emergency did not arise."

Uh-huh.

The idea that we would be dealing with a dramatic influx of illegal immigrants has some superficial plausibility, given that Bush's "reform" proposals have created an ongoing "amnesty rush." But the same was true of the Halliburton-constructed Gitmo prison facilities that are now such a valuable laboratory for the regime.

Among other loathsome purposes, Gitmo is a crucible in which military, law enforcement, and intelligence powers are being melded into an alloy essential to dictatorship. We've already seen how the Bush regime seeks to use the "military commissions" pioneered at Gitmo as the foundation for a new legal system in which those accused of any connection to terrorism can be imprisoned indefinitely, even if they are acquitted of the charges.

In light of Halliburton's contract to build detention facilities for "new programs," is it unreasonable to suspect that the regime is planning to construct a literal Gitmo Archipelago?

The New "Police Professionalism": Serious Christians Need Not Apply

Pro Libertate, December 28, 2006

Ramon Perez was a rookie police officer in Austin, Texas when he responded to a domestic violence report in January 2005. When he arrived at the address, he was greeted by a distraught woman who claimed that her elderly husband had pushed her down the stairs, leaving her with injured arms.

As he interviewed the alleged victim, the alleged assailant, an elderly man apparently in frail health, emerged from the home carrying car keys and a cup of coffee. Perez, who had called for backup, told the man to stop. As he did the backup officer, Robert Paranich "lunged" at the elderly man, nearly knocking him off his feet.

"I considered that an escalation of force," Perez later recalled.

With the suspect struggling to regain his balance, Paranich yelled at Perez to use his Taser to subdue the elderly man. To his considerable credit, Perez refused to do so, chiefly because the man wasn't resisting arrest, but also because the rookie officer was concerned that the man was so frail the electroshock device could send him into cardiac arrest.

Those considerations, incidentally, are spelled out in the Austin Police Department's Taser policy, which Perez followed exactly. In the event, Perez and Paranich were able to effect the arrest using "soft-hand" tactics. When it's possible to arrest a suspect without resort to violence, Perez later said, doing so is "the constitutionally correct thing."

A few days after this incident, Perez received what he and his attorney Derek Howard describe as a punitive transfer to the night shift. Two months later, Perez was questioned at length about the January arrest, as well as a second incident in which he acted with unauthorized fastidiousness about constitutional correctness.

He was told to report to APD psychologist Carol Logan to undergo what was described as a session of "word games" to develop better communication skills with his superiors. Perez was not told that the interview would be a "fit-for-duty review" held to facilitate the pre-ordained decision to fire him.

According to the *Austin Chronicle*, Logan confirmed that Perez had been told the meeting would focus on "word games." However, her four page report mentions nothing about that exercise; instead, it focuses "entirely on Perez's moral and religious beliefs, which Logan concludes are so strong they are an 'impairment' to his ability to be a police officer."

Perez is a self-described non-denominational fundamentalist Christian, an ordained minister who home-schools his children. This, according to Logan, produces an "impairment" of his ability to absorb new facts, to communicate with his superiors, and to deal with "feedback."

"Perez has a well-developed set of personal beliefs," wrote Logan. "These seem to be based primarily on his religious beliefs and it is obvious that he has spent a lot of time reflecting upon and developing these views."

While Logan, displaying the reflexive condescension of a career servant of the Regime, describes Perez's convictions as "admirable," she criticizes him for displaying "defensiveness" when his convictions are challenged. The firmness of Perez's moral beliefs is problematic, she concludes, because they "provide him with a rationale for explaining how his views differ with others."

Boil down Logan's assessment in a saucepan, and here's the residue: Perez was unsuitable to serve as a police officer because his values transcend the authority of the State, and his moral convictions have immunized him against collectivist thinking.

It should be noted that Perez was also troublesome because, unlike most newly minted law enforcement officers, he had two decades of adult life in the rear-view mirror before beginning his police career. He was a 41-year-old ex-engineer when he graduated from the academy, and his fellow cadets honored him with the Ernie Hinckle Humanitarian Award for compassion, integrity, and leadership on the strength of the character he had displayed.

A month after the psychologist—who actually functions as what the Soviets called a *Zampolit*, or "political officer"—rendered her assessment, Perez was given an ultimatum: He could resign from the APD and keep his peace officer's license, or be fired and lose that license, and thus be left unemployable by any other department. Perez chose the first course, while fighting with the Austin City government for a year to see the report that had led to his firing.

The triggering incident was his refusal to use a Taser on an unresisting elderly suspect; this episode revealed that Perez—who would appear to be an exemplary officer, a throwback to an era when police were peace officers, rather than heavily armed enforcers of the State's decrees—was not morally ductile. He was fired for disobeying an order from a superior that was unconstitutional and *illegal by the department's own standards.*

The official explanation is that Perez was fired for being a "substandard cop." Perez's attorney, Derek Howard, offers a more credible assessment: "He didn't fit in because of his religious belief system."

"It was concluded that my [morality] justified it [the decision to disobey], when in fact it was my commitment to policy and our training at the academy and the U.S. Constitution, and not necessarily my moral, spiritual foundation, that led me to that decision," explained Perez at a press conference earlier this month. "Being tough is a good thing. Being tough, as a cop, can save your life or someone else's. But when that toughness crosses over into civil liberties, that's where a line needs to be drawn. . . and for some officers, that's a gray area."

Like Molech and other omnivorous pagan idols sustained by lethal violence, the Regime under which we live is a very jealous god: It requires unqualified, instantaneous obedience, particularly from those in the business of enforcing its decrees.

Perez, like any Christian worthy of that designation, will render to Caesar only that to which Caesar is due—which in our system means only the power necessary to protect the lives and property of the innocent. Or, as he put it: "I do believe, if you are a police officer, you have an ordination by God to protect and preserve life." All of this resonates with the actual meaning of the much-misapplied verses in Romans chapter 13 that are often wrested by those preaching unconditional submission to State power.

So now Perez is out of a job, and Austin's branch of the Leviathan Force will fill his slot with someone willing to adapt to the Regime's priorities. In simple terms, this means it will find someone willing to shoot an unresisting elderly suspect, at point-blank range, with a Taser.

This is not the only time I've heard of a police department using psychological testing to weed out police recruits whose Christian convictions make them unsuitable to serve the Regime.

A few months ago a former professional associate of mine described how his son, who applied for a position with a Sheriff's Department in Wisconsin, was rejected after he was made to play similar "word games" with a psychologist. Despite scoring well on every evaluation, this young man was deemed unworthy to work as a deputy sheriff because of his inflexible moral views and impatience with arbitrary bureaucratic policies.

One such incident could be an anomaly, and a second a mere coincidence. Three or more, however, constitute a trend. I'm confident that a third episode of this variety could be found with relatively little effort.

2007

Death Squad in Delaware: The Killing of Derek Hale

Pro Libertate, March 25, 2007

Delaware was the first state to ratify the U.S. Constitution. It may be the first state to be afflicted with a fully operational death squad—unless a civil lawsuit filed on Friday against the murders of Derek J. Hale results in criminal charges and a complete lustration (in the Eastern European sense of the term) of Delaware's law enforcement establishment.

Hale, a retired Marine Sergeant who served two tours in Iraq and was decorated before his combat-related medical discharge in January 2006, was murdered by a heavily armed 8–12-member undercover police team in Wilmington, Delaware last November 6. He had come to Wilmington from his home in Manassas, Virginia to participate in a Toys for Tots event.

Derek was house-sitting for a friend on the day he was murdered. Sandra Lopez, the ex-wife of Derek's friend, arrived with an 11-year-old son and a 6-year-old daughter just shortly before the police showed up. After helping Sandra and her children remove some of their personal belongings, Derek was sitting placidly on the front step, clad in jeans and a hooded sweatshirt, when an unmarked police car and a blacked-out SUV arrived and disgorged their murderous cargo.

Unknown to Derek, he had been under police surveillance as part of a ginned-up investigation into the Pagan Motorcycle Club, which he had joined several months before; the Pagans sponsored the "Toys for Tots Run" that had brought Derek to Delaware. As with any biker club, the Pagans probably included some disreputable people in their ranks. Derek was emphatically not one of them.

In addition to his honorable military service (albeit in a consummately dishonorable war), Derek's personal background was antiseptically clean. He had a concealed carry permit in Virginia, which would not have been issued to him if he'd been convicted of a felony, a narcotics or domestic violence charge, or had any record of substance abuse or mental illness.

On the day he was killed, Derek had been under both physical and electronic (and, according to the civil complaint, illegal) surveillance. Police personnel who observed him knew that his behavior was completely innocuous. And despite the fact that he had done nothing to warrant such treatment, he was considered an "un-indicted co-conspirator" in a purported narcotics ring run by the Pagans.

The police vehicles screeched to a halt in front of the house shortly after 4:00 PM. The officers ordered Lopez and her children away from Derek—who, predictably, had risen to his feet by this time—and then ordered him to remove his hands from the pockets of his sweatshirt.

Less than a second later—according to several eyewitnesses at the scene—Derek was hit with a taser blast that knocked him sideways and sent him into convulsions. His right hand involuntarily shot out of its pocket, clenching spasmodically.

"Not in front of the kids," Derek gasped, as he tried to force his body to cooperate. "Get the kids out of here."

The officers continued to order Derek to put up his hands; he was physically unable to comply.

So they tased him again. This time he was driven to his side and vomited into a nearby flower bed.

Howard Mixon, a contractor who had been working nearby, couldn't abide the spectacle.

"That's not necessary!" he bellowed at the assailants. "That's overkill! That's overkill!"

At this point, one of the heroes in blue (or, in this case, black) swaggered over to Mixon and snarled, "I'll f*****g show you overkill!" Having heroically shut up an unarmed civilian, the officer turned his attention back to Derek—who was being tased yet again.

"I'm trying to get my hands out," Derek exclaimed, desperately trying to make his tortured and traumatized body obey his will. Horrified, his friend Sandra screamed at the officers: "He is trying to get his hands out, he cannot get his hands out!"

Having established that Derek—an innocent man who had survived two tours of duty in Iraq—was defenseless, one of Wilmington's Finest closed in for the kill.

Lt. William Brown of the Wilmington Police Department, who was close enough to seize and handcuff the helpless victim, instead shot him in the chest at point-blank range, tearing apart his vitals with three .40-caliber rounds. He did this after Derek had said, repeatedly and explicitly, that he was trying to cooperate. He did this despite the fact that witnesses on the scene had confirmed that Derek was trying to cooperate. He did this in front of a traumatized mother and two horrified children.

Why was this done?

According to Sgt. Steven Elliot of the WPD, Brown slaughtered Derek Hale because he "feared for the safety of his fellow officers and believed that the suspect was in a position to pose an imminent threat." That subjective belief was sufficient justification to use "deadly force," according to Sgt. Elliot.

The "position" Derek was in, remember, was that of wallowing helplessly in his own vomit, trying to overcome the cumulative effects of three completely unjustified Taser attacks.

When asked by the Wilmington *News Journal* last week if Hale had ever threatened the officers—remember, there were at least 8 and as many as 12 of them—Elliot replied: "In a sense, [he threatened the officers] when he did not comply with their commands."

He wasn't given a chance to comply: He was hit with the first Taser strike less than a second after he was commanded to remove his hands from his pockets, and then two more in rapid succession. The killing took roughly three minutes.

As is always the case when agents of the State murder an innocent person, the WPD immediately went into cover-up mode. The initial account of the police murder claimed that Derek had "struggled with undercover Wilmington vice officers"; that "struggle," of course, referred to Derek's involuntary reaction to multiple, unjustified Taser strikes.

The account likewise mentioned that police recovered "two items that were considered weapons" from Derek's body. Neither was a firearm. One was a container of pepper spray. The other was a switchblade knife. Both were most likely planted on the murder victim: The police on the scene had pepper spray, and Derek's stepbrother, Missouri resident Jason Singleton, insists that Derek never carried a switchblade.

"The last time I saw Derek," Jason told the *News Journal*, "he had a small Swiss Army knife. I've never seen Derek with anything like a switchblade."

Within hours, the WPD began to fabricate a back-story to justify Derek's murder. Several Delaware State Police officers—identified in the suit as "Lt. [Patrick] Ogden, Sgt. Randall Hunt, and other individual DSP [personnel]" contacted the police in Manassas, Virginia and informed him that Derek had been charged with drug trafficking two days before he was murdered. This was untrue. But because it was said by someone invested with the majestic power of the State, it was accepted as true, and cited in a sworn affidavit to secure a warrant to search Derek's home.

Conducting this spurious search—which was, remember, play-acting in the service of a cover story—meant shoving aside Derek's grieving widow, Elaine, and her two shattered children, who had just lost their stepfather. Nothing of material consequence was found, but a useful bit of embroidery was added to the cover story.

Less than two weeks earlier, Derek and Elaine had celebrated their first anniversary.

The Delaware State Police officers are guilty of misprison of perjury, as are the officials who collaborated in this deception. And it's entirely likely that the Virginia State Police had guilty knowledge as well.

Last November 21, in an attempt to preempt public outrage, the highest officials of the Delaware State Police issued a press release in conjunction with their counterparts from Virginia. The statement is a work of unalloyed mendacity.

"Hale resisted arrest and was shot and killed by Wilmington Police on November 6, 2006," lied the signatories with reference to the claim that he "resisted." "Hale was at the center of a long term narcotics trafficking investigation which is still ongoing."

As we've seen, Hale did not resist arrest, as everyone on the scene knew. And he was not at the "center" of any investigation; before his posthumous promotion to "un-indicted co-conspirator," he was merely a "person of interest" because of his affiliation with a motorcycle club.

Most critically, the statement—which bears the august imprimatur of both the Delaware and Virginia State Police departments, remember—asserts: "Both [State Police] Superintendents have confirmed that there was never any false information exchanged by either agency in the investigation of Derek J. Hale, or transmitted between the agencies in order to obtain the search warrant."

This was another lie.

"Delaware State Police spokesperson Sgt. Melissa Zebley conceded last week that no arrest warrant for Hale was ever issued," reported the *News Journal* on March 22. Three days after Hale was murdered, police arrested 12 members of the Pagans Motorcycle Club on various drug and weapons charges, but identified Hale at that point only as a "person of interest."

Last Friday (May 23), the Rutherford Institute—one of the precious few nominally conservative activist groups that give half a damn about individual liberty—and a private law firm in Virginia filed a civil rights lawsuit against several Delaware law enforcement and political officials on behalf of Derek's widow and parents. They really should consider including key officials from the Virginia State Police in the suit, as well.

Those who persist in fetishizing local police—who are, at this point, merely local franchises of a unitary, militarized, Homeland Security apparatus—should ponder this atrocity long and hard.

They should contemplate not only the inexplicable eagerness of Lt. William Brown to kill a helpless, paralyzed pseudo-suspect, but also the practiced ease with which the police establishments of two states collaborated in devising a fiction to cover up that crime.

According to the lawsuit, Lt. Brown, Derek's murderer, "has violated the constitutional rights of others in the past through the improper use of deadly force and has coached other WPD officers on how to lie about and/or justify the improper use of deadly force." Rather than being cashiered, Brown was promoted—just as one would expect of any other dishonest, cowardly thug in the service of any other Third World death squad.

I'm From the Government, So I Get to Kill You

Pro Libertate, February 6, 2007

Right Now, justice is being perverted in a court of law. . .[1][2]
Right Now, the truth is being obscured. . .[3]
Right Now, a mad man is wandering the streets of the town you live in. . .[4]
Right Now, our government is doing things we think only other countries do. . . .[5]

Right Now, a thuggish policeman in a country like China or Cuba is grinding a hapless victim's face in the dirt and then dragging another off to jail. En route to the detention center, the victim starts to pray, asking God to help him and to forgive his captor. This gesture is greeted with a contemptuous belch and a sneering question: "Who's this God you're praying to? Let's see your God get you out of jail."

"Once you're behind bars," the uniformed thug taunts, his features twisted into a sadistic smirk, "you'll be beaten and most likely raped."

It's not difficult to imagine something of this sort happening in some wretched Communist or Muslim country. Most Americans couldn't imagine this happening in the United States. This could be considered a failure of imagination, except for one thing: What I describe above actually happened in 1997. The assailant was a police officer in Prince George's County, Maryland, an Army veteran named Keith Washington (and a graduate of the Army's Command and General Staff College).

In the decade since that incident—which I'll describe in more detail anon—Officer Washington compiled a lengthy list of complaints for his behavior both on- and off-duty, distinguishing himself even among members of a law enforcement agency notorious for its lawlessness and corruption. On the strength of that job record, as well as fraternity ties to the County Executive, Washington was appointed Deputy Homeland Security Chief for Prince George's County.

That was the rank Washington held when he was involved in a January 24 dispute with furniture delivery men over a scratched headboard. That dispute ended with Washington drawing a gun and shooting the delivery men. The

131

department, in keeping with the Homeland Security ethos, initially charged the men Washington had shot with assault, but withdrew the charges in the interest of public relations shortly before one of the officer's victims died. Washington remains on administrative leave, rather than behind bars, which is where he would be if he weren't employed by the Regime.

In the weeks leading up to that fatal shooting, Washington had been involved in several arguments with officers of his Homeowners Association, assaulting at least two of them.

None of these developments should be a surprise to those involved in a 1997 traffic accident involving Washington and an attorney named Paul Essex.

In court testimony recounted by the *Washington Post*, Essex recalled the post-accident confrontation with Washington.

"You caused this accident!" snarled the officer.

"That's a decision for the court to make," Essex reasonably replied.

"Out here, I *am* the court," declared Washington.

When Essex disagreed, Washington placed him under arrest.

"He grabbed my arm and . . . jacked my arm up and pulled me back over to the driver's side front fender," Essex recalled.

A mechanic named David Paul Maslousky, who was a passenger in Essex's car, was thrown to the ground and arrested for "hindering" Washington in the performance of his duties, a charge that was later dropped.

During the drive to the police station, amid a constant stream of threats and invective from Washington, Maslousky began to pray. It was at that point that the officer slipped into the persona of a Soviet commissar, mocking the man's religious convictions and promising that "Bubba" would soon "have his way with you."

Maslousky later took Washington to court, winning a $210,000 damage award that was eventually overturned on appeal. The officer's defense strategy was to defend arrogance, pomposity, and aggressive hostility to the civilian public as indispensable traits for a successful law enforcement officer.

"No one has a right to a polite and cordial police officer," insisted County Attorney Andrew Murray, who represented Washington. Of the behavior on display when he was needlessly provoking Essex and grinding Maslousky into the dirt, Murray insisted: "[T]hese are characteristics that he employs . . . so that he can make order out of chaos—these are characteristics that *enable him to survive his day-to-day contact with citizens* so he can go home and see his family." (Emphasis added.)

Note this well: Washington's defense assumes that the citizenry is a threat to be subdued, and civilian life a form of chaos to which he must bring order. This is what they're teaching at the U.S. Army's Command and General Staff College, and most likely in police academies across the nation.

Washington's ascent to prominence in Prince George's County is hardly surprising to those who have chronicled the bloody, corrupt exploits of its police department. In 2001, to cite one example, Howard University student Prince Jones was killed in an execution-style police shooting, his body riddled with four bullets. The police described the incident as a "surveillance operation gone bad," insisting that Prince—a clean-cut, well-respected man with plans to marry and enlist in the Navy—was mistaken for a dreadlocked drug dealer nearly a foot shorter and substantially heavier.

This incident was regrettably representative of law enforcement in Prince George's county, which "could boast a healthy cross-section of shootings, maimings, and thrashings that would easily make the Blue Beatdowns Hall of Fame," lamented *The Washington Monthly*.

Last September, the County was hit with a verdict awarding $6.4 million in damages to Keith Longtin, whose wife Donna was kidnapped, raped, and murdered in 1999. The police took Longtin into custody and subjected him to a 38-hour "coercive interrogation"; he was allowed roughly one hour of sleep and infrequent bathroom breaks as officers worked shifts in the hope of extorting a confession. Eventually the detectives reported that the husband had confessed; he insisted that this was a lie. On the strength of that supposed confession Longtin was held in jail for 8 months—roughly seven months after DNA evidence extracted from his murdered wife's remains exonerated him.

During the 1990s, writes the indispensable James Bovard, the Prince George's County police department

> killed and maimed more people than the Unabomber and the Aryan Nation combined. They have a worse human rights record than the Federal Bureau of Investigation [which was involved in the Ruby Ridge and Waco massacres]. If they were a foreign-based entity classified as terrorists (such as Hamas), and you contributed to their cause, you would face up to 10 years in jail for supporting terrorism. Instead, they are supported with your tax dollars. They are the 1400 members of the Prince George's County police department.

Continues Bovard:

> Among the shootings the police department ruled as justified: "An unarmed construction worker was shot in the back after he was detained in a fast-food restaurant. An unarmed suspect died in a fusillade of 66 bullets as he tried to flee in a car from police. A homeless man was shot when police mistook his portable radio for a gun. And an unarmed man was killed after he pulled off the road to relieve himself."

In Maryland, as elsewhere, police officers enjoy immunity from questioning for 10 days following the use of deadly force; this interval can be, and often is, exploited by corrupt police to collude in creating a cover story.

Prince George's County abuts the Imperial Capital, and at the beginning of the decade the odor of corruption became so pervasive that the Justice Department put the police under FBI scrutiny. The elevation of Officer Washington—whose reputation was hardly a secret—to second in command of the County's Homeland Security office apparently raised no eyebrows in Washington. He's most likely just the sort of hero the Feds had in mind when they created the *Heimatsicherheitsdienst*.

---

[1] http://youtube.com/watch?v=WCkQZOnCN3k

[2] http://starbulletin.com/2007/02/06/news/story02.html

[3] http://www.downingstreetmemo.com/

[4] http://youtube.com/watch?v=Fh_3mXpDQEE

[5] http://youtube.com/watch?v=HlIKz7x6W-o

2008

Resurrection Sunday: We Are Commanded to be Free

Pro Libertate, March 23 (Resurrection Sunday), 2008

> You were bought with a price; do not become slaves of men.
> —1 Corinthians 7:23

The world was too small for Alexander, Juvenal pointed out, yet in the end he found that a small sarcophagus was sufficient. By way of contrast, the tomb could not contain Jesus, who repeatedly explained that His kingdom is not of this world. For believers, Resurrection Sunday celebrates the victory of Jesus—the only One truly entitled to be called a king—over sin and death. It should also prompt us to reflect on our duty to live as free men.

Jesus carried out his ministry in an ignominious province of a globe-spanning Empire on the descending slope of its imperial peak. Yes, several centuries would pass before Rome extinguished itself, but the republic was long dead, and the afflictions that would kill the empire were already well advanced.

Decades earlier, Scipio the Younger had wept amid the ruins of Carthage, not so much because his conscience was wounded by the pitiless destruction of an enemy, but because he foresaw a day when Rome would be on the receiving end of what it had just dealt out. Sallust would later lament that Rome's precipitous moral decline began with the destruction of Carthage in the Third Punic War.

That conflict, interestingly enough, began because Rome's long-standing rival, having been disarmed at the end of the First Punic War, abrogated the treaty in order to defend itself against incursions by a Roman ally. So we see that needless and opportunistic wars are hardly a recent invention.

By the time Jesus used a denarius to illustrate the limits of Caesar's jurisdiction ("render to Caesar that which is Caesar's" means that we are to give rulers *no more than* that which they are entitled to under God's law), the Empire had already begun the process of debasing the currency through coin-clipping. Tribute from the provinces being inadequate to sustain the empire, the imperial regime resorted to this primitive but surprisingly effective form of pre-Federal Reserve inflation—and the result, then as now, was to abet the malignant growth of government power and the wholesale corruption of public and private morals.

Clipping and adulteration of the precious metal content of Roman coinage began shortly after Tiberius (whose face disfigured the silver coin used in Jesus's parable) ascended to the purple in 14 AD "By the time he was assassinated in AD 37," write Bill Bonner and Addison Wiggin in their indispensable book *Empire of Debt*, "there were 700 million denarii in the treasury—far more than there had been at the time of Augustus's death."

Caligula, who inherited the throne, quickly wiped out this budget surplus and spent Rome into a huge deficit. When Nero came along, widespread currency debasement was undertaken once again, and it would persist until Alaric and his Goth buddies crested the seventh hill.

By the time Honorius found himself hip-deep in Visigoths, note Bonner and Wiggin, Roman currency "still bore the ancient form with the images of dead emperors pressed on it. But the value had been taken out; the currency had lost 99.98 percent of its value."

This quite understandably seems quite shocking—until we remember that since 1913, when the Regime created its official counterfeiting arm, the U.S. dollar has lost 95 percent of its value. What took Rome half a millennium—the complete devaluation of its currency—Washington has nearly accomplished in a little less than a century. It will be a miracle of sorts if the dollar survives this decade.

At the time of Jesus's ministry, Rome was mired in what Bonner and Wiggin call "a new system of *consuetudo fraudium*—habitual cheating." Romans still "remembered their Old Republic with its rules and customs," and they still "thought that was the way the system was supposed to work" long after the senate had become a vestigial body and the emperor's will supplanted the law. Willing parties to this universal, State-imposed deception, Roman citizens and subjects practiced and fell prey to private fraud of various kinds. If credit cards and sub-prime mortgages had been available at the time, Romans would have defaulted on both at rates rivaling our own.

It seems to me that this kind of behavior is to be expected when the government-issued medium of exchange is fraudulent. This is particularly true of the Roman denarius, which was designed to propagate the cult of the divine emperor: The coin used by Jesus in His parable bore the inscription, *Ti Caesar Divi Aug F[ilius] Aust Imp*—Latin shorthand for "Tiberius Caesar, divine son of the Emperor Augustus."

Which is to say that the Roman currency claimed that the emperor, depicted wearing a laurel as a token of his future exaltation, was the son of a god.

Once this is understood, Jesus's familiar saying takes on—for me, at least—a much deeper meaning than I had previously appreciated.

Writing five decades ago, theologian Roland H. Bainton points out that this debased and blasphemous currency was "Rome's best device for popularizing in the provinces the cult of the divine Emperor." Not surprisingly, Zealots and other Jewish rejectionists rebelled against the Roman currency, hammering them flat, melting them down, and stamping them with Hebrew characters. "But many of the Jews," writes Dr. Bainton, "while adamant as to the Roman standards [of morality and religion], were pliant in regard to the coins."

Among that number, perhaps, were some of the Pharisees who—with unearned confidence in their supposed cleverness—posed their trick question to Jesus: Is it lawful to pay taxes to Caesar, or not?

The import of Jesus's answer—"Render unto Caesar that which is Caesar's, and to God that which is God's"—is paraphrased by Dr. Bainton thus: "If, then, you trifle with your scruples and carry the tainted coins, give back to Caesar what he has given to you, but remember your prime allegiance is to God."

While pointedly *limiting* Caesar's jurisdiction, Jesus did not specify *how much* the emperor was entitled to. My belief is that He deliberately left that question to the individual conscience. He expects us to know when Caesar or any other ruler (or representative) has transgressed the limits of his authority, thereby attempting to lay claim on an allegiance we owe only to God.

What was the market value, circa 70 AD, of a pinch of incense? A trifle, by any standard. And speaking the phrase "Caesar is Lord" as that minuscule amount of incense was burned in front of the Emperor's likeness incurred no tangible expense. Yet the *cost* of this gesture, to Christian believers, was prohibitive, and many of them regarded death by torture a comparative bargain when the alternative was to deny their Lord, their faith, and their freedom.

Such Christians understood that Caesar was their ruler, and that they could do little to change that reality. One thing they could do, however, was to refuse to recognize them as their master. That is the demand every State eventually makes of its subjects, and it was prefigured in the blasphemous coin used by Jesus in his parable.

Does this mean that it was a form of idolatry to use Caesar's coins—that is, to participate in the imperial economic system at all? Jesus never said as much. But His parable, when understood in its historical context, clearly anticipated the time when the Roman State, which already demanded so much of the bodies of its subjects, would lay a proprietary claim on the souls of the Christians living under its jurisdiction as well. Every State, if permitted to, will eventually do the same.

Freedom, in its most elemental sense, is the power to withdraw one's consent when the State—or anyone else—lays an improper claim to one's life or property. For the Christians ruled by the Roman Empire, this meant defying terrestrial authorities by assembling in the catacombs to worship, by refusing to serve in the Empire's armies of conquest, and by refusing to worship emperors either living or dead. Thus for many of them, the only way to refuse consent was to choose the path of martyrdom.

Many early Christians who didn't suffer martyrdom understood that the State was the implacable enemy—not only to them, but to God as well. As the brilliant libertarian philosopher George H. Smith (a professed atheist) observes in an essay published by the Acton Institute, many Fathers of the early Church, while not counseling revolution, treated the Roman State as entirely illegitimate because everything it did was backed by actual or threatened use of lethal violence.

Tertullian (born in Carthage, ironically, as the son of a Roman centurion) "argued that 'all secular power and dignities are not merely alien from, but hostile to, God,'" recalls Dr. Smith. "Secular governments 'owe their existences to the sword.' All institutions of the Roman government, even its charities, are based on brute force. This is contrary to the way of Christians, among whom 'everything is voluntary.'"

What is the limit of Christian submission to a State of that description? According to Origen, explains Dr. Smith, the Christian must "'never consent to obey the laws of sin.' His first allegiance is to 'the law of nature, that is, the law of God.' The Christian will submit to secular punishment rather than transgress a divine law."

Those sentiments read like a distant ancestor of the Declaration of Independence, which properly recognized the law—God's "perfect law of liberty"—rather than any terrestrial ruler, as the power to which all must submit. In a republic, the law is king, and all political leaders exercise their authority by the grace of the governed, with the understanding that it can be revoked at any time.

It was under this vision of republican liberty (however imperfectly realized) that Americans had the opportunity to be the first people ever to carry out the divine mandate to live as free men under God's law. That right was secured through righteous rebellion against un-Godly tyranny—each man, empowered by God's law, taking up the sword against evil-doers in positions of supposed authority.

We've squandered that opportunity. Will God condescend to give us another? I don't presume to know. It is clear, however, that we've traveled a great distance down the same Roman thoroughfare to ruin, and that the Regime ruling us is ripening into the kind of Reich (that's just a fancy word for "empire," after all) that would claim jurisdiction over our souls.

Many Americans will readily pay that price, so far gone in materialism that they don't realize that a "soul" can be found in their personal inventory. Others will profess allegiance to Christ while acting as enablers and inquisitors for Caligula.

Some of us, if our country pursues its present course to its logical destination, may find ourselves caught in a predicament akin to that of Tribune Marcellus Gallio, as depicted in my second-favorite film, *The Robe*.

Like many other "bathrobe epics" of the 1950s, *The Robe* could be seen as a form of Christian midrash—in this case, a story that could have happened, but probably didn't, that draws from situations described in the Bible. In the story Marcellus is the wastrel son of a senator who is a political opponent of Caligula before Little Boots ascends to the throne. Marcellus and his slave Demetrius are exiled to Judea; there the latter becomes a follower of the Galilean Troublemaker whom the former is assigned to execute.

Eventually Demetrius leads his master to Christ, and Marcellus finds himself on trial for high treason before Caligula, newly installed as Caesar. Knowing that his words will convict him, Marcellus doesn't cavil at telling the unvarnished truth:

> If the Empire desires peace and justice and goodwill among all men, my King will be on the side of the Empire and her Emperor. If the Empire and the Emperor desire to pursue the slavery and slaughter that have brought agony and terror and despair to the world . . . if there is then nothing further for men to hope for but chains and hunger at the hands of our Empire— my King will march forward to right this wrong! Not tomorrow,

sire—Your Majesty may not be so fortunate as to witness the establishment of His kingdom—but it will come!

The verdict is as predictable as the course of a waterfall.

Caligula, who wants to make Marcellus submit even more than he wants to kill him, offers to commute the death sentence for high treason if Marcellus will renew his oath of loyalty and recant his allegiance to "this dead Jew who dared call Himself a king."

Marcellus has no trouble doing the first, reiterating his oath of loyalty and pointing out that he had never broken it. Pressed by Caligula to denounce Jesus, Marcellus stands unwavering before the Emperor and refuses:

> I cannot renounce him, Sire, nor can you. He is my king, and
> yours as well. He is the Son of God.

In the film Marcellus and his would-be wife Diana go to martyrdom, as have countless believers across the centuries. But they did this as an expression of freedom: They knew that they had been bought by a price, and chose not to be the slaves of a man claiming to be a god.

To those who don't believe, this may seem the most perfect foolishness. But those of us who believe must understand that our individual freedom may ultimately demand such a price. If we're not ultimately willing to pay it, what were we really celebrating today?

2009

Hotlined

Pro Libertate, August 12, 2009

"Grab some clothes and get into the van, *now*."

For an instant, that directive, and the tone in which it was issued, had the opposite of its intended effect: Korrin and our five older children, momentarily paralyzed by shock, looked at me in alarm. There was something in both the tone of my voice, and the expression on my face, that was new and a little frightening. None of them had seen my "game face" before. They were seeing it now.

Just seconds earlier, Korrin and I had been confronted on our doorstep by two very nice, well-dressed women who informed us that an anonymous "child endangerment" complaint had been filed with the Child Protective Services.

One of the visitors was a social worker we've known for several years, and consider a friend. The other was a stranger who introduced herself as a CPS investigator. She intended to inspect our home and speak with our children.

After being summoned to the doorstep, I had ushered our children into our house and closed the door behind me. Short of being removed by force, there was no way I was going to permit a CPS investigator to have access to our home as long as our children were vulnerable to government abduction.

"You seem like a conscientious and well-intentioned person," I quietly told the investigator, "but this is an adversarial situation, and I can't allow you to have access to my home in the absence of a warrant, and until I've consulted with legal counsel."

Although this clearly wasn't the response she had expected or desired, the investigator retained her professional composure.

"Well, that is your right," she replied. "I must advise you that I will consult with law enforcement and return later today."

"I understand," I said, shooting a quick glance at the slender silver digital recorder the investigator wasn't successfully concealing in her left hand. "I also want the record to reflect the fact that I didn't consent for our conversation to be recorded."

The investigator nodded in assent, her brows pulling together ever-so-slightly as if in puzzlement. She and her associate returned to their car and drove away. As they turned the corner I turned to Korrin and our children and ordered—yes, it was an order, not a request—them to get in the van.

"Don't bother packing," I told them in syllables drawn taut with urgency. "Just grab a couple of things and get in the van." The kids, suddenly understanding that we were at Def-Con One, quietly and quickly did as they were told.

Minutes later we were headed out of Payette County, beyond the jurisdiction of the local police and Sheriff, en route to a pre-designated safe house.

Yes, we had—as Foghorn Leghorn might put it—made plans to deal with just such an emergency.

Earlier this year, I met with a handful of close and trusted friends to discuss various crisis scenarios—from the systemic breakdown of the commercial food distribution network to the possibility that one of us might find his family targeted by the CPS. Those meetings were the idea of a good friend who is a very well-informed and astute survivalist. Relatively little was accomplished at those meetings, but as recent events testify, what little was done proved to be indispensable.

One of the participants at those gatherings (we chose a local club whose owner is defying an asinine local smoking ban; we refractory individualists need to support each other) very generously offered his home as a temporary refuge for my children in the event that the CPS came after my family. From there, working through communications cut-outs, we could make arrangements for Korrin and our children to stay in the homes of other reliable people who share our convictions.

When the balloon went up, we knew what to do. I spirited our family to my friend's house, casting frequent glances in the rear-view mirror.

"This reminds me of that movie 'Not Without My Daughter,'" commented my genius son William Wallace, our family's resident cineaste. There was no undertone of eagerness or excitement in his voice; William was scared. So was Isaiah, who quietly explained that in cases of this kind children are often taken from their parents.

That was a hard thing to say, but it needed to be said. Not surprisingly, this terrified our girls, six-year-old Katrina and four-year-old Sophia. Although he has the reflexive aversion to girls of any kind that typifies an eight-year-old boy, Jefferson wrapped his arms around Katrina and comforted her as she cried.

Once we crossed the county border, I relaxed a little bit and gave some instructions to Korrin and the kids. I told Korrin that it was important not to call our home, since caller ID would reveal the location of the safe house. I would contact them through an intermediary, and if she needed anything she was to call that person. I told the kids that they would be safe with our friends until I came to get them, but that if people from the government arrived they were to be courteously uncooperative.

The plan was for me to return to our house, tidy it up, and deal with the CPS and the police. This might mean I could face obstruction charges if they insisted on seeing Korrin and the children, I explained, so there was a possibility I would be in jail by day's end. They had to be prepared for that possibility, because I would not give the CPS an opportunity to seize our children.

Once at the safe house I called a friend who agreed to be my cut-out. Then we gathered for prayer and I went back home by a different route.

Please, Dear Lord, I prayed silently as I neared our house, *don't let it be a crime scene already.* To my relief, nobody was there.

About forty minutes later, following a minimal investment of effort, the house was tidied up. We're messy, but not unclean; no parent would be surprised to see the clutter we deal with, given that we have six small children, and no honest person would consider our unremarkable untidiness to be a threat to our children's health or well-being. But I'm well aware of CPS enforcement actions that have resulted in charges being filed against parents whose homes aren't as antiseptic as a NASA white room.

Roughly a half-hour later, while speaking on the phone to my mother, I saw a city police car drive slowly by our house, turn around, and park in front of our walkway. From it emerged a young man, clean-cut and squared away, who strode up to our front door.

Well, here we go, I thought. I was wrong—and the day took an even stranger turn.

"Who owns the vacant lot?" the young police officer politely inquired.

"Do you mean the lot next to our house?" I asked.

"No, the one behind it," he persisted.

"That's not a 'lot,' it's our backyard," I pointed out, gesturing for him to come with me to look through a nearby gate.

"Who owns this property?" asked the officer. I explained that we were renters, not owners.

"Well, there are some weeds in the backyard that apparently need to be taken care of," the officer began, his tone suggesting that he had expected to see a much bigger problem than the one confronting him. Sure, there is a row of weeds along the rear fence line of our yard (which occupies a significant fraction of an acre), but it wasn't the Amazonian jungle he had anticipated.

"I suppose the weeds along the fence line need to be cut down," the officer observed, "but that's really the responsibility of the property owner." I assured him that I intended to attend to the weeds, whether or not that was my legal "responsibility," simply in the interest of living in a presentable home. The officer took down my publicly available contact information, gave me a polite nod, and departed, leaving me to contemplate an unsettling question:

Why would a police officer visit me with a complaint about overgrown weeds *that are not visible from any of the streets that run by our house*? He couldn't have seen them from the street. Clearly, he was responding to a complaint from someone who had recently been in our backyard.

That fact may prove to be the critical clue in identifying the person who also hot-lined our family to CPS to report that our children were "endangered" by the untidiness of our living space.

Less than a half hour after the first police visit ended, an unmarked police car arrived and decanted the CPS investigator and the largest officer on the roster of the Payette City Police force—a genial man-mountain with a tonsured head, Van Dyke beard, and a ready smile. Seeing him, I simply had to chuckle: *Yes, of course they'd send **him**.*

The plainclothes officer identified himself. I replied that I had met him a couple of years earlier when he, along with practically the entire population of Payette, helped us find then-five-year-old Jefferson when he went missing. (Jefferson was found sleeping peacefully in his fortress of solitude, a secret space he created behind the headboard of a hide-a-bed.)

"I told her"—the officer began, gesturing to the CPS investigator—"that I've been in your home, and it seemed perfectly okay to me. But we have to clear up this complaint."

Since Korrin and the kids were safe, I had no objection. I invited them in and busied myself paying bills.

"Are Korrin and the children not here?" asked the CPS investigator. I told her, quite truthfully, that they had been invited to spend the afternoon at a friend's house.

About two minutes later the CPS worker and policeman were done. They explained as they left that the matter was closed but that I should contact Health and Welfare in the event that we "need any services."

"When we spoke this morning, you were very respectful," the CPS worker commented. "You did hold out for your rights, which is appropriate, but you treated me well, and I appreciated that." I smiled and said something to the effect that I try to treat people well.

This episode turned out much better than it could have.

What if I hadn't been working at home, and Korrin—who suffers from a chronic condition that leaves her exhausted and bed-ridden most of the time—hadn't been able to stave off the CPS before the house had been tidied up?

What if the CPS investigator had seen something—*anything*—"aberrant" in the behavior or appearance of our children, and decided that prudence required a more detailed examination?

What if we had been dealing with the kind of CPS investigator hard-wired to find evidence of abuse or neglect? Granted, we were blessed on this occasion to deal with someone who was sincere, polite, reasonable, and professional. That generally isn't the case in situations of this kind.

What if some combination of circumstances had resulted in a judicial order to appear at a "show cause" hearing, a procedure that almost always leads to some kind of catastrophic government intervention?

Once again, none of those things—or dozens of others, many of them worse—happened. *This* time. To us. But all of those terrible things have happened to families just like ours, because someone, for reasons only that person will know, filed an anonymous complaint with the child "protection" bureaucracy.

It's been said that one can't be a credible sportswriter unless he's actually played the games he covers, or a music critic without knowing how to play an instrument or carry a tune.

After more than two decades of writing about the disruption, or outright destruction, of families by the child welfare bureaucracy, I can finally consider myself qualified, albeit in a limited sense, to pronounce upon that subject. That's a credential I could have done without.

2010

Mass Bloodshed on American Soil: Key to Presidential "Greatness"

LewRockwell.com, November 5, 2010

Shortly after winning re-election in November 1996, Bill Clinton confided to reporters on Air Force One that his political recovery began with the Oklahoma City bombing: "It broke a spell in the country as people began searching for our common ground again."

That "common ground" was defined by unqualified submission to the central government. Mr. Clinton skillfully exploited the bombing to define "anti-government" sentiment—as supposedly displayed in the Republican conquest of the House in the 1994 midterm elections—as something akin to a criminal psychosis. "You can't say you love your country and hate your government," Clinton insisted in a Michigan State University Commencement address following the bombing. Touching on the same theme during a speech to a handpicked audience in Montana, Clinton admonished his devotees not to permit anyone to speak ill of the Regime: "When you hear someone doing it, you ought to stand up and double up your fist and stick it in the sky and shout them down."

That Bill Clinton perceived the Oklahoma City atrocity in terms of its impact upon his own political fortunes offered a useful measure of his capacity for self-preoccupation—but he is hardly unique. Indeed, the imperial presidency is designed to attract the kind of people who are eager to exploit, or precipitate, the death of thousands or millions of human beings. Clinton's immediate successor, after all, cynically used the much larger tragedy of 9/11 to similar ends. In August 2001, George W. Bush's presidency was a floundering, sputtering mess. After the Twin Towers fell, Bush was transformed into a "war president" whose will was law.

According to Mark Penn, former Hillary Clinton campaign strategist, Barack Obama needs his own OKC-style tragedy to offer him a chance to "reconnect" with the American people.

"Remember, President Clinton reconnected through Oklahoma, right?" Penn said during a November 4 panel discussion on MSNBC's *Hardball* program. "And the president right now seems removed. It wasn't until that speech [after the bombing] that [Clinton] really clicked with the American public." According to Penn, Obama needs "a similar kind" of opportunity for greatness, even if that means hundreds or thousands of mere Mundanes must die to provide it.

Gypsies, Tramps and Thugs

Pro Libertate, September 7, 2010

"This guy . . . just tried to run my husband over!" exclaimed Arkansas resident Cindy Nelson in a frantic 911 call on July 21. "Oh, my God—he's shooting at us! Oh, my God!"

A few minutes later, Fred Ensminger—the deranged assailant—placed a 911 call of his own.

"This is Diamondhead 1106," Ensminger told the suddenly swamped dispatcher. "I have been shot and I need medical at my front gate ASAP."

Ensminger is a recidivist criminal. Thanks to the fact that practically any bipedal simian with a pulse can become a police officer in Arkansas, Ensminger—who just *barely* meets those criteria—is employed by the Police Department of Diamondhead Arkansas, a gated community located south of Hot Springs.

A few minutes before Cindy Nelson told the 911 dispatcher that a "guy with a badge" was trying to murder her husband, she had passed Ensminger's pickup truck, which was parked by the side of the road.

As Nelson started to go around the truck, Ensminger—whose penchant for abusive behavior was notorious in Diamondhead—pulled out in front of her. According to an eyewitness, Ensminger "stopped suddenly," causing Nelson to slam on her brakes to avoid a collision.

According to the witness, Ensminger climbed out of his pickup truck and began to harangue Nelson. She reacted by pulling around him and proceeding down the road. An infuriated Ensminger followed in close pursuit.

With Ensminger's pickup truck looming in her rear-view, Nelson called her husband, Jerry Chambliss, and told him that she was being followed. She had no idea at this point that her stalker was an off-duty police officer.

After Nelson entered the gated community, Chambliss went into the driveway "with my arms up, palms out, hollering stop, stop, stop, what are you doing?" he later told investigators.

Ensminger gunned the pickup forward, striking Chambliss and knocking him down. He then compounded that act of attempted vehicular homicide by grabbing his 40 caliber Glock and firing several rounds into the garage. At some point Ensminger punctuated his acts of attempted criminal homicide by flashing his state-issued costume jewelry.

Chambliss raced into the house and retrieved a loaded 9mm handgun and returned fire, striking Ensminger in the shoulder and forcing the assailant to withdraw.

After Ensminger called for backup, Nelson made a second 911 call requesting a police officer. When the dispatcher replied that an officer was already on the premises, Nelson suggested that it might be worthwhile to send someone other than the person who had just perforated her home with gunfire.

"She [the dispatcher] kept telling me, 'He's not the shooter—he's a cop,'" Cindy Nelson related in an interview with Pro Libertate. "I kept trying to convince her that's what was happening—that this cop just opened fire on our home. They never did send anyone to help us, even though they did send people after he [Ensminger] called 911."

After the police arrived, Nelson continues, "they had us on the ground in handcuffs for thirty minutes. They also spent six hours searching our house— with our consent, I guess. After that they didn't even take my husband with them; they just said 'We'll call you if we need to ask some more questions.'"

Note well that right from the beginning it was clear that Chambliss had acted legally, and that Ensminger, the assailant, had committed a criminal offense. Despite this, the official stance of the Diamondhead Police Department was that Chambliss was a "suspect," and that Ensminger had fallen heroically in the line of duty.

The shootout between Ensminger and Chambliss was originally described by the Diamondhead Police and the local media as growing out of a "domestic dispute." Chief Pat Mahoney and Garland County Deputy Judy Daniel told Little Rock's Fox 16 News that they were concerned about their injured comrade, who had been stricken in the line of duty as he was "investigating" a purported episode of domestic violence.

That official lie is indigestibly rich in irony, given the fact that Ensminger—a "gypsy cop" who has been repeatedly fired and punished for disciplinary infractions and criminal acts—was himself arrested on a domestic violence charge in 2006. The victim in that assault, which took place in front of the police station in Alexander, Arkansas, was a female police officer.

"We are very happy that the officer is okay and extremely glad that the suspect is in custody," stated Deputy Daniel shortly after that heroic defender of public order tried to murder Jerry Chambliss. "It just makes it easier on everybody, the other officers, his family."

Note how this description of "everybody" refers exclusively to those employed as agents of government coercion. The "civilian" who used righteous force to repel Ensminger's criminal assault apparently didn't count. Mere Mundanes never do.

Following surgery to remove the bullet he had received as a consolation prize for finishing second in a shoot-out, Ensminger filed the predictably perjurious official report.

Like too many others in his profession, Ensminger couples functional illiteracy with an unexpected gift for storytelling. He claimed to have observed Nelson driving erratically, and that she attempted to run him over when he displayed the trinket denoting his supposed authority.

That claim was demolished by contradictory eyewitness testimony, which established that while Ensminger screamed at Nelson and wagged a finger in her direction, he never flashed his badge.

Ensminger offered a similarly mendacious version of his encounter with Chambliss. In the officer's account, he was confronted by an "angry unknown man" who slammed his hands on the hood of his car telling him to get out of the driveway.

In this depiction, Chambliss shot Ensminger without provocation, and the off-duty cop returned fire in self-defense. Once again, that account couldn't be reconciled with the evidence assembled during an investigation by the Arkansas State Police.

In his official report, state Prosecuting Attorney Steve Oliver concluded that Chambliss "was justified in using deadly physical force in the defense of himself and his wife on July 21, 2010. . . . Under Arkansas law, Mr. Chambliss was not required to retreat if he was not the original aggressor."

This of necessity means that Fred Ensminger, the "original aggressor," committed multiple acts of criminal assault, and thus be subject to prosecution—correct?

Well, no.

Oliver ruled that Ensminger displayed "poor judgment in his aggressive pursuit of Ms. Nelson to her residence but he acted with the belief that he was justified under color of law."

This unsupportable, invalid "belief" appears sufficient to exculpate Ensminger's repeated attempts to murder Jerry Chambliss. Oliver doesn't provide any other explanation for his decision not to file criminal charges of any kind against Ensminger, who not only remains free but (at least as of September

7) is reportedly still employed by the Diamondhead Police Department, even though he is currently enjoying a paid vacation (aka "administrative leave").

"Just because he has a badge he does not have the right to come down and kill citizens," Chambliss complained to Little Rock's Fox affiliate. According to Oliver, that state-issued bauble does indeed confer the authority to commit acts of discretionary murder. Oliver's report clearly suggests that if Ensminger had displayed his chintzy totem of official privilege during the highway confrontation with Cindy Nelson, Chambliss would be facing criminal charges.

"We've never had trouble of any kind with law enforcement before," Cindy Nelson remarked to Pro Libertate:

> We're well-known here, and we've always been upstanding citizens. I'm a nurse, and my husband—who served in the Navy—has been a real estate broker and a candidate for office. My husband suffered severe bruising and other injuries after being run down. We never used to lock our doors, now we have *three* locks on every door and keep our cars locked at all times.

Chambliss is also undergoing treatment for what appears to be post-traumatic stress disorder. "This guy simply terrorized us," Cindy summarizes. She and her husband have some unfortunate company in Diamondhead.

"We're scared to have him in the community, quite frankly," commented Diamondhead resident Kimberly Gilsinger, whose children were threatened by the officer while swimming in a local lake.

In late June, just weeks before Ensminger attempted to murder Jerry Chambliss, Gilsinger and her husband filed a complaint alleging that the officer had threatened to kill her son and five other local boys, the youngest of whom was ten years old.

Specifically, Ensminger allegedly said that "he would get in the water and drown every one of them if they didn't get out," Gilsinger recalled. The complaint also stated that Ensminger made a vague but unmistakable threat to shoot the kids.

(Arkansas police seem to attract child predators: Three years ago a tonsured thug named Joey Williams was captured on video choking and otherwise assaulting several young skateboarders on the streets of Hot Springs. His employer, the Hot Springs PD, ruled that his felonious assault was "justified," not that the suspense was unbearable.)

Ray Massey, President of the Diamondhead Property Association, told the Little Rock CBS affiliate that Ensminger "got a verbal reprimand and a warning" after committing what Gilsinger correctly describes as a "felony" by threatening to "harm or kill our children."

This was hardly the first criminal act Ensminger has committed in a career in law enforcement that began seven years ago.

Ensminger was fired little more than a year of being hired by the Shannon Hills Police Department. During that time he managed to shoot a suspect under dubious circumstances (the act was ruled "justified," as nearly all such shootings are) and a property theft charge. During that same busy 14-month span, reports THV-TV, "his record shows an assault case, which included a false statement to the police on Ensminger's part. That case eventually led to his firing."

He then migrated to the Alexander Police Department, where he was arrested on a domestic battery charge after he manhandled his girlfriend—a fellow police officer named April Tirado—outside the police station. Ensminger wasn't fired from that position; he was permitted to resign instead. Approximately a year later he was hired by the Diamondhead Police Department.

The Diamondhead PD refuses to release Ensminger's record, claiming that it is exempt from freedom of information laws because it is employed by a private entity, the Diamondhead Property Owners Association. It is more accurate to describe the POA as a "public-private" or corporatist body, since its police department—as prosecutor Steve Oliver points out—presumes to exercise coercive "authority" under "color of law," rather than simply protecting property rights pursuant to contract. If Ensminger were a Paul Blart-style private security guard, he would most likely be facing criminal charges.

John Frederick Ensminger, petty criminal and itinerant police officer, should be made the poster child for the problem of "Gypsy Cops"—corrupt, abusive officers who drift from one agency to another, enjoying both immunity from prosecution and unassailable job security. This problem is particularly acute in Arkansas, where no certification of any kind is required to become a police officer.

To become a licensed practicing cosmetologist in the State of Arkansas, an applicant must pass a state board examination and complete 2,000 hours of specialized training. For an investment of 600 hours an applicant can qualify to work as a manicurist or instructor.

While Arkansas strictly regulates those who cut hair or paint nails in private, voluntary transactions, it imposes no training or licensing standards whatsoever on armed people clothed in government-issued costumes and the supposed authority to inflict lethal violence on others.

"The second night I ever put on a badge and gun I was riding in my own car," recalls Crittenden County Chief Deputy Tommy Martin. At the time, Martin was 21 years old and hadn't spent so much as a minute inside a police academy classroom, notes Jill Monier of Memphis's Fox News affiliate.

"According to Arkansas state law, officers do not have to be certified for up to a year after they're hired," observes Monier. "The Commission on Law Enforcement Standards and Training says they can get an 8 month extension on top of that. So for almost 2 years, an officer can patrol the streets, by his or herself, and enforce the law without having any kind of training."

Understandably, this system is a boon to "gypsy" cops. Each time a "gypsy" cop finds a new gig in Arkansas, his 12- to 20-month grace period begins all over again; in this way, officers can be enforcing the "law" for years *without receiving certification of any kind.*

Ensminger, who couldn't legally cut hair or manicure nails in Arkansas, remains licensed to kill.

2011

Comrade Levin Seeks to "Rectify" Dear Leader's Libyan War

LewRockwell.com, March 30, 2011

A Soviet-era Russian dissident once wryly described his society as one in which the Regime could revise yesterday's weather by decree. Orwell captured this facet of totalitarianism in his description of Winston Smith's job at the Ministry of Truth, where he was employed to "rectify" the official record to bring it into conformity with the Party line:

> The messages he had received referred to articles or news items which for one reason or another it was thought necessary to alter, or, as the official phrase had it, to rectify. For example, it appeared from *The Times* of the seventeenth of March that Big Brother, in his speech of the previous day, had predicted that the South Indian front would remain quiet but that a Eurasian offensive would shortly be launched in North Africa. As it happened, the Eurasian Higher Command had launched its offensive in South India and left North Africa alone. It was therefore necessary to rewrite a paragraph of Big Brother's speech, in such a way as to make him predict the thing that had actually happened.

"This process of continuous alteration was applied not only to newspapers, but to books, periodicals, pamphlets, posters, leaflets, films, sound-tracks, cartoons, photographs—to every kind of literature or documentation which might conceivably hold any political or ideological significance," Orwell continued. "Day by day and almost minute by minute the past was brought up to date. In this way every prediction made by the Party could be shown by documentary evidence to have been correct, nor was any item of news, or any expression of opinion, which conflicted with the needs of the moment, ever allowed to remain on record."

As the exalted vanguard of the revolution, the Party must preserve its pretense of infallibility. Whatever it decrees is a self-ratifying truth, one to which any contrary historical record must yield.

160

The Regime ruling us hasn't yet reached that stage of ripeness, although Commissar Cass Sunstein is doubtless working on a way to bring that evil dream to fruition. In the meantime, those who presume to rule us have to practice piecemeal "rectification" of the kind proposed by Senator Carl Levin (D-Michigan), chairperson of the Senate Armed Services Committee.

As far as I can tell, Senator Levin is not related to the purulent little blatherskite named Mark Levin, but they—along with war criminal John Yoo—share a disdain for the Constitution's assignment of war powers. As exponents of *Fuhrerprinzip*, the Levins and Yoo all assume that the incumbent dictator in the White House has the legal authority to commit the United States Government to a foreign war without a declaration of war, or congressional authorization of any kind—and that Congress's role is either to ratify the presidential action after the fact, or to bring an end to a war by cutting off its funding.

Where the assault on Libya is concerned, there is one annoying little detail to be addressed: Comrade Obama never bothered to involve Congress in any way before ordering U.S. military personnel to attack a country that never harmed or threatened us in any way. The UN Security Council resolution that supposedly authorized this crime was issued after Congress was in recess, and hostile action was undertaken before Congress re-convened. This is complicated further by the fact that both the Dear Leader himself and his political consort Joe Biden are on record stating, in unambiguous terms, that a presidential action of this kind is grounds for impeachment (to which we should add prosecution and imprisonment).

Not being able—yet—to "rectify" the historical record by expunging the earlier statements by Obama and Biden, Sen. Levin wants to do the next best thing: issue a congressional resolution "authorizing" the war after the fact.

"I'm interested in a vote authorizing military action," Levin said yesterday (March 29)—a week and a half after that war had begun. "The president said he'd welcome it and I think it would be helpful. It'd show public support for the effort. And that's always useful."

Were this an actual constitutional republic, public support for a formally declared war, expressed through an appropriate vote by elected representatives *before* the war began, would be mandatory. Now we're told that a useless resolution issued well *after* the fact would be taken as a binding statement of "public support," which is "useful" but materially irrelevant to the actions of our rulers.

Of course, no human being has the moral authority to coerce others to make material sacrifices on behalf any government's war. What is remarkable in this case, however, is the cynical contempt displayed by the American *Nomenklatura* for what we're supposed to call the "rule of law."

When the State Breaks a Man

Pro Libertate, June 19, 2011

"How much does the State weigh?" Josef Stalin asked an underling who had been ordered to extract a confession from an enemy of his regime. Stalin understood that, given enough time, agents of State-sanctioned cruelty can break any man.

Thomas J. Ball, who committed suicide by self-immolation on the steps of New Hampshire's Cheshire County Courthouse on June 15, was a man who had been broken by the State. A lengthy suicide note/manifesto he sent to the *Keene Sentinel*, which was published the day after his death, described how his family had been destroyed, and his life ruined, through the intervention of a pitiless and infinitely cruel bureaucracy worthy of Stalin's Soviet Union: The Granite State's affiliate of the federal "domestic violence" Cheka.

Ball and his family were casualties in what he calls a federal "war on men." He wasn't exaggerating—and he has a lot of company.

The federally subsidized domestic violence industry operates a bit like the hypothetical Von Neumann Machine: Placed into a material-rich environment, it will sustain and replicate itself by destroying and assimilating everything within its field of influence. One useful sci-fi example is the robotic Planet Killer from the Star Trek episode "The Doomsday Machine"—an immense, funnel-shaped engine of destruction propelled by the remnants of the worlds it destroys (according to one deutero-canonical source, the Planet Killer uses the same material to generate replicas of itself).

That monstrous device was "self-sustaining as long as there are bodies . . . for it to feed on." The same is true, of course, of the State and all of its components—including what Dr. Stephen Baskerville calls "The Divorce Regime."

As Baskerville points out in his horrifying study *Taken Into Custody: The War Against Fatherhood*, "it is no exaggeration to say that the existence of family courts, and virtually every issue they adjudicate—divorce, custody, child abuse, child-support enforcement, even adoption and juvenile crime—depend on one overriding principle: remove the father." When a family is broken up, each child "becomes a walking bundle of cash"—not for the custodial parent, but for a huge and expanding population of tax-fattened functionaries who "adopt as their mission in life the practice of interfering with other people's children."

Thomas Ball, like millions of others, learned that the people who choose this profession have an unfailing ability to exploit even the tiniest opportunity to invade a home and destroy a family.

One evening in April 2001, Mr. Ball suffered a momentary lapse of patience with a disobedient four-year-old daughter and slapped her face. He left the house at his wife's suggestion. When he called her a short time later, he learned that his wife—"the type that believes that people in authority actually know what they are talking about"—had called the police, who told her that her "abusive" husband wasn't permitted to sleep in his own home that night. Ball was arrested at work the following day. Under the conditions of his bail, he wasn't allowed to ask his wife what had possessed her to call the police.

Years later Ball would learn that if his wife hadn't called the police and accused her husband of abuse, *she* would have been arrested as an accessory—leaving the children at the mercy of New Hampshire's utterly despicable Division of Children, Youth, and Families (DCYF).

Dot Knightly, who tried vainly for years to win custody of three grandchildren seized on the basis of spurious abuse and neglect accusations, recounts how a DCYF commissar contemptuously batted away both her pleas and her abundant qualifications to serve as a custodial caretaker: "Nobody gets their kids back in New Hampshire. The government gives us the power to decide how these cases turn out. Everyone who fights us loses."

Despairing over being wrested away from everyone he loved, Dot's grade-school age grandson Austin—who had literally been dragged screaming from his grandparents' home—tried to commit suicide. This led to confinement in a psychiatric hospital and involuntary "treatment" with mind-destroying psychotropic drugs. For New Hampshire's child-snatchers, the phrase "nobody gets their kids back" translates into a willingness to destroy the captive children by degrees, rather than allow any successful challenge to their supposed authority.

The instant the police intervened in the domestic affairs of Thomas Ball's household, his family's destruction became inevitable. The officers were required—not by law, but by official policy that followed profit incentives created by Washington—to make an arrest. In a similar fashion, and for the same reason, prosecutors are forbidden to drop domestic abuse cases under any circumstances.

Ball recalled that he was eventually found not guilty, much to the visible disgust of the be-robed dispenser of official injustice who presided at the trial. But this made no material difference: His wife—who divorced him six months after his arrest—was now a consort of the State, his children were its property. His innocence notwithstanding, Ball was given an open-ended sentence of serfdom—and the prospect of being sent to debtors' prison—through government-mandated "child support" system. Furthermore, he wasn't permitted to see his children, despite the fact that a jury had found him innocent.

"I lost visitation with my two daughters when I got arrested. One was the victim-the other was the witness. After a not guilty, I expected to get visitation with my girls. But the divorce judge . . . decreed that counseling was in order and they would decide when we would reunite."

The policy options that are rewarded by federal subsidies don't include allowing an innocent man to reunite with his children. Consigning him to the State-aligned "domestic counseling" industry—which was apparently co-designed by August Mobius and Franz Kafka—is a much more profitable alternative.

"Judges routinely use our children as bargaining chips," Ball explained. "Get the adult into counseling, continue the case for a year, and then drop it. This will open up the docket for the new arrests coming in next week. These judges that use our children are not honorable. Which is why I never use the term 'Your Honor' any more. I just call them judge."

Ball's experiences, once again, are all but identical to those endured by millions of others. Dr. Baskerville offers a potent and infuriating summary:

> A parent [generally a father] whose children are taken away by a family court is only at the beginning of his troubles. The next step comes as he is summoned to court and ordered to pay as much as two-thirds or even more of his income as "child support" to whomever has been given custody. His wages will immediately be garnished and his name will be entered on a federal register of "delinquents." This is even before he has had a chance to become one, though it is likely that the order will be backdated, so he will already be a delinquent as he steps out of the courtroom. If the ordered amount is high enough, and the backdating is far enough, he will be an instant felon and subject to immediate arrest.

The sinews of this system are the federal Office of Child Support Enforcement (OSCE) and its state-level affiliates. Some idea of the scope of the Regime's war on fathers is found in this comparison: In 2007, the Drug Enforcement Agency, the spearhead of the "war on drugs," employed a total of 4,600 armed field agents; the OSCE at the time boasted more than 60,000 enforcement agents, all of whom are permitted to carry firearms under the "Deadbeat Parents Enforcement Act."

When brought to bear against an isolated individual, the weight of this State apparatus will eventually destroy the victim. With each year, Ball's financial condition deteriorated and he became deeply mired in intractable despair. By the time he ended his life on June 16, Ball was a 58-year-old Vietnam era Army veteran who had been unemployed for two years. Owing to the fact that he couldn't pay the amount of child support extorted from him, Ball was quite likely going to be sent to jail on the following morning.

His only consolation, the company of his children, was sadistically withheld from him. The unfathomably arrogant and completely unaccountable functionaries who did so are people who have learned how to monetize the misery of the innocent.

Ball's manifesto is a work of tortured eloquence. Rather than being the chaotic outpouring of a deranged personality, the letter is cogently organized, laden with impressive amounts of detailed research, and admirably epigrammatic. The lucidity Ball displayed in explaining his decision to kill himself by the most painful method imaginable underscores not merely the depth of his despair but also of the entrenched corruption and viciousness of the people who had demolished his family.

The leitmotif in Ball's letter is the phrase "Second Set of Books," an expression that refers to the "policies, procedures and protocols" actually followed by bureaucrats and their enforcers in defiance of the "First Set of Books"—that is, the federal and state constitutions.

"You never cover the Second Set of Books your junior year in high school," Ball pointed out. "That is because we are not supposed to have a Second Set of Books." The Second Set of Books contain writings that are too holy to be inspected by mere Mundanes. Those of us who don't belong to the Sanctified Brotherhood of Official Coercion are required to behave as if there is some continuing relevance to the First Set of Books. Maintaining this official fiction is necessary in order to convince the credulous—well, those who pay attention to such matters—that it is possible to receive redress of grievances through the same system that has aggrieved them.

Like millions of other victims of the State's "domestic violence" apparatus, Ball came to understand that the system cannot be reformed from within:

> On one hand we have the law. On the other hand we have what we are really going to do-the policies, procedures and protocols. The rule of law is dead. Now we have 50 states with legal systems as good as any third world banana republic. Men are demonized and the women and children end up as suffering as well. So boys, we need to start burning down police stations and courthouses. The Second Set of Books originated in Washington. But the dirty deeds are being carried out by our local police, prosecutors and judges.

Rather than voting them out, Ball insists that it is necessary to "Burn Them Out" through arson attacks on the appropriate bureaucratic facilities.

He hoped that his self-immolation would be the symbolic spark that would ignite that revolution—just as a similar desperate act by Tunisian street vendor Mohamad Bouazizi sparked a nationwide rebellion against the fetid dictatorship ruling that country.

While I hope that God has granted rest to Ball's tortured soul, and pray for the comfort of his family, it must be said that his proposed strategy is as tragically mistaken as his suicide.

Rather than attacking the architectural manifestations of the State, we should withdraw from contact with it. In other words, don't call the police under any circumstances, and insulate your family, to the extent possible, from any contact with "welfare" bureaucracies of every kind. This will mean being prepared as parents to take appropriate evasive action when one of the State's tentacles reaches out, with malign intent, in the direction of one's children. It also means being prepared and able to employ purely defensive force where all other alternatives have failed.

Human beings have an instinctive, primordial fear of fire. Burning to death is a prolonged agony in which pain receptors operate at full capacity. The torment Thomas Ball experienced was sufficient, in his mind, to eclipse the horrors of death by fire.

On the same day that this tortured man poured gasoline on his body and struck a match, pundit Ann Coulter used her syndicated column to emit a thick stream of snotty abuse at Rep. Ron Paul and others who insist that the State must be removed entirely from any role in regulating or overseeing marriage and the family.

Hey, Ann—do you get the point now?

In Praise of "Rogue" Cops

Pro Libertate, August 1, 2011

"His death was gang-involved, the way I see it," lamented former Orange County Sheriff's Detective Ron Thomas after viewing the mangled body of his 37-year-old son, Kelly. "A gang of rogue officers . . . brutally beat my son to death."

The description of the crime is appropriate: Kelly Thomas was murdered by a thugscrum of at least six police officers on a sidewalk in Fullerton. Kelly, who had a criminal record, was a homeless adult who had been diagnosed with schizophrenia. On the evening of July 5, police were called to a street near the Fullerton bus depot by a report that someone was burglarizing parked cars.

Kelly was identified as a suspect, and was uncooperative with the police. He was tasered at least five times and beaten until brain-dead while pleading with the officers and crying out for his father. Multiple eyewitness accounts have disclosed that the beating continued—punctuated by the familiar demand that the victim "stop resisting!"—long after Kelly was on his back, motionless and defenseless.

That this was a gang-involved murder is indisputable. With all proper respect to Ron Thomas, however, the grieving father is desperately wrong about one detail: The murderers were not "rogue officers." Once the gang assault on Kelly began, practically the only thing that could have saved his life would have been the timely intervention of a rogue officer.

As an institution, the police do not exist to defend life, liberty, and property. That would be the role played by peace officers—a population that is, for all intents and purposes, extinct. Police are given the task of "enforcement"— the imposition of rules devised by, and on behalf of, the wealth-devouring class. That role includes dispensing summary punishment against people who display anything other than instant, unqualified submission to them and to the political order they embody. Any material good that is done by a police officer is a renegade act, given the nature and purposes of the institution that employs him.

In any situation blighted by the presence of a police officer, that armed functionary's first priority is not to "serve" or to "protect" anybody. Sociologist James Q. Wilson, whose writings became something akin to canonical texts for Rudolph Giuliani and other politicians and policy makers of an authoritarian bent, explains that a police officer's first priority is to "impose authority on people who are unpredictable, apprehensive, and often hostile."

That apprehension is an understandable reaction to the presence of an armed stranger of dubious character who demands unqualified submission. The hostility is predictable, entirely defensible, and generally commendable. Members of the Costumed Enforcer Class refer to it as "Contempt of Cop," and regard it as an offense subject to summary punishment through the application of state-licensed violence, frequently of a lethal nature.

Ron Thomas—who, once again, is a retired law enforcement officer himself who teaches "arrest and control" techniques—explains that the officers who murdered his son weren't attempting to arrest him as a criminal suspect, but rather "bullying" him "under color of authority" as punishment for "contempt of cop."

Incidents of this kind display a standard morphology:

A cop confronts a citizen and encounters brief, trivial, and often justified resistance. He summons "backup," and a thugscrum—which is a phenomenon similar to a criminal "flash mob," but generally more lethal—quickly coalesces and deals out hideous violence while terrified citizens look on in horror and apparent helplessness.

Any officer who doesn't play a hands-on role in beating the "suspect" will devote his attention to "crowd control"—that is, preventing intervention on behalf of the victim, and often confiscating any recording devices that might be used to gather incriminating video of the episode.

Officially sanctioned gang violence depends on a chain reaction of conformity, and often a single rogue element would be sufficient to prevent it from reaching critical mass. A "rogue cop"—that is, a peace officer devoted to protecting life, liberty, and property, rather than a dutiful law enforcer determined to uphold "authority"—would interpose on behalf of the victim.

It's difficult to know how often this happens, but we could round off that estimate to "never." This is because "rogue" cops who commit such renegade acts of lawfulness are never treated with the union-organized solicitude displayed toward "good" cops who commit acts of criminal violence against Mundanes.

Witness the case of former Austin Police Department Officer Ramon Perez, who joined the force as a 41-year-old rookie cop because of a sincere desire to protect people from crime. During a January 2005 domestic violence incident, Perez refused an order by a superior officer, Robert Paranich, to use his Taser on an elderly man who was not a threat to himself or anybody else.

Owing to the fact that the subject was a frail man of advanced years, Perez was understandably concerned that the portable electro-shock torture device would kill him. Furthermore, using the Taser in that situation would have violated the explicit provisions of the Austin PD's Taser Policy. Perez was able to resolve the situation through de-escalation, rather than by using potentially lethal force to "impose authority."

Two days later, Perez was given what could only be considered a punitive transfer to the night shift. Two months later, following a second incident in which Perez chose de-escalation over armed compulsion, he was invited to what he was told would be a "counseling" session with the APD's staff psychologist, Carol Logan. The purpose of that meeting, Perez was told, was to help him develop better "communication skills" with his fellow officers. In fact, it was a disguised "fit-for-duty review" convened to find a pretext to purge the probationary officer from the force before the "rogue cop" could infect others with his respect for individual rights.

As the *Austin Chronicle* reported, Ms. Logan's four-page report focused "entirely on Perez's moral and religious beliefs, which Logan concludes are so strong they are an 'impairment' to his ability to be a police officer."

Perez, a self-described non-denominational fundamentalist Christian, an ordained minister, and home-schooling parent, was not as morally ductile as the typical police recruit. He saw protection of civil liberties as the paramount duty of a police officer, an obligation he viewed as a literal religious vocation. For this reason Perez was seen as unsuitable for a ministry in the State's punitive priesthood.

Perez was given an ultimatum by his superiors: He could resign and retain his peace officer's license, or be terminated and lose it. This was done, once again, as punishment for Perez's "rogue" conduct—which consisted of his refusal to break the law and violate department policy.

If a "rogue" cop had intervened on behalf of Barron Bowling on July 10, 2003, the one-time cement worker from Kansas City, Kansas wouldn't be a functional invalid at the age of 37. It was Bowling's life-changing misfortune that day to be involved in a minor non-injury crash with an automobile carrying three undercover DEA agents. In a fit of juvenile impatience, the driver, DEA agent Timothy McCue, attempted to pass Bowling's car illegally on the right side of a single lane.

After the vehicles pulled over, agent McCue came boiling out of his car with a drawn gun. With help from one of his fellow heroes, McCue forced Bowling lie face-down on the pavement, despite the fact that the 98 degree heat had turned it into a frying pan. When Bowling attempted to push himself up, McCue began to punch and pistol-whip him while taunting his victim for supposedly being an "inbred hillbilly" and "system-dodging white trash." One witness to the crime reported that McCue threatened to murder Bowling. With the help of his comrades, McCue handcuffed the victim and continued to beat and kick him after he was shackled and completely helpless.

In keeping with standard procedure, the assailants accused the victim of assaulting them, which would explain why the unarmed and outnumbered "aggressor" was left with severe brain damage, persistent tinnitus, incapacitating migraines, chronic dizziness, nausea, and lingering emotional trauma that led to at least one suicide attempt.

While in police custody, Bowling was told by Officer Robert Lane that the facts of the case didn't matter; he was the one going to prison because federal agents "do pretty much what they want." Bowling's only hope to avoid prison was Detective Max Seifert, who was assigned to investigate the case—which, in practice, meant to fill out whatever paperwork was necessary to ratify McCune's perjury.

For reasons that mystified his colleagues, Seifert actually conducted an investigation. His first question was: What happened to the witness reports collected at the scene? Officer Lane told him that those documents had been "lost," because they served only to make the DEA agents "look bad."

Seifert's persistence led Deputy Chief Steven Culp chief to take him aside and order the detective to drop the matter. At the time, Seifert—who had been respected by both his fellow cops and the public at large—was less than a year from being "fully vested," meaning that he could retire with his full pension. The leverage provided by that fact provided the tacit but unmistakable "or else" that hovered above the conversation between Seifert and Culp.

To his considerable credit, Seifert continued with his investigation. After Seifert filed his report, the district attorney announced that he was dropping the charges against Bowling. Deputy Chief Culp, however, pressured the prosecutor into reinstating the case. Seifert went on the testify on behalf of the defense in Bowling's criminal trial—which resulted in an acquittal on the spurious assault-related charges—and on behalf of the victim in his federal civil rights lawsuit.

For his insistence on telling the truth, Seifert was subjected to a campaign of ridicule and abuse from his colleagues on the police force. As U.S. District Judge Julie A. Robinson pointed out in a ruling that awarded Bowling more than $833,000 in damages, "Seifert was shunned, subjected to gossip and defamation by his police colleagues, and treated as a pariah." More importantly, he was punished for insubordination by being forced into early retirement, thereby losing his pension.

None of the law enforcement officers involved in the assault on Bowling and subsequent cover-up was disciplined in any way. The only one who was punished was the "rogue" officer who had acted in defense of the truth, and of the victim's individual rights. Steven Culp, the official who ordered Seifert to participate in the cover-up and then purged him when he refused to do so, is now the Executive Director of the Kansas Commission on Peace Officers' Standards and Training. Without so much as a faint whisper of irony, Culp claims that his new job is "to provide the citizens with qualified, trained, ethical, and professional peace officers" who act "in a manner consistent with the law while being considerate of the citizens. . . ."

Residents of the Sunflower State can be confident that Steven Culp—like those in charge of recruiting and indoctrinating police officers elsewhere in the *Soyuz*—will do his formidable best to protect them from "rogue cops" like Max Seifert.

Pity the Poor, Persecuted Police

Pro Libertate, August 9, 2011

Michael Kennedy is Chief of Police in tiny Sunriver, Oregon, an unincorporated resort village in the Beaver State's Deschutes County. Kennedy insists that his police force has been terrorized for years by a marauder named Robert Foster.

"He breaks the law all the time," Kennedy insisted in a June 15, 2010 sworn deposition.

"Well, have you ever arrested him?" asked Portland attorney Frank Wesson, who was representing Foster at the time.

"I have not," admitted Kennedy.

"Has anyone in your department ever arrested him?" Wesson pressed.

Kennedy sought refuge in evasion: "Not to my knowledge, sir."

Bear in mind that Kennedy isn't supervising the LAPD; he heads an eight-member police force (supplemented on occasion by a 30-member volunteer citizens patrol) in a town of fewer than 1,500 permanent residents in which actual crime is all but nonexistent.

An honest answer would have been: No, Foster had never been arrested, because no evidence exists that he ever committed a crime. Honesty was not Kennedy's first choice, however, nor does it appear to be his strong suit. He went on to list among Foster's alleged crimes "disorderly conduct, interfering with a police officer, menacing, harassment, and stalking."

"Was he ever arrested for any of those?" Wesson persisted.

"No; fortunately for him, no," Kennedy replied. The Chief made that statement in apparent ignorance of the fact that he had just admitted, under oath, to incompetence in the administration of the law—assuming that Foster was the serial offender depicted in Kennedy's testimony and internal department memoranda.

One official report from Sunriver Officer Dree Warren to Chief Kennedy describes Foster as glaring at Sunriver police officers and emitting a sinister laugh like that of "the villain the Joker from the Batman cartoons." Surely an archfiend of that magnitude can't be allowed to prey upon the innocent people of Sunriver, and their gallant protectors!

"I'm curious, do you know why your officers wouldn't arrest Mr. Foster if they thought he was breaking the law?" asked the defense attorney.

After a brief bout of dissimulation, Kennedy tried to dismiss the question by insisting that he "can't account for what every officer is thinking."

This is true, of course. It is also entirely irrelevant. If Foster were a one-man crime wave, leaving him at large would be a grave dereliction of duty, both for Sunriver's "Finest" and their bold and intrepid leader.

Rather than instructing his officers to arrest Foster if there was evidence that he had committed a crime, Chief Kennedy, by his own account, told them "to document every time they had a problem with Mr. Foster." He did this because "Mr. Foster was harassing and stalking our officers."

After tabulating a number of "unwanted contacts" with Foster, three of Sunriver's "Finest" induced a judge to issue a Stalking Protection Order forbidding him to come within eyeshot of his cringing, terrorized "victims." Under the terms of that order, the "victims"—Officers Kasey and Tiffany Hughes (a married couple) and Sgt. Joseph Patnode—can literally arrange for the arrest of Foster any time he comes within their field of vision.

Thanks to the efforts of Robert Foster's daughter, Rebecca Kossler, I've been able to review several hundred pages of detailed information on every aspect of this controversy. This includes numerous official police reports, several sworn depositions, legal filings, photographs taken of Foster by the police during several "unwanted contacts" with Foster, and a transcribed audio recording of a July 6, 2010 traffic stop involving Rebecca Kossler's husband, Ian.

The police accounts describe Mr. Foster engaged in such suspicious activities as sitting in his pickup truck, shopping, buying gasoline, and otherwise conducting routine business that brings him within visual distance of Sun River police officers. These incidents were breathlessly described as "evidence" of some unspecified criminal activity.

Nowhere in any of the accounts provided by the supposed victims in this matter—the people with guns and badges and the purported authority to use lethal force in the name of "officer safety"—is there any evidence of an actual crime or a threat to commit the same on the part of Mr. Foster. (Chief Kennedy refused to respond to repeated requests for an interview.) However, those reports are valuable evidence of unlawful activity—the unwarranted harassment and unlawful surveillance of Robert Foster by the Sunriver Police Department.

The record of the July 6, 2010 traffic stop provides compelling evidence of a criminal conspiracy to deprive Ian Kossler of his constitutionally protected rights, and an oblique admission that the department had done the same to Robert Foster.

The officer conducting the traffic stop was Kasey Hughes, one of the "victims" who filed a stalking order against Foster. When Ian Kossler asked why he was being pulled over, Hughes replied: "You weren't wearing your seatbelt when you passed me. In fact, when you were actually following me."

"I wasn't following you," Kossler objected.

That detail is important, since Hughes, his wife Tiffany, and their supervisor, Sgt. Patnode, insisted that Foster had "followed" them on various occasions, thereby subjecting them to "coercive" or "threatening" behavior.

During his encounter with Ian Kossler, Hughes told Sgt. Patnode via radio that Kossler had been "following" him, and that he had been parked next to Robert Foster at a local restaurant called Blondie's.

"I'm gonna ask him in a minute and then . . . the fact that he is stalking me too—he can have his concealed weapons permit revoked very quickly," Hughes informed Patnode.

After returning to Kossler's vehicle, Hughes issued a citation for not wearing a seatbelt—and then brazenly attempted to provoke a confrontation.

"Keep following us around and that's what's gonna happen, okay!" sneered Hughes.

"Dude, I wasn't following you," replied a composed but puzzled Kossler.

"You were following me around," reiterated the petulant tax-feeder.

"I was not following you. . . Why are you so paranoid?" responded Kossler, whose patience was understandably beginning to evaporate.

"You stalk us and you'll lose your concealed weapons permit, too," gloated Hughes.

"I am not stalking anybody," replied the only adult who was a party to that conversation.

The order that targeted Foster amounts to a bill of attainder. Chief Kennedy and three of his subordinates have disposed of the necessity of providing evidence that Foster has ever committed a crime. Instead, they have criminalized the *person* of Robert Foster—and they won't be satisfied until they've contrived some way to put him in prison.

The traffic stop involving Foster's son-in-law establishes a pattern on the part of the Sunriver Police: Identify a troublesome person, accuse him of "stalking" them, and use that accusation to deprive him of his rights. Just a few weeks after that encounter, Foster filed his civil rights complaint—which may be the only reason why Ian Kossler hasn't been the subject of a spurious stalking order.

Foster's civil case has been submitted to third-party arbitration. Under the terms of the police department's settlement offer, Foster would be subject to a 10-year permanent stalking protection order that could not be modified, or he could choose a 5-year permanent stalking order and pay $10,000 in legal costs.

Whichever option he selected, Foster would also be required to withdraw his tort claim against the police, and the existing legal record of the case—including the damaging admissions made by Chief Kennedy—would be expunged. This would mean that the police would be able to arrest Foster for violating the stalking order at their leisure.

Incredible as it will seem to people burdened with a capacity for rational thought, the arbitrator, Bend Attorney William Flinn, is insisting that Foster accept that deal. (Like Chief Kennedy, Mr. Flinn also refused to respond to repeated interview requests.)

"I know Bob feels that, had he accepted the [settlement] offer, the police still would have found some way to construe episodes of his future conduct as stalking," Flinn wrote to Foster's current defense counsel on July 11. "But, I don't think that was a good reason to reject the offer." Four days later, Flinn reiterated his demand that Foster submit to a settlement that was manifestly not in his best interest, telling his attorney that "there is virtually no chance that Bob will prevail in court, despite your excellent trial skills and *some evidence of paranoia/lack of candor on the part of the police*." (Emphasis added)

A more appropriate term to describe the "lack of candor" Flinn refers to is "perjury."

Not only are the Sunriver police paranoid, according to Flinn, but in his opinion they also pose a threat of potentially lethal violence. That's an eminently defensible assessment—one that Flinn fashioned into an argument that Foster should submit to their demands.

"The skirmishing between the Sunriver police and Bob Foster has been going on for over five years," wrote Flinn to Foster's lawyer. "So far, no one has resorted to the use of weapons, but it appears the risk increases with every new encounter. If I were the judge hearing this case, my priority would be to defuse the situation before it gets violent. No judge wants to be blamed, in retrospect, for passing up an opportunity to prevent armed conflict and the loss of life."

In his sworn deposition, Chief Kennedy admitted that Foster has never been seen carrying a firearm. The only threat of violence in any of those encounters is that posed by the armed children under Kennedy's supervision. That threat can, and should, be defused by ordering Kennedy and his kiddie patrol to withdraw their complaint and leave Foster alone, unless there is evidence that he's actually committing a crime. Instead, the "mediator" is making common cause with people he describes as dishonest and potentially violent—and who are engaged in something that can properly be described as extortion.

The fearsome figure who causes Sunriver's "Finest" to lose bladder control is a wiry, soft-spoken 51-year-old entrepreneur who runs a hot tub installation and maintenance company. A lifetime resident of rural Oregon, Bob Foster is the kind of blessed troublemaker who carries copies of the U.S. Constitution in his pickup truck, but—unlike nearly everybody else in Deschutes County—rarely carries a rifle in his gun rack, a fact Chief Kennedy artlessly tried to obfuscate in his sworn testimony.

Foster is blunt but not abrasive. He is a devoted grandfather. He is also an accomplished guitarist whose irreproachable taste in classic rock is demonstrated by the fact that his favorite band is Thin Lizzy. Most importantly for the purposes of the present discussion, Foster is an outspoken critic of what he describes as Sunriver's ruling political clique.

Before 2008, Sunriver was one of the few places in the known universe where police were required by law to act as peace officers, rather than law enforcers. Although they were permitted to arrest people for crimes against person and property, they were forbidden to act as armed tax farmers by detaining and mulcting motorists who violated Oregon's invasive seatbelt law, or who committed other infractions that would result in traffic fines elsewhere.

"No seatbelt? No citation. No tail light? No ticket. In too much of a hurry? Not to worry," reported a March 3, 2007 AP story from Sunriver. "Sgt. P.J. Beaty watches people in this upscale development breaking traffic laws, and sees plenty of them. But he can't pull them over. A man swerved head-on into Beaty's lane, and then back out again and Beaty couldn't law a glove on him."

Owing to the fact that Sunriver was actually governed by a private homeowners association, its streets were exempt from most of the obnoxious enactments used as pretexts for roadside shakedowns by police. As local reporter Susan Lawson of the Sunriver *Scene* told Pro Libertate in a May 2007 interview, "if someone were robbing the mini-mart up the road the police would obviously have the power to arrest the suspect. The police are simply not permitted to enforce a very small number—it's either six or eight—of laws dealing with minor traffic infractions, because our roads are the equivalent of private property."

This was an unconscionable state of affairs, according to the SROA, which prevailed on Oregon State Rep. Gene Whisnat to sponsor H.B. 3445, which extended police "authority" to include roads and streets on "premises open to the public that are owned by a homeowners association. . . ." That measure was passed, and another freedom-promoting "loophole" was closed. But that wasn't the end of the matter.

In 2003, the Sunriver Owner's Association (SROA), which functions as a municipal government, had created a special service district within Deschutes County. In 2008, following passage of H.B 3445—which put the police in the business of collecting revenue at gunpoint—the SROA enacted a special multi-million-dollar tax assessment for the special service district.

Bob Foster, who has lived in the area nearly all his life and is a well-respected local businessman, became a conspicuous presence at public meetings, where he would politely but forcefully express his opposition to the service district and the tax assessment.

Like any small town dependent on tourism, Sunriver is acutely sensitive to economic trends. During one public meeting in which the town's economic challenges were discussed, Foster suggested that the SROA could save several millions of dollars each year by seceding from Deschutes County, thereby canceling the expensive service district agreement. He also recommended that the duties of the police be scaled back to their pre-2007 role, and that Sunriver contract with a nearby town called La Pine for emergency services.

"That's the kind of talk that made me Public Enemy Number One," Foster told Pro Libertate during a lengthy interview. He is a legitimate threat to the Sunriver Police—not to the physical safety of any of its officers, but to the agency's continued access to a steady stream of plundered revenue. This is why every gesture or public utterance by Foster is treated by the Sunriver Police as evidence of his criminal intent.

In an October 8, 2010 petition seeking the extension of the stalking protection order, Officer Kasey Hughes accused Foster of making "violent and aggressive" statements that displayed a "distorted perception" of the police department. Among those supposedly criminal utterances was "You're a public servant, I'm your boss." On another occasion Foster "referred to the Sunriver Police as 'the local Gestapo'"—an assessment which, given the department's behavior, barely qualifies as hyperbole.

Foster "appears to be a highly volatile person," simpered Hughes, accusing him of "obsessive behavior that could turn to aggression at any point." Besides, Foster "has access to guns," pouted Hughes, who—unlike his supposed persecutor—carries one with him at all times.

A report filed by Officer Hughes a few weeks before submitting that petition suggests that he, not Foster, is hostage to bizarre obsessions. Hughes described how he and two other officers were responding to a citizen complaint at the Crossroads Gas Station in Sunriver when he saw Foster "sitting at a table directly in front of his truck," writing in a notepad. A few minutes later, while interviewing a local resident, "I saw Foster standing outside his vehicle, staring at me," Hughes continued. "I also noticed him washing his windshield very slowly."

Foster's "threatening" behavior was supposedly noticed by the individual Hughes was interviewing. "Man, he's eye-f**king you," the resident told Hughes, according to the officer's unsupported account. According to the report, this incident was enough to frighten Hughes away—although, oddly enough, his supposed stalker "was still at the gas pumps when I left."

If Robert Foster is compelled to accept the Sunriver Police Department's settlement offer, Hughes would be able to transmute a peculiar sexual fantasy of that kind into a criminal complaint. He or either of the other two "victims" would also be granted a license to stalk Foster and *have him prosecuted for violating the permanent stalking order.*

Robert Foster's experience can appropriately be described as "Kafkaesque"—but it is not unique. There are uncanny similarities between his story and recent developments in Quartzsite, Arizona, another small rural town (population circa 3,600) that is largely dependent on tourism. In recent months, something perilously close to open warfare has erupted between the Quartzsite Town Council and its reform-minded Mayor, Ed Foster (the shared surname is another striking coincidence).

Foster is convinced that the Council has engaged in corrupt and dubious bookkeeping. His suspicions were sharpened by the Council's refusal—in defiance of municipal ordinances and state law, and with the support of Police Chief Jeff Gilbert—to allow him access to the appropriate records. On several occasions, the Mayor and several other prominent critics of the Council have been arrested or harassed by the police in transparent acts of retaliation. This led ten members of the Quartzsite Police Department to file a public protest denouncing Gilbert's abuse of "authority." The Council has responded by declaring a state of emergency, suspending all but three members of the police force, and placing the dissenting officers under a gag order.

One member of Quartzsite's Town Council, Joe Winslow, persuaded Justice of the Peace Karen Slaughter (a retired sheriff's deputy with no legal education) to issue an injunction against a local businessman named Michael Roth, who was accused of "harassing" and "threatening" Winslow by shooting him dirty looks and speaking to him disrespectfully. The court order requires that Roth surrender his firearms to Chief Gilbert and his praetorian guard—not because of anything the citizen has done, but because the offended Council member, who admits to purchasing a shotgun, describes himself as "more concerned about my reaction to his aggression than anything else."

In other words: This Mundane has frightened me and made me angry, so he must be disarmed before I either kill him or have one of my armed minions kill him on my behalf. There is little, if any, material difference between that demand and the terms being forced upon Robert Foster.

A third case of a similar kind is unfolding in Renton, Washington, where police and the City Attorney seek to arrest and prosecute an anonymous parodist who created several animated cartoons mocking the scandal-plagued police department.

The videos "target specific members of the City of Renton and Renton Police Department with the intent to embarrass and emotionally torment the victims," asserts police investigator Ryan Rutledge in a July 11 affidavit filed in the Superior Court for King County. Rutledge contends that the videos—which by any rational definition constitute politically protected speech—are covered by the Washington State "cyberstalking" statute. In an example of what would be irony were it not related to the institutionalized corruption called "government," the Renton Deputy Police Chief Tim Troxel was given a trivial reprimand for ordering an off-duty police officer to stalk his wayward girlfriend.

Although no institutional or personal names were mentioned in the cartoons, Rutledge reports that "three individuals have come forward and identified themselves as being the persons targeted by embarrassing and emotionally tormenting comments about past sexual relationships or dating relationships that were discussed within some of these videos." Once again, the "offense" in question consisted of making public comments that hurt the feelings of corrupt public officials.

One case of this type can be regarded as an anomaly; two can be described as coincidence; however, three or more examples constitute a pattern.

Wherever they can get away with it, police are using wiretapping statutes to prosecute Mundanes who record their public behavior. Now local police, and the entrenched political elites they serve, are using anti-stalking and anti-harassment laws to disarm and criminalize their critics. We can expect depraved ingenuity of this kind on the part of the tax-devouring class as the retreating economic tide lays bare layer after layer of official corruption—from Washington to Wall Street to City Hall.

Framing Steele: A Case Study of Sovietized American "Justice"

Pro Libertate, October 12, 2011

Yes, I'd give the Devil the benefit of the law—for my own safety's sake.

> —Sir Thomas Moore, as depicted in "A Man for All Seasons"

When Edgar Steele was told on the morning of June 11, 2010, that his wife Cyndi had been killed when her SUV was run off the road in Oregon, his first reaction, understandably, was shock. That reaction mutated into panic minutes later when FBI Agent Michael Sotka told Steele that his mother-in-law had also been shot and killed.

"He wanted to contact family members and find out if they were okay," testified State Trooper Jess Spike, who was at Steele's home in Sagle, Idaho when the dire tidings were delivered. Asked by Agent Sotka who might have perpetrated those crimes and "who his enemies were," Steele named "a number of organizations that may have been against him," Spike continued. "There was like the Anti-Defamation League, Southern Poverty—there were one or two others. I don't recall the acronyms or names of them."

Trooper Spike was referring to the Southern Poverty Law Center (SPLC), which bankrupted the northern Idaho-based Aryan Nation white supremacist group in a 2000 lawsuit. Steele, a controversial lawyer who described himself as the "Attorney for the Damned," had represented the Aryan Nation in court, thereby earning the abiding enmity of the SPLC and its allies, including the Anti-Defamation League—both of which are quasi-private affiliates of the Homeland Security apparatus.

In addition to his legal work, Steele was a polemicist on behalf of worldview that can fairly be characterized as white supremacist. The author of a book entitled *Defensive Racism*, Steele disavowed aggressive violence. This wasn't true of at least some of his detractors: Prior to June 11, 2010, Edgar Steele had received death threats that the FBI had traced back to the so-called Jewish Defense League, which has been implicated in more than a dozen domestic terrorist incidents in the United States.

183

In the months leading up to June 11, Steele had endured a near-fatal heart attack. On the morning he received the news, he was still recuperating from a second health crisis, a nasal aneurysm that had left him hospitalized just a few weeks earlier. So he was in pretty fragile condition as horrible news accumulated suggesting that his enemies were laying siege to his family. But that wasn't the final shock he was to endure on that crowded morning: Agent Sotka suddenly announced, "Your wife is not dead . . . you're under arrest."

As Sotka hauled the stunned and shaken Steele from his home, the FBI Agent encountered Dr. Allen Banks, a local biochemist family friend who had arrived that morning to help Steele haul a load of lumber from the Home Depot in nearby Coeur d'Alene.

Brandishing a recorder, Sotka triumphantly told Banks: "We've got everything we need right here." A few hours after being led to believe that his wife and mother-in-law had been murdered, Steele was charged with hiring a local handyman named Larry Fairfax to kill them.

Trooper Spike would later admit in court that there was nothing in the June 11 conversation that indicated Steele's guilt. The elaborate fiction created by Sotka was a "ruse" intended to get Steele to incriminate himself. Rather than reacting to a confession or a critical disclosure by Steele, Sotka arrested him when it became clear that he "wasn't going to crack," Trooper Spike recounted on the witness stand.

As it happens, within four days of arresting Steele, the FBI had a confession from a suspect who admitted to placing a pipe bomb on the automobile Cyndi Steele drove to Oregon City to visit her cancer-stricken mother: Larry Fairfax himself, who had reportedly carried out the plot with unnamed "accomplices." The bomb was accidentally discovered when Mrs. Steele took the van to a Jiffy Lube. Fairfax, who we're told approached the FBI on June 9 to report that Steele had hired him to murder his wife and mother-in-law, hadn't disclosed the existence of the pipe bomb.

Fairfax, who had done some remodeling work on the Steele home, was supposedly asked to carry out the double murder for $25,000 that would come from an insurance pay-off. (Fairfax wasn't aware that Steele had canceled his wife's insurance policy two years earlier.) This arrangement was supposedly made on May 27, just a few weeks after Steele had been hospitalized for his second life-threatening aneurysm.

Prior to Steele's arrest, Fairfax had cashed in roughly $10,000 in silver. Edgar and Cyndi claimed that Fairfax—who knew where the family had cached precious metals on their property—had stolen the silver. Fairfax insists it was part of the pay-off for his role in the murder plot. All that is known for certain is that the silver had belonged to the Steeles before Fairfax cashed it in.

It is likewise known for sure that Fairfax—with the help of his still-unknown accomplices—built the pipe bomb and placed it on the undercarriage of Cyndi Steele's vehicle. Edgar Steele's only connection to the pipe bomb was a recorded June 10 conversation with Fairfax in which the phrase "car bomb" was spoken. Fairfax and the FBI insisted that the conversation made reference to an earlier, unrecorded agreement between the two of them that Fairfax would kill Cyndi Steele and her ailing mother.

During his testimony in Edgar Steele's trial, Agent Sotka admitted that the FBI had given Fairfax and James Maher $500 and that "we decided to send Mr. Fairfax over to Portland in case Mr. Steele asked for a phone call from him." That call, according to Agent Sotka, was intended to be Steele's alibi, proving that he was nowhere near the scene of the crime when it occurred.

A stronger case can be made that this call was designed to be the finishing touch on the frame the Feds had constructed to entrap Steele. By calling from Oregon, Fairfax would create an interstate "nexus" that supposedly justified federal charges against Steele. It's important to note that this element of the case against Steele involves something he *didn't* do—namely, contacting Fairfax in Portland—while Sotka admitted under oath that it was the FBI that sent Fairfax to Portland.

Last May, following a trial that lasted less than a week, a federal jury convicted Steele on four counts, including conspiracy to commit murder. He faces a mandatory minimum of 30 years in prison—which, owing to his age and fragile health, is a life sentence. The prosecution case that resulted in that sentence is miraculously untainted by reliable evidence.

The alleged victim, Cyndi Steele, has been her husband's most consistent and vocal defender, despite what she has described as intimidation by Agent Sotka. The so-called pipe bomb was little more than a stage prop incapable of exploding—a fact withheld by the Feds until the day after Steele's trial ended, when it was introduced, without Government objections, during Larry Fairfax's sentencing hearing.

Fairfax, who manufactured a supposedly "lethal" weapon of mass destruction as part of a plot to murder two innocent people, was charged with possession of an "unregistered firearm" and given a sentence of 27 months in prison (with credit for time served), followed by three years of supervised release. He was ordered to pay Cyndi Steele—his victim—a total of $900 in compensation. That detail eloquently testifies of the contemptuous hostility the Feds have for the uncooperative "victim."

As with so many other prosecutions of this kind, this case shouldn't have been in federal court in the first place.

Edgar Steele "did not 'cause' anyone to travel in interstate commerce," points out his attorney Wesley Hoyt in a motion for a new trial. "Government informants Larry Fairfax and James Maher were dispatched from Idaho on June 11, 2010 by the Government, not the defendant. They were paid $500 by the FBI to travel to Oregon . . . so that FBI Agent Sotka could have Fairfax call Mr. Steele from an Oregon prefix"—thereby creating a supposed "jurisdictional link" to justify a federal prosecution.

This is a familiar FBI tactic: Where there is no clear federal "nexus," create one through a letter or an interstate telephone call. In the 1991 case *U.S. v. Coats*, the Fourth Circuit Court of Appeals ruled that an FBI-instigated interstate phone call that "was contrived by the Government for that reason alone" did not provide the desired "jurisdictional link."

The FBI's claim that Steele had actually hired Fairfax to kill his wife depends on two dubious pieces of evidence, neither of which is sufficient alone but that supposedly validate each other: The ambiguous and disputed recording of a conversation between Fairfax and Steele on June 10, 2010, and Fairfax's testimony.

During the trial in Boise, the defense repeatedly objected to the introduction of the recording, and the Government-provided transcript, on the basis that they were offered without "foundation."

Addressing that objection, Federal District Judge Lynn Winmill ruled that "if he [Fairfax] testifies that he has listened to it and it accurately sets forth what was said at the time, then that is the foundation." In its closing arguments, the prosecution heavily emphasized the claim that the recordings likewise "corroborated" Fairfax's account. The problem here is that both of those pieces of "evidence" are terminally flawed—and since each of them is thoroughly impeachable, they can't be used to validate each other.

The chain of custody necessary to authenticate the recordings breaks down at the very first link. Fairfax's demonstrated dishonesty (the Feds were forced to admit that he was "not completely forthcoming" about the pipe bomb) makes him unsuitable as a corroborative witness regarding their reliability. "In order to authenticate the records, the Government presented the testimony of an admitted liar . . . who during trial stated that on June 9, 2010 he lied to the FBI when he did not tell them about the existence of a bomb on Mrs. Steele's car," notes the motion for a new trial.

FBI Agent Sotka claimed that Fairfax and Steele were under constant surveillance on the Steele family's property while the recorded conversations took place. However, the discussion took place in a barn, while the two of them were concealed from view. Since the device concealed on Fairfax was a recorder rather than a "wire," nobody heard the conversations as they actually occurred.

On the witness stand Agent Sotka described how he downloaded the digital audio file from the recording device onto an FBI computer in Coeur d'Alene with a special proprietary software program. From there, the file was reportedly uploaded to a database at an FBI lab in Virginia. Sotka did this without listening to the recorded conversation. He then copied the file onto a compact disc, from which the file was re-copied onto a second disc. At that point, according to Sotka, he purged the original digital file from the recording device, since "part of the procedure is to delete the conversation and have the recorder clear for the next time you need to use it."

Sotka appears to be selectively fastidious about following FBI procedures, since he did all of this by himself, without having a second Agent present, as dictated by Bureau policy. What this means is that the recordings heard by the court—and that had been played to Cyndi Steele by Agent Sotka prior to the trial—were, at the very best, a third-generation copy of the original digital file, which was destroyed by Sotka without being heard by himself or anybody else.

When the version of the recording was played for Cyndi Steele, the alleged victim and target of the purported murder-for-hire plot was not convinced that what she heard was an actual conversation involving her husband. Furthermore, the version of the recording played in court contained an odd repetitive clicking noise, which the prosecution insisted was the sound of "Tic-Tacs" rattling in Fairfax's pocket. That noise, which wasn't present on the pre-trial version, is the kind of audio artifact that can result when a recording is digitally assembled from several different sources.

Dr. George Papcun, a forensic scientist who has served as an expert witness and law enforcement consultant for several decades, detected numerous "transients" and other anomalies—by one count, roughly 300 of them—in the pre-trial version of the FBI recordings. Dr. Papcun concluded that there was "a reasonable degree of scientific probability that [the recordings] do not represent a true and valid representation of reality and they are unreliable." That assessment provides ample, if not unassailable, grounds for reasonable doubt, especially in light of Dr. Papcun's credentials.

After finishing his undergraduate degree in mathematics at the University of Arizona, Papcun went on to earn a Master's Degree in Formal Linguistics and a Ph.D. in Linguistics (with a specialization in Acoustic Phonetics) from UCLA. As a graduate student, Papcun was awarded Ford Foundation and National Defense education fellowships; his professional work earned an award from Johns Hopkins University and a place on the R&D-100 list of top achievers in "Technological Innovation." He has been an advisor to local, state, and federal law enforcement agencies, including the Department of Homeland Security, and an expert forensic witness in numerous high-profile cases.

Not surprisingly, the prosecution attempted to exclude both Dr. Papcun's report and his testimony from the trial. On May 2, Judge Winmill held a hearing to determine whether the defense would be permitted to present Papcun's testimony. At the time, Papcun was vacationing in Bora Bora, and Winmill initially ruled that he could testify via video conference on the following day. However, the prosecution complained that this arrangement would be unacceptable, since it wouldn't permit them to "confront" the witness—a right that is guaranteed to the defendant, not the prosecution, by the Sixth Amendment to the U.S. Constitution.

On May 3, Judge Winmill, exhibiting his habitual, undisguised bias in favor of the prosecution, dutifully reversed his ruling and issued an entirely whimsical demand that Dr. Papcun be physically present in Boise, Idaho no later than 8:30 AM the following morning—Wednesday, May 4—in order to testify at the trial.

Since neither teleportation nor sub-orbital commercial flight is presently available, the earliest Papcun could be available was Thursday, May 5. Papcun was willing to interrupt his vacation, and the defense was willing to pay the expense. However, Judge Winmill—who was consistently flexible in meeting the prosecution's demands—maintained that there wasn't sufficient wiggle room in his schedule to permit Papcun to testify on Thursday. None of this would have been necessary, of course, if Winmill had simply stuck to his initial ruling and permitted Dr. Papcun to offer fully interactive testimony by way of a video conference held at the nearest U.S. consulate.

Judge Winmill's earnest concern for the supposed right of the prosecution to "confront" Dr. Papcun stands in stark contrast to his indifference to Edgar Steele's constitutionally protected right to confront a key prosecution witness,

Ukrainian resident Tatyana Loginova—whom Steele had contacted as part of what he and his wife Cyndi both described as his research into the Russian "mail-order bride" scam.

Steele's daughter Kesley testified under oath that both she and her mother were aware of that research, and often joked about it. That account was confirmed from the witness stand by family friend Allan Banks, who said that Steele had told him about contacting several women from the former Soviet Union as "part of a legal case."

The question of motive was probably the biggest of the numerous weaknesses in the prosecution's case: Why would a man who had just recovered from a near-fatal aortic aneurysm seek to murder the wife whose personal care had been indispensable to his recovery?

The prosecution confected a story in which Steele—a senior citizen in fragile health—was secretly trolling the Web in search of a nubile young girlfriend, and had developed a schoolboy crush on Miss Loginova.

Loginova's testimony was critical to the prosecution's case, and the "right to confront" protected by the Sixth Amendment required that Steele and his counsel be given an opportunity to cross-examine her. However, Winmill permitted the prosecution to enter into evidence a videotaped deposition conducted via video conference with the aid of a Russian language translator. Loginova's story included a claim that Steele had promised to visit her in Ukraine in August 2010.

While the Edgar Steele jury was permitted to hear Loginova's videotaped testimony, it was not permitted to hear the testimony of Dr. Robert Stoll, who had spent several hours in Steele's company on June 10—the day he supposedly planned to murder his wife. Dr. Stoll, a local veterinarian, has filed an affidavit recounting how he had discussed Steele's health problems and how he was impressed by "the manner of Edgar's tender affection for his wife and family. I believe that this man's intent . . . when I visited him was not to kill anyone, especially his wife."

To understand the deeply prejudicial nature of Winmill's rulings in this regard it's necessary to take into account the composition of the jury: In a case involving an alleged plot by a husband to murder his middle-aged wife, the jury consisted of eleven women and one man.

The panel that emerged from voir dire was ideal for the prosecution's theory of the case, which could have been the plot from any of several dozen made-for-TV movies of the kind broadcast incessantly on the "Lifetime" cable network: The scheming, unfaithful husband, driven by ego and what remains of his mid-life libido, plots to murder his long-suffering wife in order to take up with a pneumatic trophy bimbo.

Edgar Steele is a widely despised figure. His legal practice was devoted to defending the rights of similarly marginalized and disreputable people out of the conviction that "it is the . . . politically incorrect whose rights are first infringed and then eliminated," as he pointed out in a speech he delivered in Jekyll Island, Georgia almost exactly two years before his Stalinist show trial in Boise.

Actually, the comparison to the Soviet-era Russian legal system is unfair, given that a defendant hauled before a Soviet criminal tribunal actually enjoyed a small but measurable chance of acquittal.

After the Bolsheviks seized power in 1917, the jury system—which had been established under Alexander II in 1864—was abolished and replaced with "People's Courts" composed of a judge and a panel of two to six Party-appointed "assessors" who heard all of the evidence and decided all questions of both fact and law. The assessors "became known as 'nodders' for simply nodding in agreement with the judge," wrote federal Judge John C. Coughenour in an article published by the *Seattle University Law Review*. "People's assessors virtually always agreed with judges; acquittals were virtually nonexistent. . . . [U]nlike our adversarial system, the Soviet inquisitorial criminal justice system neither prioritized nor emphasized the rights of individual defendants, but instead paid homage to the interests of the state."

What Judge Coughenour describes as a contrast between the Soviet and American legal systems is actually one of the strongest points of similarity. Lew Rockwell recently pointed out that in the pseudo-legal proceedings referred to as "trials" by the federal Leviathan, the defendant "wins once every 212 times"—a respectable approximation of "never." During the late Stalin era, Soviet procurators were ordered to achieve a 100 percent conviction rate; their counterparts in contemporary U.S. federal courts have essentially accomplished that feat. This is because the federal system, like its Soviet predecessor, is designed to serve the interests of the State—and federal juries are typically purged of anyone unwilling to play the role of "nodder" in a show trial.

During jury selection in the Edgar Steele "trial," Assistant U.S. Attorney Traci Whelan, who presided over the prosecution, carefully scrutinized potential jurors for what she called "hidden biases" against "the United States Government." Neither Whelan nor Judge Winmill was willing to abide the presence of any juror who understood that the jury's role is to force the government to overcome the constitutionally prescribed "bias" in favor of the defendant. They needn't have worried.

In Idaho, the most "anti-government" state in the *Soyuz*, the Feds were able to win a murder conspiracy conviction in a case without a victim, a murder weapon, or a motive, using only a doctored audio recording and the self-exculpating testimony of an admitted liar who confessed to manufacturing and planting the non-functional bomb. Andrei Vyshinsky would be suitably impressed.

2012

Restore the Right to Resist

Easy Rider magazine, February 2012

"This guy's a douche. Let's f**k him up."

That exhortation fell from the sneering lips of a Sheriff's Deputy about two minutes into an unprovoked assault on Darrin Ring in the front yard of his home near Waverly, Tennessee.

Ring's supposed offense was to hesitate in confusion when Deputy James McCord told him to take his hands out of his pockets, although his hands weren't in his pockets at the time. McCord and two other deputies seized Ring, threw him into the snow, stripped him naked, and beat him repeatedly. The blows were punctuated with the familiar refrain employed by both rapists and police: "Stop resisting! Quit resisting!"

Another officer, Joseph Parnell of the Waverly PD, arrived with a Taser and ordered the victim to lie still, then commanded him to roll to his stomach—and then inflicted multiple Taser strikes to punish the victim for non-compliance.

Ring, who had suffered broken bones, several bruised ribs, and a punctured lung, was shackled hand and foot and dragged to the county jail. Denied medical care, Ring was beaten, kicked, and Tasered again while still in handcuffs. He was then charged with aggravated assault on an officer and held behind bars for five months before being released.

In his official report, McCord claimed that before the assault began, Ring "stepped away from me, creating more distance between us. He then stood straight and angled his body toward me. . . ." The assault was therefore necessary "for the safety of myself and the other deputies on the scene."

McCord, like all police officers, was taught to depict body language of that kind as an "aggressive posture." Like all police officers, he was also taught to lie. The criminal charges derived from McCord's lies might well have stuck had it not been for the dashcam video. Ring has filed a lawsuit, and a grand jury is considering criminal charges against the officers involved in the beating.

If Ring had actually fought back, this attempt at self-defense would most likely have been regarded as the supposed crime of "resisting arrest"—despite the fact that the arrest was illegal, and the force used to effect it constituted an unambiguous criminal assault.

"It appears to be a nearly universal rule in American jurisdictions that when a suspect responds to an unconstitutional search or seizure [including an arrest] by a physical attack on the officer, evidence of this new crime is admissible notwithstanding the prior illegality," decreed the Idaho State Supreme Court in the 2008 decision *State v. Lusby*.

What this means is that when a common citizen exercises what is called "violent self-help" to prevent a criminal trespass or assault by a cop, the *victim* is liable to prosecution.

That perverse principle was reiterated in a recent federal court decision awarding Arkansas resident Derrol Kirby a single dollar in nominal damages for an incident in which he was needlessly beaten, choked, and Tasered by police. The court ruled that Kirby's passive resistance was an "intervening cause of his injuries," thereby absolving the assailants of any further liability.

For centuries, Anglo-Saxon common law recognized a right to resist unlawful arrest. Two key precedents in the Queen's Court of England—*Hopkin Huggin's Case* (1666) and *Queen v. Tooley*, (1710)—note that bystanders have a right, if not a duty, to intervene forcefully to prevent an unlawful arrest or other criminal violence by the police. In a 1900 ruling entitled *John Bad Elk v. U.S.*, the Supreme Court recognized that an innocent man can employ lethal force to repel an unlawful arrest.

In *Terry Glenn Miller v. State of Alaska* (1969), that state's Supreme Court admitted that "The weight of authoritative precedent supports a right to repel an unlawful arrest with force." Unfortunately, that indispensable right has been supplanted with a supposed duty on the part of the citizen to submit to whatever criminal violence the State's punitive caste sees fit to inflict on him.

Restoring legal recognition of the right to resist arrest is a matter of singular urgency—unless we're content to live in a society in which the police have an unqualified liberty to "f**k up" anybody they consider a "douche."

Restoring the Right to Resist: An Exchange

Easy Rider magazine, March 2012

The following brief essay was written in reply to a letter from a subscriber to Easy Rider magazine who objected to my essay on restoring the right to resist arrest.

The core of Mr. Matt Faulk's complaint with my essay is found in the following sentence: "The author compares law enforcement to rapists, states that all police officers are taught to lie, and encourages violent resistance against those tasked with the increasingly dangerous and difficult duty of being a police officer in America."

I will address each of those three complaints separately:

> Until recently, women facing the prospect of sexual assault were admonished: "Don't resist—it will only make things worse." Thankfully, rape victims are now expected to fight back—but victims of police assault are required to endure, with abject meekness, the criminal violence committed by the assailants (usually more than one is involved). Furthermore, a woman who fights back when sexually assaulted by a cop may be prosecuted for resisting arrest or assault on a police officer. Gregory Babbitt, an attorney representing the State of Michigan before that state's Supreme Court, admitted as much during oral arguments last October 4. Adam Skweres, a Pittsburgh cop recently charged with several sexual assaults in the line of duty, told one of his would-be victims that if she attempted to flee she would be arrested for resisting arrest.

> "Police lie. It's part of their job." Thus began an essay entitled "Training Cops to Lie," written by former prosecutor Val Van Brocklin and published in the November 16, 2009 edition of the online journal Officer.com. In his 2005 memoir *Breaking Rank*, former Seattle Police Chief Norm Stamper testifies that the training referred to by Ms. Van Brocklin has been quite

196

effective: "Cops lie. Most of them lie a couple of times per shift, at least" (Pg. 129). Stamper insists that there is value in what might be called situational dishonesty, but he has no use for the kind of routine truth-shading or outright perjury that has become tragically commonplace in contemporary law enforcement.

As I noted in the essay, there is abundant judicial recognition of the fact that Anglo-Saxon common law recognizes the right to resist unlawful arrest—if necessary, through the use of lethal force (the Supreme Court's 1900 *John Bad Elk v. U.S.* decision remains the definitive precedent on the subject). Legislation currently being considered in Indiana, Minnesota, and New Hampshire would restore legal protection for that right, which is a development as welcome as it is overdue.

Does Mr. Faulk believe that police have an unqualified right to commit criminal violence against civilians? Apparently so, given his blithe dismissal of the case of Darrin Ring, the innocent Tennessee resident who was left with broken bones, bruised ribs, and a punctured lung after being needlessly beaten and tasered by a gang of police officers who—as one of them said—simply wanted to "f**k him up."

There's no use "analyzing" that incident, Faulk insists, because "it doesn't matter who was right or who was wrong." This only makes sense if we assume that Ring, as a mere Mundane—that is, someone who doesn't belong to the exalted brotherhood of official coercion—doesn't have any rights the police are required to respect.

Mr. Faulk is zealous to defend police who "do an honorable job"—yet he takes inconsolable offense when criticism is directed at those who dishonor the profession by committing criminal assaults on the innocent and then compounding those crimes with perjury. Restoring legal protection for the right to resist unlawful arrest would pose no threat to genuinely honorable peace officers—individuals devoted to protection of life, liberty, and property, rather than unionized bullies bearing government credentials.

The Pseudo-Courage of Chris Kyle

Pro Libertate, February 5, 2012

That kind of courage, which is conspicuous in danger and enterprise, if devoid of justice, is absolutely undeserving of the name of valor. It should rather be considered as a brutal fierceness outraging every principle of humanity.

—Cicero, The Offices, Book I Chapter XIX

As a sniper with the Navy SEALs in Iraq, Chris Kyle was shot twice and wounded on several other occasions. He is credited with 160 confirmed kills. He received several commendations. Of his fierceness there is no reasonable doubt. Whether his exploits display courage is an entirely separate question.

American Sniper: The Autobiography of the Most Lethal Sniper in U.S. Military History, the ghost-written memoir for which Kyle claims primary authorship, offers convincing testimony that Kyle not only failed to display genuine courage in Iraq, but was incapable of recognizing it when it was exhibited by desperate patriots seeking to evict the armed foreigners who had invaded and occupied their country.

The insurgents who fought the American invasion (and the few "allied" troops representing governments that had been bribed or brow-beaten into collaborating in that crime) were sub-human "savages" and "cowards," according to Kyle.

"Savage, despicable evil," writes Kyle. "That's what we were fighting in Iraq. . . . People ask me all the time, 'How many people have you killed?'. . . The number is not important to me. I only wish I had killed more. Not for bragging rights, but because I believe the world is a better place without savages out there taking American lives."

None of the American military personnel whose lives were wasted in Iraq had to die there, because none of them had any legitimate reason to be there. From Kyle's perspective, however, only incorrigibly "evil" people would object once their country had been designated the target of one of Washington's frequent outbursts of murderous humanitarianism.

The insensate savagery of the Iraqi population was supposedly illustrated by the first kill Kyle recorded as a sniper, while covering a Marine advance near Nasiriyah in March, 2003.

"I looked through the scope," Kyle recalls. "The only people who were moving were [a] woman and maybe a child or two nearby. I watched the troops pull up. Ten young, proud Marines in uniform got out of their vehicles and gathered for a foot patrol. As the Americans organized, the woman took something from beneath her clothes, and yanked at it. She'd set a grenade."

Kyle shot the woman twice.

"It was my duty to shoot, and I don't regret it," Kyle attests. "The woman was already dead. I was just making sure she didn't take any Marines with her. It was clear that not only did she want to kill them, but she didn't care about anybody else nearby who would have been blown up by the grenade or killed in the firefight. Children on the street, people in the houses, maybe her child. . . ."

Of course, if the Marines hadn't invaded that woman's neighborhood, she wouldn't have been driven to take such desperate action—but Kyle either cannot or will not understand the motives of an Iraqi patriot.

"She was . . . blinded by evil," Kyle writes of the woman he murdered from a safe distance. "She just wanted Americans dead, no matter what. My shots saved several Americans, whose lives were clearly worth more than that woman's twisted soul."

Were Kyle just a touch more literate, he might recognize the term *untermenschen*, a German expression that encapsulates his view of the Iraqis who took up arms to repel foreign invaders. From his perspective, they were incurably inferior to their "liberators" and possessed of an inexplicable hatred toward their natural betters.

For some reason many Iraqis resented the armed emissaries of the distant government that had installed Saddam in power, built up his arsenal and apparatus of domestic repression, and then conferred upon the inhabitants of that nation the unmatched blessing of several decades of wars, embargoes, airstrikes, disease, and the early, avoidable deaths of hundreds of thousands of children.

"The people we were fighting in Iraq, after Saddam's army fled or was defeated, were fanatics," Kyle insists. "They hated us because we weren't Muslim. They wanted to kill us, even though we'd just booted out their dictator, because we practiced a different religion than they did."

Actually, most of them probably wanted to kill Kyle and his comrades because they had invaded and occupied their country. They were prepared to use lethal force to protect their homes against armed intruders who had no right to be there. Ironically, Kyle's book offers evidence that he understands that principle; he simply doesn't believe that it applies to Iraqis.

In one incident described by Kyle, he and several other U.S. personnel raid an Iraqi home, in the basement of which they discover a mass grave containing the bodies of several soldiers and Marines. For several panic-stricken moments, Kyle is understandably terrified by the thought that he might find the lifeless body of his younger brother, a Marine who had also been deployed to Iraq.

With obvious and vehement disgust, Kyle cites the "murdered young men whose bodies we had pulled out" of that basement grave as evidence of the bestial nature of the enemy. He exhibits no interest at all in the fact that tens of millions of Iraqis have seen friends and family meet violent, avoidable deaths as a result of the wars and sanctions imposed on their country by Washington.

Untermenschen, apparently, aren't entitled to experience grief and rage— much less the right to defend their homes and families against aggressive violence.

After returning from his first combat tour in Iraq, Kyle recalls, he was rudely roused from slumber one morning when the burglar alarm went off. Although this was a malfunction rather than a real emergency, Kyle's reaction was revealing.

"I grabbed my pistol and went to confront the criminal," he recalls. "No son of a bitch was breaking into my house and living to tell about it."

Why was it "evil" for Iraqis to feel exactly the same way about the foreign sons of bitches who broke into their country and wrecked the place?

Later in the book, describing a stalking exercise during his training to become a sniper, Kyle recounts how he "heard the distinct rattle of a snake nearby."

"A rattler had taken a particular liking to the piece of real estate I had to cross," Kyle recalls. "Willing it away didn't work. . . . I crept slowly to the side, altering my course. Some enemies aren't worth fighting."

Exactly: The only enemies worth "fighting," apparently, are those who aren't capable of hurting you when you trespass on their turf.

The Gadsen Flag—featuring a coiled rattlesnake and the directive "Don't Tread On Me"—was, and remains, the best symbolic expression of authentic American patriotism. Genuine American patriots can understand why patriots of other countries would feel similar attachments, and be similarly inclined to repel foreign invaders. This is why they will never support any war that puts other Americans in the position of killing foreign patriots who are defending their own homes.

A rattlesnake defending its territory earns Kyle's respect; an Iraqi patriot fighting on his home soil with his back to his home and the face to his enemy, however, is "blinded by evil" and not truly human.

"They may have been cowards, but they could certainly kill people," observes Kyle of the guerrillas. "The insurgents didn't worry about ROEs [Rules of Engagement] or court-martials [sic]. If they had the advantage, they would kill any Westerner they could find, whether they were soldiers or not."

If that charge (made on page 87 of Kyle's book) is accurate, it might reflect the fact that the Iraqi resistance (as well as the tactics of foreign guerrillas who joined the fight) was playing according to ground rules established by the U.S. early in the war.

On page 79, Kyle describes the Rules of Engagement that his unit followed when they were deployed to Shatt al-Arab, a river on the Iraq-Iran border: "Our ROEs when the war kicked off were pretty simple: *If you see anyone from about sixteen to sixty-five and they're male, shoot 'em. Kill every male you see.* That wasn't the official language, but that was the idea." (Emphasis in the original.)

Those orders were of a piece with the studied indifference to civilian casualties that characterized the "Shock and Awe" bombing campaign that began the war. In preparing that onslaught General Tommy Franks and his military planners were guided by a computer program that referred to civilian casualties as "bugsplat." Franks had no compunction about ordering bombing missions that would result in what the computer projections described as "heavy bugsplat." After all, aren't the lives of American military personnel "clearly worth more"—to use Kyle's phrase—than those of the Iraqi civilians, who were mere insects to be annihilated?

In one of her occasional contributions to Kyle's book, his wife Taya rebukes people who criticize the bloodshed wrought in Iraq by her husband and his colleagues: "As far as I can see it, anyone who has a problem with what guys do over there is incapable of empathy." The trait she describes isn't empathy; it's a variation on the kind of preemptive self-pity described by Hannah Arendt in her study *Eichmann in Jerusalem*.

Referring to those who killed on behalf of the Third Reich, Arendt observed:

> What stuck in the minds of these men who had become murderers was simply the notion of being involved in something historic, grandiose, unique ("a great task that occurs

201

once in two thousand years"), which must therefore be difficult to bear. This was important, because the murderers were not sadists or killers by nature; on the contrary, a systematic effort was made to weed out all those who derived physical pleasure from what they did. . . .

This was true even of those who belonged to the SS: Even those in the Reich's killer elite were not able to suppress their conscience entirely. Thus the

trick used by Himmler—who apparently was rather strongly afflicted by these instinctive reactions himself—was very simple and probably very effective; it consisted in turning these instincts around, as it were, in directing them toward the self. So that instead of saying: "What horrible things I did to people!," the murderers would be able to say: "What horrible things I had to watch in the pursuance of my duties, how heavily the task weighed upon my shoulders!"

Kyle's memoir is remarkable chiefly for the complete absence of the kind of moral anguish Arendt describes among the SS. Kyle eagerly participated in a patently illegal and entirely unnecessary war of aggression against a country that never attacked, harmed, or threatened the United States. He killed scores of people, terrorized thousands more. As Kyle tells the story, he reveled in the experience, and regrets only that he wasn't able to slaughter more of the "savages" who surrounded him.

During Kyle's last deployment to Iraq, his unit—Charlie Company of SEAL Team 3—assigned themselves the nickname "The Punishers," appropriating as their insignia the Death's Head logo used by the psychotic comic book character of the same name.

Interestingly, a group of police officers in Milwaukee had exactly the same idea. They also adopted the "Punisher" logo, which they displayed on their police vehicles and wore on knitted caps as they prowled the street in search of asses to kick.

The most memorable exhibition of what they regarded as valor came in October 2004, when a thugscrum of "Punishers" beset a male dancer named Frank Jude, who was nearly beaten to death because he was suspected of stealing a badge.

After throwing Jude to the ground, the Punishers severely beat, kicked, and choked him—then put a knife to his throat and jammed a pen into one of his ears. The victim survived the assault, but was left with permanent brain damage. The officers later claimed that this amount of violence was necessary to "subdue" Jude—who was never charged in connection with the incident. The jury in the criminal trial accepted that claim and acquitted the officers—who were later found guilty of criminal civil rights violations.

During his service in Iraq, Kyle occasionally functioned as a law enforcement officer of sorts. He was involved in dozens of raids against the homes of suspected "insurgents," many of whom were arrested on the basis of uncorroborated accusations by anonymous informants.

He allows that many of the people dragged off in shackles were entirely innocent, but maintains that he wasn't ever troubled by that fact; he was just doing his "duty."

Shortly before the war began, Kyle was part of a SEAL unit tasked to enforce UN sanctions against Iraq by intercepting tankers leaving the country with unlicensed oil deliveries. On one occasion, he boarded a tanker commanded by a commercial sea captain who "had some fight in him, and even though he was unarmed, he wasn't ready to surrender."

"He made a run at me," Kyle continues. "Pretty stupid. First of all, I'm not only bigger than him, but I was wearing full body armor. Not to mention the fact that I had a submachine gun in my hand. I took the muzzle of my gun and struck the idiot in the chest. He went right down."

If Kyle had been a warrior, rather than a bully, he would have admired the authentic courage displayed by the smaller, unarmed man who fought to protect the ship and cargo entrusted to him.

How would he act if the roles were reversed—if he were the over-matched man trying to defend private property from a group of state-licensed pirates claiming "authority" from a UN mandate? We'll never know the answer to that question, because Kyle's "courage" is of the sort that only manifests itself in the service of power, and in the company of those enjoying a prohibitive advantage over their victims.

Kyle's "service" continues, even though he's retired from the military. He is president of Craft International, a Homeland Security contractor involved in training domestic law enforcement agencies. It's quite likely that Kyle's outfit will soak up a considerable portion of the roughly $1.5 billion dollars the Obama administration seeks to hire military veterans of Iraq and Afghanistan to work as police, emergency personnel, and park rangers.

How to Become a "Stalker" in Oregon: Criticize the Police

Pro Libertate, April 22, 2012

What does it take to be officially designated a "stalker" in the State of Oregon?

In a recent decision the State Court of Appeals ruled that a bully can subject a terrified elderly woman to a years-long campaign of harassment, intimidation, and physical violence without being saddled with a stalking protection order (SPO). Two years ago, the same court ruled that an individual can commit repeated acts of property damage, coupled with physical assaults and even an explicit death threat, and not qualify for stalker status.

Apparently, the only guaranteed way to earn the unwanted title of "stalker" in the Beaver State is to criticize the local police and the corrupt municipal cabal it serves. That's a reasonable inference to draw from the bizarre experience of Sunriver, Oregon resident Robert Foster, whose stalking case involving the Sunriver PD and the Sunriver Owners Association (SROA) is scheduled for trial on Tuesday, April 24.[1]

Roughly two years ago, Foster—a well-established and widely respected local businessman who operates a hot tub service company—was designated a stalker in an ex parte proceeding. Since that time he has been arrested twice for the supposed crime of coming within eyeshot of one of the timid, shivering creatures who supposedly live in bladder-loosening fear of Foster—Sergeant Joseph Patnode and Officer Kasey Hughes.

Foster has never said or done anything to harm either of those proud, intrepid members of the Brotherhood of Coercion. Prior to the arrests made pursuant to the spurious stalking protection order, Foster had no criminal record of any kind. Over the past two years, Foster has been treated as a prisoner in his own hometown. At one point last fall he was driven into out-of-state exile for three months to avoid arrest as he prepared for a January 26 court date.

Rather than convening the trial on the appointed time at the designated location, the presiding Judge conducted a series of sidebar conferences with the parties in her chambers while dozens of people waited for several hours in a crowded, poorly ventilated courtroom. In the far corner of the small room could be seen a poorly-disguised Detective from the Deschutes County Sheriff's

Office, who furtively took photographs of everyone who had gathered to support Foster.

In the middle of the courtroom had assembled practically the entire Sunriver Police Department. All of them but Hughes and Patnode were in uniform and wearing body armor. They were also wreathed in the unmistakable aroma of pure, unfiltered fear. This shouldn't surprise us: These are people who profess to be terrified by the mere sight of a skinny, mild-mannered, unarmed, 51-year-old businessman whose only weapon is a finely whetted wit.

Bob Foster and his daughter, Rebecca Kossler, were as eager for their day in court as the Sunriver PD was to avoid it—a fact that says everything we need to know about the relative merits of their respective cases. If Foster's accusers were telling any portion of the truth, they wouldn't be exhausting every dilatory tactic known to man in an effort to avoid testifying under oath in an adversarial setting.

In defiance of State Law, the original SPO was granted without a mandatory hearing at which Foster could contest it. His court appearance on January 26 was the first time he was able to speak for himself in a judicial proceeding. Rather than permitting Foster the opportunity to tear apart the specious case against him, the presiding judge attempted to fashion a modified order under which Foster would be granted the supposed privilege of a judicial hearing before the "victims"—Officers Patnode and Hughes—could arrange for his arrest.

The Sunriver PD faction refused to drop the charges against Foster because, as they explicitly told the judge, they were concerned that he would sue the department for the taxpayer-subsidized harassment he has experienced.

Assuming that his persecutors could be held personally liable, rather than socializing the costs of their criminal foolishness, Foster would be entitled to sue them into penury: During the past two years he has spent more than $200,000 contesting the patently false and unambiguously malicious accusation that he had been stalking the local police.

In sworn pre-trial depositions, neither of the "victims" of Foster's purported stalking was ever able to describe an instance in which he did or said anything so much as suggesting violent intent. The same is true of former Sunriver Police Chief Michael Kennedy, who—as we will see—has since lost his position and offered several key disclosures regarding what can only be called a criminal conspiracy against Foster.

Foster's supposed victims are armed individuals claiming a license to use lethal force at their discretion—and who supposedly dissolve into puddles of petulant panic at the sight of him. Pedro Erazo's victim, by way of contrast, was a senior citizen named Kathryn Reitz, whom he repeatedly harassed, threatened, and physically assaulted at the Goodwill convenience store in Hillsboro, Oregon.

Over the course of two years, Erazo and his cohorts would descend on the thrift store in pursuit of severely discounted books to re-sell online. Three times a day, employees would wheel out large bins full of merchandise, including books. Heedless of rudimentary courtesy, Erazo's group would shove aside other shoppers—and, on occasion, store employees—in order to scoop up armloads of books whose barcodes would be read by a handheld digital scanner. Any potentially valuable volumes would be piled in a cart.

Reitz attracted Erazo's malign attention by voicing disgust over his behavior. He retaliated by following her around the store, barraging her with insults and threats.

"You should be afraid of me," Erazo sneered at the terrified 64-year-old woman. "They're not going to stop me. I can do whatever I want."

As it happens, the thrift store chain's management *did* stop him: Erazo is now banned from 40 stores in Northwest Oregon and Southwest Washington. At Reitz's request, Washington County Circuit Court Judge Donald Letourneau imposed a stalking order against Erazo, who was one of several people to complain about the tactics he employed.

Another frequent shopper who testified on behalf of Reitz recalled that Erazo had instructed his goons to "shadow me, follow me. If I would go here, then [he told them] 'go with her,' and then a person would come and . . . just follow me wherever I would go . . . stand right next to me, elbow me, make it incredibly uncomfortable."

Despite the fact that Erazo and his gang had clearly engaged in aggressive and violent behavior, the Oregon Court of Appeals overturned the stalking order. Oregon state law requires at least two "contacts" in which the victim would have a "reasonable apprehension" regarding his or her physical safety. While Erazo had physically assaulted Reitz on one confrontation, and assailed her with insults and threats during numerous others, a second violent "contact" would be necessary in order for his behavior to qualify as "stalking" under state law.

In a similar case from 2010 (*Swarringim v. Olson*), the Court of Appeals dealt with a neighborhood dispute that escalated to property damage (vandalism to the petitioner's home and automobile) as well as violence and death threats.

In one confrontation, Swarringim's 14-year-old son was knocked flat on his back by Olson's 18-year-old son, Matthew, who also warned that he knew people "who will slit [the boy's] throat."

Stipulating to the facts as related by the Swarringim family, the Court of Appeals threw out the stalking order, maintaining that the evidence was insufficient to establish that the actions of Olson and his son had caused "reasonable apprehension for personal safety" on the part of the victims.

Obviously, it is difficult to make a stalking order stick in the State of Oregon, even when the subject of the order has committed acts of criminal violence and made explicit death threats. The designation of "stalker" is reserved for truly dangerous people like Bob Foster, whose sole offense was to make the police uncomfortable.

Foster was a prominent opponent of both the SROA and the proposed Special Services District (SSD), which was created in 2008 and inflicts an annual cost of several million dollars on Sunriver home owners.

Sunriver—although a lovely place—isn't really a town; it is a shopping mall with a thyroid condition. The Census Bureau considers it to be part of nearby Bend. Until 2008, its streets were not considered "public conveyances," but rather private roads accessible to the public. This meant that the Sunriver PD couldn't write traffic citations, much to the frustration of those who coveted the revenue.

In 2007, the SROA successfully lobbied Oregon State Rep. Gene Wisnat to sponsor H.B. 3445, a bill custom-tailored for Sunriver that extended police "authority" to include roads and streets on "premises open to the public that are owned by a homeowners association. . . ." The following year, the SROA enacted a special multi-million-dollar tax assessment for a special service district (SSD) it had created in 2002. The SSD now included a fully functional police department, which immediately became a huge nuisance to local business owners and the visitors upon whom the local economy depends.

"The police constantly harassed people in my parking lot," recalled Connie Hutcherson, former owner of RJB's restaurant, in an interview with a private investigator. "They would do drive-throughs looking for DUIs. . . . I lost a lot of business because of them. Customers would tell me, 'We'd love to come in more, but we're scared.'"

On more than a few occasions, an aggravated Hutcherson confronted the officers in her parking lot. "They didn't care for me much," she wryly observed.

No Quarter

In her interview with the investigator, Danyl Dahl described a March 2009 episode in which the deli delivery van she was driving was stopped by two Sunriver officers who—in response to a trivial traffic infraction—approached her with guns drawn and faces drawn taut with irrational rage.

"Do you want to get arrested today?" one of them snarled at the perplexed and terrified woman. "Do you want to go to jail today?"

"These people were hired by the Sunriver Owners Association," Dahl pointed out. "They think they can do anything they want."

The Sunriver police were just as inhospitable to visitors—something Shawn Vickers, who was stopped for speeding, witnessed first-hand. During the traffic stop, a tourist riding a bicycle stopped and began taking photos of the police vehicle.

"The officer lost control," Vickers related to the investigator. "He was like, 'Halt! You do not have my permission to take my picture! Freeze! Do not move!' And then he . . . was very agitated, he did not know what to do. . . . At some point, I thought he was going to draw his gun."

"Are you kidding me?" exclaimed an astonished Vickers, who was still seated behind the wheel of his vehicle. This provoked another outburst: "He was like, 'Freeze! Put your hands where I can see them! Do not move!' He moved about 6–7 feet from me. He never turned his back to me." As it happened, the bicyclist was a visiting sheriff's deputy from Los Angeles County who collected photographs of police vehicles. Upon learning of the tourist's identity, the officer regained at least a portion of his composure. For several anxious moments, however, "I thought this guy was going to lose it and draw down on one of us," Vickers reports.

A Sunriver resident who identified herself only as "Vicki" told the investigator about a similar incident she witnessed in October 2010 involving three Sunriver police officers who swarmed a car containing an elderly couple "with guns drawn and pointing at them." The elderly couple weren't armed fugitives; at worst they had committed a minor traffic infraction. Yet they were threatened with lethal violence by a police department determined to manufacture work for itself.

April Gossling, who operated the Villagio Espresso shop, recalled an April 2011 incident in which three Sunriver Police officers pulled over a group of teenagers who were found with alcohol and marijuana. She overheard the police "threatening them—telling them how much trouble they were in, and how they needed to report to them" regarding drug and alcohol use by other kids.

209

One of the officers wasn't satisfied merely to cultivate a group of informants: He prevailed on one of the underage girls to supply him with her phone number in a conversation involving the suggestion of "sexual favors," Gossling testified. During this lengthy encounter, Gossling overheard an emergency call on the police radio that was blithely ignored by the officers.

Unremitting harassment by the Sunriver PD led at least one resident to flee the town.

"I was a victim of such continuous harassment by the Sunriver PD that I eventually simply moved," former Sunriver resident Jared Lewis told Pro Libertate. "I was so fearful of them every time I left my house. . . . I was routinely followed, harassed and stopped by Sunriver PD for absolutely no reason for a period of three years."

In some cases, Lewis reports, Officer Kasey Hughes—one of the two gallant defenders of public order who filed a stalking order against Foster—followed him "for miles at a time before stopping me." In one particularly crowded day, Lewis was stopped four times by four different Sunriver PD officers.

"The most disturbing aspect of this was that after dozens of stops per month, I finally reached a point of approaching the [now former] chief to complain and was not only rebuffed, but it was revealed to me by the chief that *none* of my stops was recorded," Lewis recalled. "He essentially told me that his officers had never stopped me and that I was a liar."

Obviously, many Sunriver residents recognized that the police department—and the quasi-private municipal cabal running it—constituted a large, festering problem. However, only Bob Foster was willing to confront those responsible for it.

In public meetings, Foster denounced the Service District as an unnecessary expense that consolidated the grip of the village's insular ruling elite. He proposed abolishing the District and contracting with nearby La Pine for emergency services—an arrangement that would have saved Sunriver home owners a great deal of money and reined in the power of the SROA.

In reprisal, the SROA concocted a plot to silence the civic-minded businessman. This is not a matter of speculation: The key player in that conspiracy, former Sunriver Police Chief Michael Kennedy, has provided an admirably candid summary of that conspiracy in a March 8 letter to the Deschutes County Commission.

Kennedy wrote that letter to file a grievance with the Commission after being fired on February 16 in what he described as an act of retaliation by a corrupt and unaccountable municipal government whose official dealings are as opaque as the proceedings of the North Korean Politburo.

"The Sunriver Owners Association has pressured the Sunriver Police Department as well as me to perform unlawful and unethical acts . . . which we have refused," wrote Kennedy. "It is my firm belief that my firing was a direct result of my refusal to act on their unethical requests."

The conspiracy to railroad Bob Foster on "stalking" charges was prominent among those "unethical" acts to which Kennedy refers.

After growing weary of what was described as Foster's "unwanted attention," Kennedy approached the SROA and requested "that Bob Foster be trespassed from the SROA/Police building," the former Chief recalled. This would mean that Foster wouldn't be able to attend public SROA meetings, or file a police complaint, without being subject to arrest.

Kennedy's suggestion, if acted on, would have been an act of petty, officious retaliation, but it wasn't a criminal conspiracy. What the SROA suggested does meet that description.

> After meeting with the board, the SROA board president, Bob Nelson, and Bob Wrightson, who are both also on the Service District board, came to my office and told Sergeant Patnode and I [sic] that they would not be trespassing Bob Foster. . . . [H]owever, their legal counsel had a better solution. . . . A short time later, our legal counsel advised that we would be filing a stalking order against Bob Foster. . . . At the request of legal counsel, I contacted Sergeant Patnode and Officer Kasey Hughes to see if they would be willing to have the stalking orders filed on their behalf. They subsequently agreed and the stalking orders were filed.

Unfortunately for the SROA, Bob Foster "didn't immediately roll over," Kennedy recalls. Instead, he gave notice that he intended to file lawsuits against the SROA and the Service District—which, as Kennedy points out, are essentially the same entity.

"The current management structure of the Sunriver Service District puts entirely too much control in the hands of a small segment of the community,"

Kennedy explained to the County Commission. "The end result is that *a private home owners association has effective control over the operations and funds of a public taxing district*." (Emphasis added.) That same entrenched cabal uses the Sunriver PD as its enforcement arm and revenue-extraction mechanism.

Seeking to limit the potential damage from the lawsuit, the SROA "appeared to be attempting to withdraw Service District protection from the two officers" it has used to file stalking orders against Foster.

In an executive session, SROA Board President Nelson "said something to the effect of 'Why is the Service District financing these stalking orders, when this is clearly a civil matter between these two officers and Bob Foster,'" Kennedy recalled:

> I reminded him that we had asked those officers if they would be willing to file the stalking orders at the request of legal counsel. . . . I advised him that if asked, that is how I would have to testify in court. After that, SROA appeared to further distance themselves from the case, even though *they were the ones who initially started us down the path of filing the stalking orders*. (Emphasis added.)

In those paragraphs, Kennedy made at least three critical admissions:

- The private SROA, in defiance of conflict-of-interest laws, controls a public taxing district and the police department—just as Bob Foster had predicted it would.
- The stalking case against Foster was instigated by the SROA, with the connivance of the police department; it had nothing to do with any criminal conduct on Foster's part.
- The SROA and Service District were using funds extracted from Sunriver tax victims to finance its vendetta against Foster.

Kennedy's final performance evaluation by the SROA commended him for taking the lead "in seeking to support and protect [his] officers when harassment by a stalker reached the point where legal action had to be taken." The SROA's assessment of Kennedy changed abruptly after the predictable scene in which the Chief told them, in effect, "If I go down, I'm taking you with me."

After Kennedy was cashiered, he was reportedly given a severance package of $100,000—a rather extravagant amount for a minor bureaucrat who managed a tiny police force in a tranquil resort community with a permanent population of fewer than 1,000 people. If the SROA's intention was to buy off Kennedy, they badly underestimated the price of his silence—and misunderstood the magnitude of his admissions against interest.

Kennedy insists on being reinstated as Sunriver Police Chief. He also demands the resignation of five directors of the SROA, and the disbanding of the special service district. That last demand is another vindication of Bob Foster, who made the same proposal five years ago—thereby provoking the lengthy and expensive campaign of criminal harassment in which Kennedy eagerly participated until it became personally risky to him.

Disbanding the service district is necessary but insufficient. The only adequate remedy would be to add Sunriver, Oregon to the lengthening roster of small towns that have been relieved of the burden of a municipal police department. Chances are, Kind Reader, that the city in which you live would benefit from the same kind of "neglect."

---

[1] The trial was never held.

Judicially Authorized Rape: The Newest Weapon in the Prohibitionist Arsenal

Pro Libertate, June 13, 2012

Under Utah state law, "object rape" consists of the involuntary "penetration, however slight, of the genital or anal opening of another person who is 14 years of age or older, by any foreign object, substance, instrument, or device. . . ." This act constitutes a form of aggravated sexual assault for which the penalty is a prison term of no less than ten years, followed by lifetime enrollment in the sex offender registry.

As 22-year-old Utah resident Stephan Cook discovered, the crime of object rape—like any other offense against person or property—can be transmuted into a policy option when it's committed pursuant to a government decree.

While attending Snow College in Ephraim, Utah, four years ago, Cook and a friend were smoking cigarettes near a parked car when they were accosted by several police officers. Following the standard script, the officers—who, let us not forget, were trained to lie—claimed to smell marijuana and demanded to search the car.

Cook and his friend emptied their pockets and consented to a pat-down search. They permitted the officers to search the interior of the car several times with a drug-sniffing dog. Eventually a glass pipe was found in the trunk. Rather than arresting Cook, who was a passenger in the car, the officers ordered him to drive to a nearby police station, supposedly to save his friend the expense of an impound fee.

There was neither probable cause nor reasonable suspicion to justify the search of the car. By ordering Cook to drive to the station, the police made it clear that they did not believe that he was under the influence of marijuana.

Furthermore, Cook didn't own the car, a fact that severs the thinnest thread connecting him to the glass pipe found in the trunk.

Yet the officers persisted in their effort to manufacture an offense. Cook was detained and informed that he would have to undergo a drug test. When the police demanded that he sign a waiver of his rights, Cook—whose parents are police officers—repeatedly and explicitly demanded access to an attorney.

"I asked for an attorney because I didn't know if this was right," Cook recalled in a television interview. "Once I did that, they said 'We're getting a

214

search warrant so we're going to have your urine by the end of the night.'" A "bodily fluids warrant" was issued "authorizing" the cops to obtain a urine sample. It did not, however, specify that the sample could be taken by force. Lindsay Jarvis, Cook's attorney, informed Pro Libertate that the warrant was issued by a judicial "commissioner," rather than a judge.

Since the police considered Cook sufficiently sober to drive, they clearly weren't facing exigent circumstances. Even if we make the unwarranted assumption that the police were entitled to take a urine sample, they had the luxury of collecting one at leisure—but this wouldn't have satisfied whatever prurient interest they had in inflicting unnecessary pain on a teenage male.

Cook's abductors took him to the Sanpete Valley Hospital, where Nurse Ratched told them "to hold my shoulders and she undoes my pants and wipes me down with iodine, catheterized me and took my urine," the victim recalls.

Ms. Jarvis points out that the purpose of this procedure was clearly punitive, not investigative: "Rather than employ a simple blood test, they're forcibly catheterizing these people."

This satisfies another element of the statutory definition of object rape: The act was committed with the "intent to cause substantial emotional or bodily pain to the victim."

After sexually assaulting Cook, the offenders charged the victim with possession of marijuana and resisting arrest. Even before the matter was brought before a judge, Cook was also slapped with immediate disciplinary action by Snow College.

"The commissioner who issued the warrant was also on the college disciplinary board," Jarvis observed in a phone interview with Pro Libertate. "So his student account was immediately put on hold until he completed a two-month class on alcohol and drug abuse. He wasn't able to complete his midterms, or register for the following semester. This cost him a lot of money on what amounts to wasted tuition."

Rather than being prosecuted, two of the officers who sexually assaulted Cook—Chad Huff and Justin Aagard—have been promoted. Huff is now Chief of Police in Fountain Green, Utah, and Aagard has been appointed to the same post in nearby Moroni City. In the interest of civic integrity, the municipal governments of Fountain Green and Moroni City should post a warning informing visitors that their respective police departments are under the direction of violent sex offenders.

Cook, who was forced to take a plea, has filed an $11 million lawsuit against Sanpete County. This has drawn the predictable shoulder-shrug response from county attorney Peter Stirba. "My client officers certainly did not do anything wrong," Stirba declares, insisting that "the officers were acting pursuant to a lawful court order requiring catheterization of Mr. Cook."

Leaving aside the fact that no document or directive can make the act of object rape "lawful," the warrant to which Stirba refers was issued by a county functionary who had no legal training of any kind—and it did not *require* catheterization. The painful and degrading procedure was inflicted on Cook for the purpose of punishing him for invoking his rights, and to terrorize his friend into compliance: After witnessing what had been done to Cook, the owner of the vehicle surrendered a urine sample "voluntarily."

The gratuitously vicious nature of this episode is further underscored by the fact that although Cook was booked into jail after being violated, the urine samples were never tested, and no record was made of his visit to the hospital.

"What they did was wrong—and I'm pretty sure they're doing it to other people," Cook observes. Indeed, there's reason to believe that object rape of this variety has become a preferred tactic in the "war on drugs."

"It was like I had been raped . . . and all those guards were helping," testified Haley Owen Hooper of her own "forced catheterization" by Sevier County deputies in December 2004.

Hooper (known at the time as Haley Owen) was a 20-year-old who stood about 5'1" and weighed about 105 pounds. She was pinned beneath a thugscrum of at least four officers—one of whom later gave a self-serving estimate that he weighed 260 pounds. As she struggled beneath a half-ton of tax-subsidized suet, her pants and underwear were removed so a licensed practical nurse could insert the catheter.

A few seconds before the assault began, Hooper had pleaded for the deputies to draw blood instead of sexually violating her.

"I screamed, 'Why can't you just take my blood?'" Hooper testified at trial. "The guy in the black cowboy hat said, 'The judge wants urine. We're going to take urine.'"

That was a lie, of course. A magistrate had issued a "body fluids" warrant, but it did not specify a urine sample. Furthermore, the affidavit requesting the warrant was "weak and misleading," in the words of federal District Judge K.K. McIff. The officer claimed that Hooper, who was arrested following a traffic stop, was "belligerent and uncooperative . . . fidgety and nervous," behavior that he described as "consistent with the use of a central nervous system stimulant." He also claimed that the stop was conducted because it was "known by the officers that Haley [Hooper] didn't have a drivers [sic] license."

The trained liar who filed that affidavit carefully avoided the fact that the "traffic stop" was actually carried out by the Central Utah Narcotics Task Force, who thought that the car was being driven by another person. It wasn't until the vehicle was stopped that the officers realized that Miss Hooper was behind the wheel. She had committed no traffic infractions to justify the stop. Her agitated behavior—which included treating her captors to some pungent epithets—was not evidence of drug use, but the predictable result of being surrounded by more than a half-dozen strangers who pointed guns at her and barraged her with threats and profane, abusive language.

Judge McIff's Memorandum Decision recalls that when the officers demanded to search the vehicle, Hooper "challenged the officers' authority" by refusing to cooperate. They replied that "they knew more about the law than she did and that they could search anyway." Although nothing incriminating could be found, Hooper's "contemptuous" attitude simply couldn't be countenanced— so she was taken to a nearby hospital for summary punishment in the form of sexual humiliation.

The only suitable description of what was done to Hooper is "gang rape"— albeit through the use of an object. Just before that crime was committed, the perpetrators, seeking to preserve the fiction that what they did was legal, placed a phone call to the court clerk to ask if the warrant would apply to both blood and urine. That phone call wouldn't have been necessary if, as the rapist in the black cowboy hat claimed, the judge had instructed them to collect urine.

The clerk, who allegedly conferred with the judge, supposedly said that the warrant would include the forcible extraction of a urine sample. There is no way to know whether that conversation took place, because no printed or audio record was made of the phone call.

In July 2010, federal District Judge Dee Benson dismissed Hooper's lawsuit against the Task Force on the grounds of "qualified immunity." This means that as things presently stand, police in Utah are free to commit object rape in order to teach an object lesson to Mundanes who commit the unforgivable offense called "contempt of cop." Similar conditions prevail elsewhere in the *Soyuz*.

Last September, a federal district court for southern Indiana dismissed a lawsuit filed by Jamie Lockard, who was subjected to a forced catheterization following a traffic stop for supposedly running a stop sign in March 2009. Officer Brian Miller, once again sticking to the preferred script, claimed that he smelled alcohol on Lockard's breath. A Breathalyzer test returned a BAC of 0.07—which is under Indiana's legal limit.

Rather than apologizing for his unwarranted intrusion and bidding Lockard good evening, Miller demanded that Lockard submit to a chemical test. When the motorist refused, Miller abducted (or, as he would say, "arrested") him, filled out a pre-printed application for a search warrant, and faxed it to the local judge. Since this happened at 12:10 AM, it's not unreasonable to believe that the warrant Miller obtained was the product of a less than rigorous judicial deliberation.

After Lockard was taken to Dearborn County Hospital, Miller demanded that he provide a sample. Since he was unable to pee on command, Lockard was charged with "obstruction"—a class D felony—because "he refused to voluntarily give a urine sample," according to Miller's report. Miller and another officer, Michael Lanning, pinned the victim down while a nurse prepared the catheter.

Originally, the nurse planned to use a straight size 16 Foley catheter. After Lockard pointed out that he suffers from an enlarged prostate, she switched to a smaller Coude catheter. This didn't improve things for the victim: Lockard described the pain he experienced as "just as if somebody would take a burning hot coal and stick it up your penis."

For several weeks after the incident, Lockard suffered severe burning sensations and other symptoms described by a physician as "consistent with clinical prostatitis." After spending some time in jail, Lockard was forced to take a plea for reckless driving. He was given a 180 day suspended sentence, 180 days' probation, a $100 fine, and assessed $165.00 in court costs.

Lockard's lawsuit was dismissed on the familiar, and incurably specious, grounds of "qualified immunity." The ruling took note of more than a half-dozen precedents involving forced catheterization, all of which grant studiously ambiguous permission for police to violate people suspected of harboring "evidence" in the bloodstream. Significantly, two of those precedents—*Sparks v. Stutler* and *Levine v. Roebuck*—involved forced catheterization of inmates by prison officials. In each of those cases, a district court judge ruled that the procedure was an impermissible violation of the individual—only to be reversed by a federal judge who decreed that members of the State's punitive caste enjoy "qualified immunity" to commit object rape, at least with a judge's consent.

The events described in *Lockard v. Lawrenceburg*—the case offering the most detailed examination of the issue of object rape by police officers—occurred in Indiana. That state recently enacted a measure recognizing the innate right of innocent people to use lethal defensive force against police officers who commit criminal aggression against their persons or property. I'd like to believe that those two developments are related.

A Snitch in Time

Easy Rider magazine, June 2012

Derek Hale was sitting on the front porch step of a friend's home in Wilmington, Delaware when an unmarked police car and a blacked-out SUV arrived at around 4:00 in the afternoon on November 6, 2006. No more than ten minutes later, Derek would be dead.

Roughly a dozen armed men—all of them dressed in black and displaying no police insignia—surrounded the front porch. Derek, who had been talking to homeowner Sandra Lopez and her two young children, stood to his feet with his hands in his hooded sweatshirt. One of the cops ordered Derek to remove his hands from his sweatshirt. No more than a second or two later, according to eyewitnesses, Derek was hit with the first of what would be seven Taser strikes.

Derek slumped sideways went into convulsions. Ordered to put his hands up, Derek struggled to comply, but found himself paralyzed. So he was struck with a second Taser blast that drove him to the side and induced him to vomit in a nearby flower bed.

"Not in front of the kids," Derek pleaded. "Get the kids out of here."

"That's not necessary!" exclaimed eyewitness Howard Mixon, a contractor who had been working nearby. "That's overkill! That's overkill!"

One of the officers swaggered over to Mixon and threatened him: "I'll f*cking show you overkill!" he snarled, threatening the witness with a gun. Meanwhile, Derek—left to wallow in a puddle of his own vomit—was desperately trying to comply with the demands of his assailants.

"I'm trying to get my hands out," Derek gasped. Horrified, his friend Sandra screamed at the officers: "He is trying to get his hands out, he cannot get his hands out!"

Acting with the serene confidence that his victim couldn't harm him, Lt. William Browne of the Wilmington Police Department—who was close enough to seize and handcuff Derek, if this had been necessary—shot him at point-blank range, sending three .40-caliber rounds into his chest.

After a typically self-exculpatory "investigation," Delaware Attorney General Beau Biden issued a report claiming that multiple taser strikes were necessary to overcome the victim's "resistance to arrest so he could be taken into custody without injury to himself or to the officers." This doesn't explain why Browne simply gunned down the paralyzed and helpless man. But this is a trivial matter, insisted the Wilmington city government when it approved a $975,000 settlement with Hale's widow Elaine in December 2010: "We . . . know that our officers acted properly and professionally."

Derek was not a criminal suspect. A member of the Pagans Motorcycle Club, Derek—a recently discharged Marine and veteran of multiple combat tours in Iraq—had traveled from his home in Virginia to Delaware in November 2006 to participate in a Toys for Tots promotion. He wasn't aware that he had been under surveillance for weeks as part of a federally coordinated investigation of the club.

Several Pagans had been recruited by the Feds to serve as informants. One of them, James "Pagan Ronnie" Howerton, was recruited by the FBI in 2004. While being paid hundreds of thousands of dollars as an undercover Fed, Howerton became the club's sergeant-at-arms. In 2009, the Feds breathlessly announced that they had compiled a massive indictment against the Pagans as an interstate criminal conspiracy—only to see that document deflate into a small number of relatively trivial charges against specific members of the club. The "criminal enterprise" claim boiled down to the accusation that the Pagans had committed a federal offense by running a raffle.

Howerton was always a dubious asset: Before receiving hundreds of thousands of dollars to serve as a snitch for the FBI, he had been convicted of second-degree murder. Wes Hudnall, an informant for the Bureau of Alcohol, Tobacco, and Firearms who posed as a Pagan recruit, was a chronic drug abuser who had been diagnosed with severe mental problems. Hudnall eventually committed suicide by hanging himself in a jail cell.

Derek Hale was an honorably discharged Marine veteran with no criminal record and a stable family. He was not under investigation for criminal conduct. Why was a paramilitary strike team sent to arrest him? The officials who exonerated Hale's murderers refuse to say, but the most reasonable explanation is that the task force intended to intimidate him into becoming an informant.

Feds fish for snitches in any available pool of petty offenders. Their preferred lure is the promise of a "downward departure" in sentencing (called the "5K option" by prosecutors) if the guy they've hooked can help them reel in bigger fish.

Andrew C. White, a former prosecutor for the Maryland U.S. Attorney's office, describes the "5K" option as the "nuclear weapon" in the federal arsenal. It's also a handy time-saver for work- and risk-averse law enforcement officers: Rather than building cases based on shoe-leather investigative work, they can simply create a stable of informants and "cooperators" and manufacture drug cases *ex nihilo* using their "witnesses" as ventriloquist's dummies.

Various state and federal agencies also train full-time personnel to work as undercover informants. William Queen, an undercover agent for the Bureau of Alcohol, Tobacco, and Firearms, spent roughly 30 months infiltrating the Mongols Motorcycle Club. Although less than minuscule in membership (approximately 350 members are found in the U.S. and Mexico), the Mongols have a formidable reputation.

After Queen's undercover assignment ended in May 2000, a nationwide raid by ATF Special Response Teams and various law enforcement agencies against Mongol members across the country "netted some seventy illegal firearms, including handguns, machine guns, and assault rifles, as well as explosives; seventeen stolen motorcycles; two kilograms of cocaine; significant quantities of marijuana and methamphetamine; and tens of thousands of dollars in cash."

That isn't much to show for an operation that cost millions of dollars and nearly destroyed Queen's family. As if seeking to compensate for the operation's trivial achievements, Queen describes the Mongols as if they were a huge and growing domestic terrorist organization:

> While they are wearing that patch, they are untouchable to the
> world at large. No one can make trouble for them without
> bringing down the fury of the whole Mongol Nation.

The same description applies to a much larger, better-funded, and more dangerous armed brotherhood—government law enforcement agencies, both local and federal. Ironically, Queen himself makes exactly the same point.

"Living full-time as an outlaw gave me a perspective few law-enforcement officers ever get to experience," he writes. "I was often more at risk from my supposed brothers in blue than from my adopted brothers in the gang. Just as there were some decent qualities—loyalty, love, respect—among the outlaw bikers, there were some law-enforcement officers who were little more than outlaws with badges."

Anybody who disputes Queen's assessment should discuss the matter with Derek Hale's widow and fatherless children.

Comrade Obama's Doxology: Praise the State, Ungrateful Individualist Infidels!

LewRockwell.com, July 16, 2012

Addressing a partisan crowd during a campaign stop in Roanoke, Virginia, President Obama hymned the praises of government as the provider of all good things, while rebuking business owners for their supposedly misplaced belief that they "build" wealth as individuals:

> If you were successful, somebody along the line gave you some help. There was a great teacher somewhere in your life. Somebody helped to create this unbelievable American system that we have that allowed you to thrive. Somebody invested in roads and bridges. *If you've got a business—you didn't build that.* **Somebody else made that happen.** The Internet didn't get invented on its own. **Government research created the Internet so that all the companies could make money off the Internet**.

In Obama's collectivist reading of U.S. history, it was through government intervention—not individual initiative—that "we created the middle class."

"We rise or fall together as one nation and as one people," he insisted. "You're not on your own, we're in this together."

Like most people of his ideological bent, Obama either cannot or will not distinguish between *society*—which is created through peaceful commerce and other forms of private cooperation—and the *state*—an anti-social artifact built on conquest, coercion, and confiscation of wealth. Government produces nothing; it is an exercise in pure consumption and, usually, the destruction of capital. As Nietzsche famously said, everything the State has is stolen.

Barack Obama—whose brow has never been moistened by the sweat of honest labor—knows literally nothing about creating wealth and value. As a politician, however, Obama is deeply committed to "community organizing"—that is, the creation of government-focused coalitions devoted to the forcible redistribution of the wealth that is created through the exertions of private producers.

Speaking as a state legislator in a 2001 radio interview, Obama distinguished between his variety of "community organizing" and the work of civil rights activists in the 1950s and 1960s. The earlier efforts, he pointed out approvingly, sought to overcome the "negative" concept of liberties—that is, freedom from state control and protection against abusive of individual rights by government agents—but was too wedded to the idea of pursuing its social revolution through the courts.

As Obama pointed out:

> the Supreme Court never ventured into the issues of *redistribution of wealth*, and the more basic issues of political and economic justice in this society. . . . [O]ne of the, I think, tragedies of the civil rights movement was, because the civil rights movement became so court-focused, I think there was a tendency to lose track of the *community organizing* and activities on the ground that are able to put together the actual *coalitions of power* through which to bring about *redistributive change*. And in some ways we still suffer from that. (Emphasis added.)

As a paladin of the parasite class, Obama characterizes his tax policies as a matter of "ask[ing] for the wealthy to pay a little bit more"—as if an official demand backed by armed government agents were akin to Oliver Twist's plaintive request for a second helping of porridge, and that the shakedown needed to fund Washington's redistributive designs would only apply to the "wealthy."

"Sovereign Citizens" and Government's Monopoly on Crime

Pro Libertate, September 20, 2012

Robert Paudert refers to May 20, 2010—the day his son Brandon was killed—as the "worst day of my life, ever." Given that losing a child is the worst thing that can happen to a parent, Paudert isn't exaggerating.

Brandon Paudert was an officer in the West Memphis, Arkansas Police Department. At the time Brandon was killed, Robert was the town's police chief; Brandon's partner, Officer Bill Evans, was his cousin.

Until about 11:00 AM on that fatal day, Officers Paudert and Evans, who were assigned to the narcotics interdiction team, had maintained surveillance on what they considered to be a "suspicious" rental truck. It turned out that the vehicle wasn't being used to ferry narcotics; it was filled with household possessions belonging to a pleasant grandmother who was probably puzzled by the unwanted attention she had received from the local police.

Chief Paudert, who had been called to the scene, chided his son and his nephew and told them to "get off their butts and back on the interstate," where they had a better chance of finding a vehicle carrying contraband—or perhaps a sizable amount of cash that could be seized and "forfeited." Crittenden County, where West Memphis is located, has become notorious for this officially sanctioned variety of highway robbery.

A few minutes after hitting the highway, Evans spied a white minivan with unusual license plates and conducted a traffic stop. He called Brandon to back him up as he went to interrogate the driver, 45-year-old Jerry Kane. Within a few minutes a scuffle ensued, and Kane shoved the officer into a ditch.

Jerry Kane was not a drug smuggler. As an adherent of a loosely organized movement referred to as "sovereign citizens," he insisted on exercising his freedom to travel without obtaining government licenses, permits, and similar bureaucratic impedimenta. A former long-haul trucker, Kane traveled the country in a minivan organizing seminars in which he taught dubious methods of avoiding foreclosure.

Shortly before the fatal encounter in West Memphis, Kane had been arrested—and fined $1,500—for driving without a license in New Mexico. His

225

money was dissipating even as trouble with law enforcement continued to accumulate.

When the traffic stop degenerated into a shoving match, Kane's 16-year-old son, Joseph, emerged from the minivan armed with an AK-47. Evans reached for his sidearm, but before he could draw he was shot several times. Taking cover behind his vehicle, Brandon got off several shots before he, too, was fatally wounded. Roughly two hours later, the Kanes were killed in a shootout with police that took place in a Walmart parking lot.

The funeral for Brandon Paudert and Bill Evans was attended by hundreds of police officers from several states. "I hope that no parent has to suffer through what we've been through," Chief Paudert commented a few weeks after that sorrowful observance.

There is nothing worse than the death of a child, and every parent who has experienced such an unfathomable loss is entitled to sympathy. It's worth pointing out that there is no record of Chief Paudert extending condolences to Debra Farrow, the mother of 12-year-old DeAunta Farrow, who was murdered by one of the officers in his employ.

DeAunta Farrow, who was unarmed and was not a criminal suspect, was fatally shot on June 22, 2007 by West Memphis Police Officer Erik Sammis. The twelve-year-old was walking home from a convenience store at about 9:30 PM with his 14-year-old cousin, Unseld Nance.

Sammis, who was commander of the Special Response Team (the West Memphis equivalent of a SWAT team), had staked out the neighborhood. He and Officer Jimmy Ellis were parked in a dark gray, unmarked pickup truck. They were wearing gray shirts, camouflage pants, and black bulletproof vests. They did not wear badges or other police insignia visible from the front.

As the two boys entered an apartment building, one of the officers saw what he thought was a gun in the waistband of Farrow's pants. In fact it was a plastic toy. The officers came boiling out of the truck, ordering the kids to hit the ground. According to Nance, neither Sammis nor Ellis identified himself as a police officer. Nance also insisted that Farrow, whose hands were raised and whose toy gun remained in his waistband, "was fixing to get on the ground when they shot."

Within seconds of screaming at DeAunta to hit the ground, Sammis fired two shots.

"It's a toy gun," the fatally wounded youngster told Sammis as he bled to death.

Nance was taken into custody and interviewed the same evening by the Arkansas State Police. Sammis, who sought shelter in the protection of the "Garrity" rule—which dictates that disclosures made by a police officer can only be used for departmental investigations, rather than criminal prosecution—didn't speak for the record about the incident until a month later.

Roughly five months after DeAunta Farrow was killed, a special prosecutor announced that there was "insufficient evidence" to charge Sammis with a crime. Debra Farrow filed a wrongful death lawsuit that was immediately challenged on the grounds of "qualified immunity"—the incantation deployed by police and prosecutors to shield themselves from the consequences of culpable misconduct.

In a 2009 ruling, the U.S. Eighth Circuit Court of Appeals, observed that:

> the officers approached Farrow and Nance without identifying themselves as police officers . . . the toy gun was tucked in Farrow's pants throughout the entire confrontation . . . Sammis only said to drop the gun and get to the ground, and . . . Farrow may have raised his hand or hands while trying to get to the ground before Sammis shot him twice without warning.

Since those facts "could establish the excessive use of force," the court concluded, it would be improper to grant the officers' request for a summary judgment on the basis of "qualified immunity." In April 2011, a federal jury in Jonesboro, Arkansas found in favor of Sammis and Ellis, accepting their claim that the summary execution of an unarmed, cooperative 12-year-old who was not a criminal suspect was, in some sense, "reasonable."

Sammis, it should be pointed out, was responsible for training other members of the West Memphis PD in the use of deadly force. Chief Paudert described his work in that role as "outstanding."

"It's tragic, but in my mind, it's not wrong," Sammis had told investigators during his belated debriefing in July 2007. "I did what I had to do to survive and protect my partner. I feel confident that any officer in the same position would have done the same thing I did."

Here's an important question: If Sammis was justified in gunning down a terrified, unarmed, compliant 12-year-old, why was it *morally* wrong for Joseph Kane to shoot an armed police officer who was perceived as threatening his father?

It might be said that the late Jerry Kane was a con artist, and that his previous run-ins with various law enforcement agencies suggested criminal tendencies. Whatever could be said about the merits of Kane's seminars, there is no evidence that he was a thief. Driving without government-assigned "privileges" may be unwise—as Kane's experiences demonstrate—but this can't be described as a "crime" in any rational sense of the word.

Sammis, by way of contrast, had a lengthy history of violent misconduct, including behavior that can honestly be described as criminal.

Before finding employment in West Memphis, Sammis was a "gypsy cop" with a predictably troubled record. He had been reprimanded—and then fired—by the North Little Rock PD for making "untruthful statements." After a short stint in Gould, Sammis was hired by the West Memphis PD. His background investigation noted that Sammis, who was notoriously untruthful and had problems with his temper, would need careful "supervision."

In 1998, Sammis unleashed an attack dog on a non-violent suspect. Witnesses described the attack as sadistic and unprovoked. The victim required 75 stitches, and the city government discontinued use of K-9 "officers" because of the episode. A year later, Sammis was suspended for a day without pay after insisting on wearing his "battle dress uniform" rather than a conventional patrol uniform. A few months later he was investigated for "abuse of authority" following a "confrontation" with security guards at a Pilot Truck Stop.

At the time of the shooting, Sammis was facing at least two lawsuits for abusive conduct, one of them growing out of an incident in which he was part of a police wolf-pack that beat and handcuffed a man named Tim Howard. After Howard was restrained, Sammis—according to witnesses—grabbed Howard by the hair and unloaded a canister of pepper spray directly into his face. When Howard's mother pleaded with Sammis to stop, the officer slugged the 48-year-old woman in the face, and then assaulted Howard's father as well. Eventually the lawsuit was settled out of court.

Sammis resigned from the West Memphis PD in December 2007, weeks after the special prosecutor had announced that no charges would be filed against him.

"The FBI/DOJ investigation, the Arkansas State Police investigation, the independent prosecutor investigation, and the WMPD internal investigation have all cleared me in this tragic event," Sammis wrote in his resignation letter. "I am leaving this department knowing that I did the right thing."

The "right thing," according to the officials who reviewed the incident, was to shoot and kill an unarmed 12-year-old boy who was not a criminal suspect and posed no threat to anybody.

As a representative of the State's coercive caste, Sammis had an unqualified right to kill DeAunta Farrow, and the child had an unambiguous duty to die. The child's killer is not required to express remorse. The grieving mother isn't even entitled to official sympathy from the Police Chief who hired that killer, insulated him from accountability, praised his performance, promoted him, and extolled him as a role model to others on the force.

The only substantive "reform" to occur because of the killing of DeAunta Farrow was a municipal ordinance banning the possession of toy guns.

Owing to the fact that DeAunta Farrow was black, and Sammis is white, the child's shooting was exploited by Al Sharpton and similar figures in the Indignation Industry's race-baiting affiliate. One "civil rights" group was conspicuous by its absence: The so-called Southern Poverty Law Center (SPLC), the lucrative quasi-private secret police agency founded by the degenerate fraud named Morris Dees.

The DeAunta Farrow case—the murder, by an abusive white cop, of a poor black child—would appear to be perfectly tailored for a "civil rights" group focusing on issues of poverty and racial injustice. This is especially true in light of the fact that in the years prior to DeAunta's murder, the West Memphis PD had been hit with a half-dozen lawsuits alleging civil rights violations, and had lost five of them.

Obviously, West Memphis was a target-rich environment for the SPLC. Yet the group didn't pay any attention to the town until after Officers Paudert and Evans were killed in an encounter with "sovereign citizens"—that is, political dissidents of a kind who figure prominently in the SPLC-defined official demonology.

In December 2007, the West Memphis City Council passed a resolution calling on Bob Paudert to resign, along with Officers Sammis and Ellis.

"Why should I resign?" responded Chief Paudert. "I haven't done anything wrong."

When Paudert finally resigned in 2011, he treated it as a personal triumph that he hadn't been "run out of town" by his critics—including, one assumes, the mother of DeAunta Farrow. He was immediately hired by the Bureau of Justice Assistance, a division of the same "Justice" Department that found no "civil rights violation" in Erik Sammis's killing of DeAunta Farrow. He has become an SPLC-promoted evangelist, touring the country to "make sure others who wear the badge don't get murdered by a group of domestic terrorists," in the words of a news account.

"We as law enforcement officers must recognize this very real threat, so we can protect ourselves," Paudert said in an SPLC propaganda video. He insists that "sovereign citizens" should be regarded as a pervasive threat to officer safety. This refrain is joined by the SPLC and the FBI, who—by way of demonstrating the "deadly threat" posed by the estimated 300,000 members of the "sovereign citizens"—point out that eight police officers have died in encounters with people regarded as "sovereign citizens" since 2000.

Although police agencies diligently record the death of every officer, there is no comparable tally of "the precise number of people killed by the police, and the number of times police use excessive force," noted Fox Butterfield of the *New York Times* about a decade ago. An abortive effort was made in the mid-1980s to collect and publish that data, but was quickly discontinued because "the figures were very embarrassing to a lot of police departments," observed James Fyfe, a professor of criminal justice at Temple University.

The SPLC describes "sovereign citizens" as people who believe that they alone "get to decide which laws to obey and which to ignore." Some people thrown into that category have circulated worthless financial instruments; others conduct business in a "peculiar dialect" that is deliberately opaque and understood only by a small, self-selected population.

If that description were considered accurate, it would be difficult to distinguish the behavior of "sovereign citizens" from that of the exalted personages who call themselves the "government." Such people take refuge in arcane language to justify law-breaking, including the routine practice of monumental financial fraud involving the public treasury.

The SPLC accuses "sovereign citizens" of emitting "verbal fog" as a way to distract attention from their schemes. One wonders if anybody with that organization has ever been exposed to the artful gibberish that dribbles down the chin of Federal Reserve Chairman Ben Bernanke every time he makes a public effort to justify the activities of his criminal cartel.

The SPLC depicts "sovereigns" as lawless people who are primed to kill and utterly remorseless in dealing with those they regard as enemies. If this is the case they're guilty of mimicking the government they despise.

Disinterested application of the SPLC's definition would lead us to conclude that Barack Obama is the most dangerous "sovereign citizen" on the planet, given his assertion of the power to imprison or kill anybody on the face of the earth. The SPLC's zeal for the sanctity of the law, and its compassion for "people of color," didn't inspire the organization to protest the presidentially ordered murder of 16-year-old Yemeni-American Abdulrahman al-Awlaki, who was killed by a CIA-operated drone.

Decades ago, the immortal Albert Jay Nock pointed out that a public functionary who calls himself an "official" will routinely commit acts that any objective, moral observer would describe as crimes. Such a person can do such things "without any sense of responsibility, or discomfort, simply because [he acts] as an official and not as a man." In this fashion, "once could commit almost any kind of crime without getting in trouble with one's conscience"—or with the public, once it has been properly indoctrinated regarding the mystical concept called "authority."

"Sovereign citizens" supposedly believe that acts of force and fraud are transmuted into justice when accompanied with the proper conjurations. How would that differ, in principle, from the behavior of the governing "officials" on whose behalf the SPLC labors? If "officials" can commit acts of aggressive violence, on what moral basis do we condemn similar behavior on the part of private individuals who declare themselves "Sovereign" as well?

When a "Sovereign" kills a police officer, the SPLC—speaking on behalf of the entire police state apparatus—commands us to mourn and rend our garments. When Officer Erik Sammis guns down a 12-year-old African-American, or Barack Obama slaughters a Yemeni-American teenager with a drone-fired missile, the SPLC maintains a reverent silence in the face of what it must regard as the sacramental exercise of the government's transcendent authority—while it quietly adds names to its ever-expanding roster of dissidents and heretics.

"He's a Constitutionalist"

Pro Libertate, October 9, 2012

"Bear! There are guys with guns outside!" shouted Marcella Cruz to her husband as she looked out the kitchen window of their farmhouse in Letha, Idaho.

Timidly opening the kitchen door, Marcella—a small, slender, middle-aged woman—spied a large man carrying a gun and wearing a tactical vest.

"Don't go back into the house," the stranger ordered Marcella as the woman instinctively retreated into the safety of her home.

At roughly the same time, another intruder armed with an assault rifle pounded on the front door.

"Come out!" he demanded.

As Marcella tried to shut the kitchen door, the first intruder—who outweighed her by at least 100 pounds—grabbed her by the left wrist and started to pull the terrified woman from the house.

"Why are you dragging me out of my home?" asked the terrified woman. "Why would you be pulling me out of my home?"

"Open the door," insisted the assailant, using his weight advantage and leverage to extract the woman, who had braced herself against one side of the door while clinging desperately to the other with her right hand. As she lost her grip, the left side of Marcella's body scraped painfully against the door frame before she was thrown to the ground.

One of the invaders finally identified himself.

"Bear! Step out—Sheriff's office!" bellowed the Berserker packing an assault weapon.

"What's the matter?" asked Michael Gibbons—known as "Bear" to his friends—as the exasperated farmer opened the front door. "What is the problem?"

"Who else is in the house?" demanded one of the invaders.

"Nobody," replied Bear.

"You guys having a fight this morning?" inquired the armed man, his finger still poised on the trigger.

"We had an *argument*," Bear replied, his voice tinged with incredulity. "What's going on?"

"We'll let you know in a sec," the armed man replied in a dismissive tone. "For right now, go to your knees for me. Face away from me."

With those words, the armed stranger—who had not established any legal justification for invading the couple's property—ordered Bear to assume the *coup de grace* position.

At this point, Bear—who had just seen his wife assaulted at gunpoint—had every reason to think that he might be murdered, and no legitimate reason to believe that the marauders were actual peace officers. After all, anybody can buy weapons and body armor, and official-looking insignia.

The raiding party was composed of Gem County Sheriff's Deputies, but their behavior was that of a home invasion gang, rather than a group of peace officers.

"What is this about?" Bear demanded from his knees as a deputy handcuffed him.

"We're going to tell you—now's the time to shut up!" sneered the goon with the assault rifle.

A more honest answer would have been, "Now's the time to invent a justification for the raid."

After being handcuffed behind his back, Bear was ordered to get up.

"Why is this happening?" Bear demanded to know.

"I said get *up*!" answered one of his captors, who, with the help of another, hoisted the tiny man off the ground—and then promptly dropped him on his tailbone. Bear suffered a severe back injury that has left him incapacitated.

With Bear in handcuffs and Marcella being detained, a small group of officers, led by Sheriff Chuck Rolland, conducted a warrantless search of the home on the pretext of "clearing" it.

As the video record of the search illustrates, the officers were not looking for a concealed threat to their safety. They made little effort to clear the corners or to inspect potential hiding spots. However, they were very interested in finding evidence of marijuana use—lifting and sniffing ashtrays and going through personal effects. After going upstairs they found what they believed to be a "grow room."

"We'll have to get a warrant for this," one of them remarked.

"We found your grow room," Lt. Timony told Bear after the officers emerged from the home a few minutes later.

"You found our tomato plants!" Bear responded, pointing out that the supposedly suspicious "grow room" was actually an aquaponics system of the kind he had described to an indifferent Emmett City Council just a few months earlier.

Although Bear admitted that he does occasionally use marijuana to treat lingering chronic injuries—the most serious of which he received, ironically, as a police officer when he was stabbed by a shoplifter in 1982—he hadn't smoked any that morning.

Marcella had let him sleep in that morning, and Bear had gotten up just a short time before the police materialized on his property. In that brief period, however, he and Marcella had one short, inconsequential verbal spat of the kind every couple occasionally experiences.

The argument was overheard by a neighbor who—displaying a sense of civic responsibility more appropriate to East Germany than western Idaho—called the police.

Bear and Marcella have lived in Letha, an unincorporated town near Emmett, Idaho, for about two years. They are organic farmers, like most of their neighbors. Unlike at least one of their neighbors, the couple is determined to mind their own business.

On the morning of August 16, a neighbor who identified herself as "April" overheard the couple's argument and called 911 to report that she thought Bear was "beating" his wife.

Because the neighborhood is located near the county line, the cellphone call was originally directed to the dispatcher for the Payette County Sheriff's Office, who relayed the information to her counterpart in Gem County.

In making the handoff, however, both dispatchers clearly understood one critical fact: *There was no indication that weapons were involved in the alleged domestic dispute*, or even to be found in the household. This meant that the proper response to the report, according to established policy, was a low-key "welfare check."

Why, then, did the Gem County Sheriff's Office choose to mount a SWAT-style raid against Bear and Marcella? The short answer is that the couple was the victim of "political profiling": They were identified as a threat to "officer safety" on account of their perceived political opinions.

"Are you familiar with these guys?" asked a deputy identified in the 911 recordings as "Officer 57."

"Negative," answered another deputy designated "Officer 56."

"I am, and it's affirmative, there is [sic] weapons," continued Officer 57. "He is—or at least was—anti-law enforcement. We've had issues with him. He's a Constitutionalist."

Idaho is one of the few states in the Union where most people would consider the term "Constitutionalist" to be a plaudit rather than a pejorative.

That epithet—which Officer 57 spat out in audible disgust—was the reason why Bear would soon find himself on his knees with his back to a deputy whose finger was caressing the trigger of an assault rifle.

The illegal search of the couple's home yielded no evidence of drug dealing, so the raiding party had to be satisfied with writing a misdemeanor citation for possession of drug paraphernalia. Before they left, however, Detective Rich Perecz couldn't resist the opportunity to upbraid the victims for displaying insufficient docility.

"Perecz knelt down next to me, showed me his badge and said, 'What is this?'" Bear related to me during an interview in his living room. "I said, 'It's your badge.' He said, 'Can you tell me why your wife wouldn't come out of the house when I told her to?' Those guys didn't identify themselves as the Sheriff's Office until *after* they had dragged Marcella out of our house. All we knew was what she said when she saw them coming through our corn field—they were men with guns."

Perecz briefly attempted to preserve the pretense that an act of domestic violence had occurred at the couple's home.

"He asked me, 'Why are your wife's knuckles all scraped up?'" Bear recounts. "He was trying to get me to admit that I had beat my wife. He apparently knows nothing about living and working on a farm. Of course Marcella's hands get scraped from time to time; we *work* for a living, after all."

The official police report notes that Marcella Cruz showed "no evidence of battery" at the end of the incident. (Interestingly, Marcella was not identified as a "victim" in that report.) Photographs taken two days later showed that her left arm and side were disfigured with large bruises that had been inflicted by Detective Perecz when the officer yanked her out of her kitchen doorway.

If Marcella's husband had been responsible for those bruises, he would be facing felony domestic violence charges. Under Idaho law (Chapter 9, 18-903 and 18-905[b]), Perecz's actions constitute aggravated assault.

In an email, I asked Perecz this question:

"By physically seizing a small, unarmed, terrified woman who was not a criminal suspect, and injuring her in the process, didn't you commit an act that can be fairly characterized as criminal battery, as defined in Idaho law?"

Despite repeated requests, Perecz has declined to answer that question, or provide any other information about the incident.

In his official report, Lt. Dave Timony states that the officers were advised that Bear and Marcella were "possibly armed and may be extremely confrontational to authority."

By way of email, I asked Lt. Timony to elaborate on that claim:

> What was the basis of that characterization? Is it the policy of your department to compile political or ideological "profiles" of people who have had encounters with law enforcement in Gem County? Has your department undergone training/indoctrination regarding supposed threats posed by people characterized as "constitutionalists"?

Like Detective Perecz, Lt. Timony has refused to reply to my inquiries.

It is true that Bear and Marcella had previously had unpleasant dealings with the Gem County Sheriff's Office—and with Detective Perecz, in particular.

More than a year ago, Marcella contacted the Sheriff's Office to report that a man calling himself "Greg Hall," who had lived with them for an extended period, had stolen money and jewelry from them. Marcella provided me with copies of email messages in which she and Detective Perecz had discussed the theft—including the suspect's specific location, which at the time was just across the Snake River in Ontario, Oregon.

"He told me that he couldn't help us, because the suspect had fled the jurisdiction," Marcella related to me. "But it's not as if he couldn't pick up a telephone and inform the Malheur County Sheriff's Office, or the Ontario Police. The bogus 'domestic violence' report that led to the raid on our home was originally received by Payette County and relayed to Gem County. It's not as if these people can't talk to each other."

It's worth pointing out as well that inter-state law enforcement cooperation in the Treasure Valley—an area encompassing towns on both sides of the Idaho/Oregon border—is quite commonplace. This is especially true of narcotics enforcement, which is a far more profitable racket than legitimate efforts to protect persons and property from criminal violence.

"Now that you know we didn't have a fight, why don't you pack up and go away?" asked Bear following the illegal search of his home.

"Oh, we can't do that," one of the deputies insisted. "We're here now, and we have probable cause."

What they had—or, at least, thought they had—was an opportunity to seize Bear and Marcella's home and farm through "civil asset forfeiture." That tantalizing prospect evaporated when it became clear that the couple was cultivating organic tomatoes, rather than marijuana.

"The Gem County Sheriff's Office wasn't at all interested in helping us when we were victims of a crime," Marcella summarizes. "But they were ready and eager to attack our home when they were given an excuse."

That excuse was a report made by a neighbor who, according to Bear and Marcella, is part of a neighborhood clique who resents the couple for reasons they can't understand. The woman they identify as the leader of that clique has accused the couple of stealing water from the irrigation co-op. That charge is rejected by the co-op's elected water master, Marvin Richardson (a long-established organic farmer and prominent political activist who had his name legally changed to "Pro-Life").

The malicious imagination of a hostile neighbor transmuted a brief and trivial marital argument into evidence of "domestic violence." The vicious opportunism of the Gem County Sheriff's Office magnified the incident into a pretext for a paramilitary raid that resulted in an act of felonious battery against Marcella.

In a country where gratuitous SWAT raids frequently result in state-sanctioned murder, this is a potentially fatal combination—especially when the subject of the raid is designated a "Constitutionalist" and thus regarded as an Enemy of the State.

2013

Ed Flynn: Milwaukee Crime Lord, Citizen Disarmament Advocate

Pro Libertate, February 27, 2013

Police Chief Ed Flynn of Milwaukee believes that his department is at war with the gun-owning public. In his February 27 testimony before the Senate Judiciary Committee, Flynn claimed that "in the last 20 years we've been in an arms race" with private citizens who supposedly out-gun the police.

Flynn testified in support of a proposed federal ban on so-called assault weapons. But in the past he has made it clear that he considers a Mundane carrying a firearm of any kind an unlawful enemy combatant subject to detention and forcible disarmament.

"My message to my troops is if you see anybody carrying a gun on the streets of Milwaukee, we'll put them on the ground, take the gun away, and then decide whether you have a right to carry it," Flynn said a few years ago in response to a statement from Wisconsin Attorney General J.B. Van Hollen recognizing that residents of the state have a right to carry firearms openly.

Flynn clearly sees himself as commanding an army of occupation. In practical terms, he is less a warlord than a crime lord who presides over an officially sanctioned street gang.

Like most petty dictators of his ilk, Flynn is protected by a praetorian guard that will retaliate against people who speak ill of their dear leader. In November 2009, his "troops" arrested a local gadfly named Bob Braun, who had committed the unpardonable sin of publicly embarrassing Commissar Flynn.

Braun and a friend picketed Milwaukee Police headquarters carrying signs describing Chief Flynn, who admitted to an extra-marital affair with a sycophantic reporter, as an adulterer. Citing the relevant section of Wisconsin law, Braun demanded that Flynn be prosecuted—a sentiment shared by many Milwaukee residents. Instead, Braun was arrested by Sgt. Mark Wagner and charged with disorderly conduct. The citation falsely claimed that Braun, a devout Christian, repeatedly told Sgt. Wagner to perform an anatomically impossible sexual act.

When the case was heard before a jury, the only witnesses the prosecution could produce were Wagner and two fellow police officers—whose travel and subpoena fees were paid by Braun. The jury quite sensibly concluded that the officers—who are, let us not forget, trained liars—were perjuring themselves in the service of the adulterer who commands them.

Given the abysmal character of the chief who commands the Milwaukee PD, it shouldn't surprise us to learn that the department has been a haven for uniformed sexual predators.

In July 2010, a single mother in Milwaukee (whose name has not been publicly disclosed) was raped by Officer Ladmarald Cates. After someone vandalized the woman's home, she made the common mistake of calling the police in the entirely unfounded belief that they would be of help. Cates was the first on the scene.

Acting on instinct and experience, the predator recognized an exploitable opportunity. The officer ordered the boyfriend to go to a nearby convenience store to buy some bottled water. Once he had isolated the victim, Cates maneuvered her into the bathroom, where he put her "on the ground" by forcibly sodomizing and raping her.

Immediately after the assault, the woman—barefoot and wearing tattered clothing—ran screaming from the house. Cates stormed out of the building and grabbed the victim by the waist, causing her feet to strike his partner. This gave the officers an excuse to arrest the battered and traumatized woman for "assaulting an officer."

The victim was taken to jail and held for 12 hours before receiving medical aid. After the hospital visit, she was sent back to jail for four days before being released without charges.

This was not Cates's first assault—but the department wasn't willing to take disciplinary action of any kind until DNA evidence corroborated the rape victim's account. Instead of prosecuting Cates, Flynn fired him for "idling or loafing on duty." In January 2012, Cates was convicted of federal civil rights charges and sentenced to 24 years in prison.

Flynn would insist that Cates isn't representative of his officers. This is true, but not in the sense Flynn would have us believe. What makes Cates an anomaly is not the fact that he was a purulent thug, but rather that he was actually punished for his crimes: The Milwaukee Police Department holds down the number two spot in the national police brutality rankings. Its distinguished contributions in the field of state-sponsored crime include a lengthy and growing list of suspicious deaths of people in police custody.

Cates was not the only uniformed sexual predator in Milwaukee who earned headlines in 2012.

Last September, four of Flynn's "troops" who had followed his orders with exceptional zeal were charged with felonies for assaulting and strip-searching citizens both in the street and in district stations. In one case, three officers restrained a victim—one of them putting him into a choke hold, while another held a gun to his head—while a third jammed a hand into his rectum.

The ringleader of this rape gang, Officer Michael Vagnini, was charged with 25 counts of sexual assault and related crimes.

In a press conference after charges were filed, Flynn professed to be "disgusted" by the conduct of his minions.

"Crime cannot be fought with criminality," warbled the costumed functionary who had publicly abetted criminal violence against innocent citizens—and who has actually protected an undisguised street gang within his department.

This hyper-violent clique adopted the logo of a nihilistic comic book character called the "Punisher," and they brazenly displayed the insignia on their police vehicles and their uniforms as they prowled the street in search of helpless people whom they could "put on the ground." Among the formidable figures targeted by the Punishers was a male dancer named Frank Jude, who was nearly beaten to death in October 2004 because he was suspected of stealing a badge.

After putting the terrified male dancer "on the ground," the Punishers severely beat, kicked, and choked him—then put a knife to his throat and jammed a pen into one of his ears. The victim survived the assault, but was left with permanent brain damage. The officers later claimed that this amount of violence was necessary to "subdue" Jude—who was never charged in connection with the incident. The jury in the criminal trial accepted that claim and acquitted the officers—who were later found guilty of criminal civil rights violations.

Former Milwaukee Police Officer Jon Bartlett, the ringleader of the gang beating, was eventually convicted—along with six others—on federal civil rights charges. An internal affairs investigation conducted by MPD Commander James A. Galezewski produced a detailed description of the Punishers in official reports filed on two separate investigations—one in 2005, the other in 2007. He also described his findings at length in a sworn deposition in November 2010.

One training supervisor and at least one active-duty police officer were identified as current members of the gang. Nonetheless, as late as January 2011, Flynn insisted that the existence of the gang was merely a matter of "rumor." A reasonable surmise would be that Flynn wasn't engaging in conscious deception;

after all, the moral gradient separating his normal "troops" from the berserkers who belong to the "Punishers" gang isn't very steep.

Every city police department is an armed gang organized to implement the will of the municipal corporation that employs them. Under the rule of Ed Flynn the Milwaukee PD has become one of the most malodorous outfits of its kind in the Midwestern United States. He and his "troops" appear to be determined to validate every syllable of Albert Jay Nock's famous capsule description of the State:

> Everyone knows that the State claims and exercises [a] monopoly of crime . . . and that it makes this monopoly as strict as it can. . . . It punishes private theft, but itself lays unscrupulous hands on anything it wants, whether the property of citizen or of alien. . . . Of all the crimes that are committed for gain or revenge, there is not one that we have not seen it commit—murder, mayhem, arson, robbery, fraud, criminal collusion and connivance.

If Ed Flynn presided over a police agency in Latin America or Africa, his deeds would be chronicled in the annual human rights reports issued by the State Department, which diligently catalogs the offenses of every regime but the one ruling us.

Flynn's misbegotten reign in Milwaukee reminds me of a comment made by Isaac Lappia of Amnesty International in Sierra Leone at the 2001 UN Small Arms Conference at the world body's headquarters.

The UN's proposed international firearms treaty—which, in updated form, will likely be signed later this year by Barack Obama—was intended to disarm civilians. However, as Lappia pointed out, his organization's studies proved "incontrovertibly that small arms are . . . used in many more countries to facilitate serious crimes by law enforcement personnel—including police, prison authorities, paramilitaries, and the army—where they commit persistent human rights violations, including rape, torture, 'disappearances,' and arbitrary killings."

This reads like a profile of the department Ed Flynn commands—and it's on the basis of a record of this kind that Flynn was invited to testify on behalf of the Obama regime's citizen disarmament initiatives. *Res ipsa loquitur.*

"For Your Protection"

Pro Libertate, March 5, 2013

There is no situation that cannot be made instantly and immeasurably worse through police intervention. A splendid illustration of this principle is found in a recent ruling from the Arkansas Court of Appeals.

According to the court, police were entitled to arrest, tase, and beat a teenager who had done nothing more sinister than speak to his mother on the street in front of their home. A police officer accosted the young man—who, as a juvenile, is identified only by the initials "R.R."—after he saw him approaching a woman who was walking a dog.

The officer, who belongs to a social cohort of people who are distinguished primarily by their timidity, claimed that he was "concerned for the woman's safety." His fears should have been allayed when it was established that the woman was the teenager's mother.

If the cop had been an actual peace officer, he would have tipped his hat and left. But he was a law enforcer—that is, someone through whose dark ministrations innocent people are transformed into "criminals"—and so he insisted on detaining and interrogating the entirely harmless youngster. To that end he sent for "backup," and a thugscrum soon coalesced around the puzzled and terrified teen.

As the Court of Appeals summarizes, R.R. was "tasered several times, removed from the backseat [of a police vehicle], thrown to the ground, tasered again, kicked, handcuffed, and arrested." All of this was done because the young man "moved around and wrestled around while the officers held him on the ground, making it difficult for the officers to put the cuffs on him."

Because he didn't permit himself to be shackled like a slave in front of his own home because he had been seen speaking to his mother, the teenager committed the supposed crime of "refusing to submit to arrest."

The trial court in the case also acknowledged that the victim was "a fine young man, an excellent student, and active in sports, clubs and church activities." The judge reportedly expressed dismay that "an innocent situation . . . just completely got out of hand"—which is, once again, the familiar and entirely predictable outcome when members of the State's enforcement caste materialize. Despite these superficial expressions of regret, the Judge sentenced the victim to serve one day in detention—thereby leaving him with a criminal record because he had been on the receiving end of a state-aggravated assault.

Like most communities in its section of the country, Pope County, Arkansas, where that incident occurred, is thickly populated with Evangelical Christians, whose numbers probably include most elected officials, prosecutors, judges, and police officers. At some point in Sunday School they probably read the 22nd chapter of the Book of Acts, which describes how the Apostle Paul, accused of disturbing the peace, was arrested by Roman occupation soldiers and taken to a local barracks to be questioned under scourging.

As the interrogator was preparing to whip the apostle, Paul pointed out to the centurion in charge that it was illegal to flog a Roman citizen unless he had been tried and convicted of a crime. This objection caused the interrogator to desist immediately, and prompted the officer in command to express the fear that he could face criminal charges because he had chained—that is, handcuffed—a Roman citizen.

Every day in this supposedly free country, police commit an act that was impermissible for their antecedents in imperial Rome: In the name of "officer safety," they handcuff American citizens who are not criminal suspects while conducting investigations. Police also routinely inflict summary punishment—using batons, Tasers, pepper spray, or other means—against those who resist being detained without cause. Within a few years police will have at their disposal handcuffs that can impart electrical shocks to detainees.

In an 1894 essay published by *The Strand Magazine*, Inspector Maurice Moser of Scotland Yard wrote that the earliest historical mention of handcuffs was in the fourth century BC, "when soldiers of a conquering Greek army found among the baggage of the routed Carthaginians several chariots full of handcuffs, which had been held ready in confident anticipation of a multitude of prisoners."

"My personal experience of handcuffs is small, because I dislike them," wrote Inspector Moser of the restraints. He pointed out that in Belgium, which at the time was the seat of a substantial empire, "the use of handcuffs by police is entirely forbidden."

Like most police officers of his era, Moser was a relatively civilized man who found the act of shackling another human being to be barbarous and punitive. Handcuffing a human being certainly doesn't enhance the safety of the person being restrained. Nor does it relieve police anxieties about the all-encompassing threat to that most sacred of considerations, "officer safety."

Witness the large and ever-growing number of cases in which officers—almost always in the plural, of course—beat, tase, pepper-spray, and even shoot suspects who have already been handcuffed.

Last summer, police in Aurora, Colorado indiscriminately handcuffed and detained scores of people for the space of more than four hours following an armed robbery at a branch of Wells Fargo bank.

According to Officer Frank Fania, drivers and passengers in the vicinity "were handcuffed, then were told what was going on and were asked for permission to search the car. They all granted permission, and once nothing was found in their cars, they were un-handcuffed."

Once the victims were handcuffed, of course, they had no choice but to grant "permission" for their abductors to paw through their vehicles. What if they had withheld consent? What if they had refused to endure the indignity and injury of being handcuffed in the first place?

Fania insisted that the mass arrests were necessary and justified because it was a "unique" situation. But it's more honestly described as mass application of the standard approach to "protective" detention of individuals who are not criminal suspects.

Owing to the semantic deviousness of police and prosecutors, citizens are increasingly unsure of their status when they are accosted by police: Are they under arrest, or subject to "investigatory detention"? If the citizen isn't formally under arrest, is he free to leave? Can police draw their guns and threaten a citizen with lethal force if he is not formally under arrest?

That last question has been addressed in a recent ruling by Louisiana's Fifth Circuit Court of Appeal, which held that those circumstances do not constitute a formal arrest—at least when the legitimacy of that arrest is questioned by the defendant.

On June 8, 2010, Robert Carter of Jefferson Parish, Louisiana parked outside a convenience store. Acting on a tip from a snitch that Carter would soon arrive at the location to conduct a drug deal, two undercover detectives had kept the lot under surveillance. After Carter parked his car, the detectives used their unmarked vehicles to cut off his escape and approached him with guns drawn.

In a panic, Carter threw his car into reverse, severely damaging the unmarked car behind him.

During his bench trial, Carter claimed that the arrival of two armed men— one of whom admitted in testimony that they didn't clearly identify themselves as police—made him fear for his life. After being convicted of felony malicious property damage, Carter—a second offender—was sentenced to 20 years in prison. On appeal, Carter insisted that the arrest was unlawful.

In a remarkable achievement in judicial sophistry, the appeals court ruled that what it called an "investigative detention" is *not* an arrest—while insisting that Carter had no right to leave what the trial judge called "the arrested place [where] he's supposed to remain." In practical terms this means that cops are permitted to detain any citizen at gunpoint without such an action qualifying as an "arrest"—and therefore being subject to the restrictions supposedly guaranteed by the Fourth and Fifth amendments. Once the individual is detained, he can be shackled at the discretion of the officer—and then beaten, jailed, and prosecuted if he objects.

The act of handcuffing another human being is a serious injury. When not done to restrain someone who has actually harmed another human being, handcuffing is a morally impermissible form of aggressive violence. It is meant to be a tangible demonstration of superiority that requires the victim to submit to the supposed authority of the aggressor. It is designed and intended to humiliate the victim. This is why it is done even to six-year-old inmates of government schools who are dragged away by police officers, nonagenarians who are abducted at gunpoint for neglecting to pay traffic tickets, or pregnant female inmates who are chained while giving birth.

This is also why police who are charged with crimes are often spared being handcuffed out of "professional courtesy"—which in some cases has actually imperiled the arresting officer.

In the American *Soyuz*, any of us, at the whim of an armed stranger in a government-issued costume, can find himself being treated in the same way that the Carthaginians treated captured prisoners of war. At least Carthaginian soldiers didn't insult the intelligence of their victims by insisting that they were being shackled for their own "protection."

The Stalinist in the White House

Pro Libertate, March 6, 2013

In the fashion of Caesar thrice refusing the crown even as he assumed dictatorial powers, tyrants will occasionally engage in self-aggrandizement disguised as self-deprecation. Barack Obama offered a moment of that kind last week when, in reply to a question about the budget sequester posed by a media sycophant, he said, "I'm not a dictator."

Obama wasn't serious, of course. He does consider himself a dictator, albeit one whose term in office is limited, at least for now.

Obama might not lock the doors of the Oval Office and force Republican congressional leaders to carry out budget negotiations, but—as his Attorney General made clear in a letter to Senator Rand Paul—he considers himself duly empowered to carry out the summary execution of U.S. citizens on American soil if he deems such action necessary.

In testimony before the Senate Judiciary Committee today, Holder made it clear that the president he serves answers to nobody, and is bound by no laws, in carrying out extra-judicial killings, either within U.S. borders or beyond them. Expressing a point of view familiar to students of Soviet Russia under the reign of Stalin, Holder maintained that the purpose of the law is to prevent anybody—whether an individual citizen, a judge, or a legislative body—from restraining the exercise of presidential will.

"Do you believe Congress can pass a law prohibiting [the President] to use lethal force on U.S. soil?" Senator Chuck Grassley of Iowa asked Holder. If we still resided in something resembling a constitutional republic, that question itself would be perverse: Congress wouldn't need to pass a law to prevent something that the law doesn't authorize the president to do.

Furthermore, as civil liberties activist Marcy Wheeler points out, Grassley's question wasn't intended to suggest a general prohibition against "targeted killings," but rather one that "would apply only where a person did not present an imminent threat." In other words, Grassley was willing to concede that the president could order summary executions after addressing some trivial formalities about the dire necessity of such action.

But even this would be too restrictive, according to Holder.

"I'm not sure that such a bill would be constitutional," he told Grassley. "It might run contrary to the Article II powers that the President has." In other

248

words, Holder is claiming that the President, as Commander-in-Chief of the military, can order the military (or, presumably, the CIA) to carry out an extra-judicial execution of a U.S. citizen on American soil—and Congress would be forbidden by the Constitution (whatever that word means to Holder and his ilk) from preventing such action.

Domestic use of the military as a law enforcement agency is forbidden by the Third Amendment and the Posse Comitatus Act. This means nothing to the budding Stalinist occupying the Oval Office.

For the Obama-centric Left, as it was for the Bush-centric Right, the U.S. President is the "Living Constitution." His power is limited only by the resources at his command, and the extent of his sadistic imagination. Thomas Jefferson—in an essay promoting what we are told is the subversive and un-American doctrine of "interposition"—warned that "confidence in men" is a "dangerous delusion" that is fatal to liberty. Today, collectivists of the Right and Left insist that this is true only on those occasions when power is exercised by people associated with the other faction.

Perhaps this is an unfair and overbroad characterization. There are some prominent figures who can abandon partisan attachments in defense of principle. Regrettably, this usually means that party labels are discarded in favor of an unabashed embrace of the non-partisan Warfare State, and the principles being applied are entirely depraved. Witness the fact that many conservative commentators, rather than condemning Obama for assuming the powers of a literal dictator, have actually applauded him. Among them is John Bolton, who represented the Bush administration in the United Nations, who admits that Obama's drone strike program "is consistent with, and derived from, the Bush administration approach to the war on terror." In Bolton's opinion, the drone-killing program is "entirely sensible."

Channeling the spirit of a Stalin-era Communist Party apparatchik, South Carolina Republican Senator Lindsay Graham has proposed a resolution applauding the administration's drone-killing program and urging all of his Republican colleagues to express their support. Graham has explicitly commended the administration for the summary execution of U.S. citizen Anwar al-Awlaki, who was murdered (no other word is suitable) by a drone strike in Yemen without ever being charged with a crime. Graham hasn't said whether he considers the murder of Anwar's 16-year-old son Abdulrahman to be a similar triumph of statecraft.

More remarkable still was the reaction of John Yoo, a former Bush-era Justice Department functionary who now teaches law at the University of California-Berkeley. Seven years before Eric Holder claimed that Congress has no authority to rein in Obama's power of discretionary killing, Yoo breezily claimed that no law or treaty could prevent President Bush from ordering the sexual mutilation of a child in order to extract information from the victim's parents.

Yoo employed a *Wall Street Journal* op-ed column to criticize the Obama "white paper" that sets out the guidelines for drone attacks—not because it gives unaccountable discretionary killing power to the president and his subordinates, but because it supposedly extends due process to "enemy combatants." Yoo complains that the paper "suggests" that U.S. citizens like Anwar al-Awlaki "enjoy due process rights. By doing so, it dissipates the rights of the law-abiding at home."

Presumably, Yoo's concerns have been placated by Holder's unflinching assertion that the president has unqualified authority to murder Americans anywhere, for any reason he deems suitable.

Senator Angus King of Maine has proposed the institutionalization of the drone program through creation of a special court that would be modeled after the tribunal that issues warrants under the Foreign Intelligence Surveillance Act (or FISA). The FISA court, significantly, issues warrants after surveillance has begun. In similar fashion, Senator Young's proposed court would review decisions to carry out drone strikes after the missiles had flown and the targeted individual had been killed. This proposal has been criticized by some congressional Republicans—once again, not because it represents a concession to tyrannical power, but rather because it supposedly inhibits the exercise of that power, if only by acknowledging that the power is subject to some form of independent scrutiny.

Until the filibuster staged by Senator Paul—who, despite his plentiful shortcomings, has proven that he has learned much from his heroic father—no Senate Republican had rejected the Stalinist premise that the President can order the summary execution of U.S. citizens. What about the Professional Left—the people who, like then-Senator Obama, were so agitated over the Bush administration's crimes against the Bill of Rights? They're too busy debating such weighty matters as the proper honorific by which to address the Dear Leader, or helping the Southern Poverty Law Center draw up "kill lists" of domestic "extremists."

About a week ago, State Department spokeswoman Victoria Nuland insisted that Washington would maintain its embargo of Cuba because the regime ruling that island continues to be a "state sponsor of terrorism." Unlike the Regime for which Nuland speaks, the Cuban government doesn't occupy a foot of foreign territory, nor does it use robot aircraft to rain death from the skies on neighborhoods halfway around the world.

In its 2011 human rights report on Cuba, the agency that issues Nuland's paycheck described its government as a "totalitarian state" ruled by a military hierarchy that routinely commits criminal violence against the innocent. All of that is true, of course. Interestingly, the document admitted that in 2011, "There were no reports that the government or its agents committed arbitrary or unlawful killings." The same cannot be said of the Regime that employs Nuland, which in the same year murdered hundreds of people in Pakistan, Afghanistan, and Yemen. Among those "arbitrary [and] unlawful killings" were the summary executions of at least three U.S. citizens, including a 16-year-old boy. And now the chief law enforcement officer of the Obama Regime insists that the "law" would forbid Congress to restrain the Dear Leader from carrying out the extra-judicial killings of U.S. citizens.

While it's true that Cuba remains mired in poverty and still lives under the reign of a thoroughly despicable ruling clique, we really must confront this question:

By what standard is the government of Cuba totalitarian, if the Regime in Washington is not?

"Ominous Threats" and Murderous Zeal

Pro Libertate, March 15, 2013

"There are, in increasingly frightening numbers, cells of angry men in the United States preparing for combat," warns an unusually strident house editorial by the *Los Angeles Times*. "They are usually heavily armed, blinded by an intractable hatred, often motivated by religious zeal."

That description was not applied to the masked, armor-clad Berserkers who kick down doors in the early morning or late at night and terrorize families over non-violent "offenses." Nor was it offered in reference to the militants who have purchased more than 1.6 billion rounds of ammunition—much of it hollow-point rounds unsuitable for military use—while distributing armored vehicles and other military hardware to their adherents in practically every city nationwide. The *Times* didn't direct that rhetorical salvo at the people who are openly discussing plans to fill America's skies with robot planes that can—and will— be used as weapons platforms.

The *Times* editorial collective focused its indignation upon a much safer target—namely, "white, right-wing Americans, all with an obsessive attachment to guns, who may represent a greater danger to the lives of American civilians than international terrorists."

The statist screed makes passing reference to what it calls "the massacre of a bizarre sect by federal agents in Waco, Texas," twenty years ago—without passing moral judgment on the "massacre" in question.

Slaughtering religious eccentrics is a venial offense compared to the grave heresy committed by those who speak ill of the Holy State, since their "blather"—*not* the murderous actions of those who impudently presume to rule us, mind you—"tends to get under the skin of the Timothy McVeighs of the world."

Once again: Immolating harmless people in a church is a perfectly proper thing, assuming that this act of mass murder is carried out by the consecrated hands of the State's enforcement caste, but *referring* to it as mass murder is the sort of thing only an incipient terrorist would do.

In recent days, we've heard that the Obama Regime—which is running out of plausible foreign enemies—is seeking to broaden the scope of the "war on terror" to include "offshoot" groups that are connected only by rumor to al Qaeda (which was always more of a brand name than an actual organization). Terror

Warriors need not fret; ere long we'll harvest the nettles that have been so plentifully sown by the Regime's implacable aggression abroad. In the meantime, however, the *Times* suggests that the "war on terror" should re-direct its focus inward.

Citing the most recent missive from the self-appointed Stasi at the Southern Poverty Law Center, the *Times* claims that there are 1,360 proto-terrorist groups—sneeringly denounced as "patriots," "constitutionalists," and "sovereign citizens"—scattered throughout the *Soyuz*. "These groups should be closely monitored, with resources adequate to the task, even if it means shifting some homeland security money from the hunt for foreign terrorists," concludes the paper.

Reconfiguring the "war on terror" from an imperialist venture into a domestic purge was the central idea of a letter sent by the SPLC to the Department of Homeland Security. "On October 25, 1994, six months before the Oklahoma City bombing, we wrote Attorney General Janet Reno about the growing threat of domestic terrorism," wrote SPLC President Richard Cohen to Attorney General Eric Holder and Homeland Security Secretary Janet Napolitano:

> Today, we write to express similar concerns. In the last four years, we have seen a tremendous increase in the number of conspiracy-minded, anti-government groups as well as in the number of domestic terrorist plots. As in the period before the Oklahoma City bombing, we now also are seeing ominous threats from those who believe that the government is poised to take their guns.

Mr. Holder recently claimed that it is illegal for Congress to forbid the President to order summary executions. Thus it's remarkable that Cohen would discern "ominous threats" in the rhetorical bluster of an inchoate movement, but nothing objectionable about the fact that the Obama administration routinely carries out extra-judicial killings abroad—and will not rule out the possibility of doing so here at home, as well.

Where the depiction of "threats" is concerned, the SPLC is notorious for rendering models of T-Rex-scale monsters from small and undistinguished bone fragments—witness the fact that one of the "militant" groups listed in its most recent index of domestic enemies is an anti-war knitting circle led by an ailing senior citizen.

It doesn't take a similar feat of ideological imagination to see something of an "ominous threat" in the following remarks from Democratic Congresswoman Louise Slaughter, a devoted opponent of civilian gun ownership, in an interview on Al Gore's cable network:

> The idea of fighting the federal government with an AR-15 . . .
> I know that is an idea a lot of people have—if they ever look,
> as I have, at what the federal defense budget is, I think they
> would disabuse themselves of that notion right away.

Allusively, but unmistakably, Rep. Slaughter was referring to the prospect of making war against the people of the United States—which, as it happens, meets the specific constitutional definition of "treason." Only those who have lost interest in living, or who have acquired an interest in auto-erotic asphyxiation, would hold their breath awaiting SPLC's condemnation of the vulgar threat that emerged from the tax-devouring gullet of the appropriately named Rep. Slaughter.

Echoing the central theme of Cohen's letter to the Feds, SPLC spokesman Mark Potok, "We are in a scary moment. It is very much reminiscent, at least to me, of the months leading up to the Oklahoma City Bombing." This is indeed quite ominous—not because the SPLC has correctly gauged the public mood, mind you, but because the group was deeply involved in the Fed's PATCON false flag operation that precipitated the OKC bombing. The FBI spent the last decade running COINTELPRO-style provocation operations against American Muslims. There's every reason to suspect that they're busy seeding informants and provocateurs in every cohesive group of right-wing dissidents they can find.

The SPLC-derived *Los Angeles Times* editorial—which could be digested into the phrase, "The conspiracy theorists are plotting against us!"—brings to mind an incident in the early 1980s in which East German officials arrested a group of human rights activists for "defaming" the state by claiming that it suppressed freedom of speech. As Tony Cooper, an instructor in terrorism negotiation at the University of Texas-Dallas, pointed out in 1995, the Regime in Washington is perfectly capable of such totalitarian behavior.

"I see the formation of a curious crusading mentality among certain law enforcement agencies to stamp out what they see as a threat to government generally," Cooper told the *Washington Post* in 1995. "It's an exaggerated concern that they are facing a nationwide conspiracy and that somehow this will get out of control unless it is stamped out at a very early stage."

Never forget: A "conspiracy theorist" is someone who notices things without official permission—and a "terrorist" is anybody who challenges the government's monopoly on violence.

Resistance is Dangerous; Submission is Frequently Fatal

Pro Libertate, March 24, 2013

Resisting arrest is not a crime. It is a common-law right, the exercise of which is treated as if it were a crime.

The act of resistance was transmuted into a criminal offense chiefly through judicial activism, rather than legislation. Courts that seek to criminalize resistance have generally made the pragmatic argument that resistance is more dangerous than submission. We've long since reached the point where the reverse is often the case.

Until 1942, when the Interstate Commission on Crime published the Uniform Arrest Act, every state recognized and protected the right to resist. Under the still-controlling U.S. Supreme Court precedent, *John Bad Elk vs. U.S.*, a citizen faced with the prospect of unlawful arrest—that is, an armed abduction—has a legally protected right to use any appropriate means, including lethal force, to defend himself.

The *Bad Elk* ruling came in 1900. Thirteen years later, the New Mexico State Supreme Court, in *Territory v. Lynch*, tried out a line of sophistry that would become part of the standard refrain in judicial rulings six decades later:

> The law . . . calls upon the citizen to exercise patience, if illegally arrested, because he knows he will be brought before a magistrate, and will, if improperly arrested, suffer only a temporary deprivation of his liberty.

In other words: If a cop seeks to abduct you without legal justification, you should submit in the serene confidence that your deprivation of liberty will be temporary and trivial. I have referred to this as the "Rapist Doctrine," since rapists and police officers are the only assailants whose victims are encouraged to submit.

One hundred years after the New Mexico State Supreme Court published that ruling, the case of New Mexico resident Stephen Slevin demonstrates that this assurance is a cynical lie.

In 2005, Slevin—who was battling depression and driving a car lent to him by a friend—was stopped for driving under the influence. He was put into a special cell reserved for people suspected of being suicidal. After three days, he was transferred to solitary confinement—where he remained for two years.

Although some may regard the traffic stop to be considered justified, and the initial arrest to be defensible, what happened to Slevin offers a stark and compelling demonstration of what can happen to anyone who finds himself immured in one of the Regime's penal facilities. What was done to him is indistinguishable from the kind of criminal abuse associated in the public mind with prison facilities in Cuba and North Korea. More importantly, it is entirely typical of what happens in jails and prisons here in the putative Land of the Free.

Prolonged solitary confinement is a form of torture. In Slevin's case, isolation was compounded with aggressive neglect as he literally rotted in his cell.

Despite repeated pleas for medical attention, Slevin developed skin fungus and bedsores. Deprived of dental care, Slevin was eventually forced to extract a tooth by himself. His toenails grew so long that they curled under his feet, his hair and beard grew to be long and unkempt, and he lost fifty pounds.

As his body decayed, Slevin's mind degenerated. Already depressed at the time of his imprisonment, Slevin fell prey to hallucinations.

"I have not slept in days," Slevin wrote to a nurse a couple of weeks into his solitary confinement. "I'm in a deep depression." He also mentioned a lack of appetite, and that he was being afflicted with "weird and bizarre" dreams.

"I'm afraid to close my eyes," he wrote in a plaintive letter to the jail's "nurse practitioner," an official with a bachelor's degree in psychology and no medical credentials or experience. The "nurse" responded by prescribing a dose of sedatives.

The habeas corpus guarantee requires that anyone arrested by the police be quickly brought before a judge and either formally charged or released. Slevin, who was sent to solitary after failing to post $40,000 in bail, was never given a judicial hearing. If it weren't for the intervention of his sister, who became concerned after Slevin stopped replying to her letters, Slevin would have died in jail without ever being charged with a crime.

Once he was released, Slevin filed a lawsuit against Dona Ana County. After a five-year legal struggle, Slevin was awarded $22 million by a federal court—one million dollars for every month he had been unlawfully incarcerated.

The county, which refused to discipline anybody responsible for Slevin's imprisonment and torture, and refuses to answer questions about the crime committed against that man, protested that the civil judgment was excessive, and eventually agreed to a $15.5 million tax-funded civil settlement. This may still seem like an extravagant amount until it's understood that the 59-year-old victim suffers from terminal lung cancer.

"The law cannot restore an arm, an eye, or a life; it can and does restore freedom," wrote Ralph D. Smith of the University of New Mexico School of Law in a 1967 law school journal essay. His point was that "self-help" by citizens confronted with the prospect of unlawful arrest is impermissible, because they are dealing with people—that is, police officers—who have legal sanction to kill them if they resist.

"Life and liberty, though equally precious, cannot be viewed on the same plane where self-help is concerned," Smith continues. "Liberty can be secured by a resort to law, life cannot." A good case can be made for the proposition that Slevin's illegal incarceration was terminal. Furthermore, unjust deprivation of liberty for *any* length of time is a grave and ineffaceable injury.

"If one is unlawfully arrested today, his period of confinement is likely to be brief," wrote Smith, offering a glib assurance of the kind that comes easily to those who are paid well to defend the indefensible. "In the seventeenth and eighteenth centuries"—that is, the period in which British courts handed down rulings explicitly recognizing the common law right to resist arrest—"bail was usually unattainable. Today, it is freely granted for most offenses. Requirements of a prompt hearing and arraignment before a magistrate also serve to protect today's citizen from a lengthy unjustified detention."

None of that was true in the case of Stephen Slevin, who suffered the theft of two years that were stolen from a life that was further abbreviated by the unpunished abuse of those who illegally imprisoned him.

During the less-enlightened times in which courts recognized that citizens had the right to avoid illegal arrest and detention, Smith continues, an improperly detained individual could be confined for months, and then "re-incarcerated until he had paid certain fees demanded by the jailer, the clerk of the assize, clerks of the peace, and the like." What he describes is exactly the same arrangement that prevails today in a probation and parole system that encourages probation and parole officers to find excuses to "violate" their charges as often as possible in order to recycle them through the mechanism.

"Seventeenth and eighteenth century prison conditions might well induce resistance to arrest, if only to keep out of jail," observes Smith. The same was true not only in the case of Stephen Slevin, but also that of California resident Daniel Chong, who was held, handcuffed, in isolation and darkness, for five days without being charged with a crime in April of last year.

Chong was deprived of food, water, and bathroom facilities. When he was finally released, Chong—who had begun to suffer from hallucinations—asked his captors to kill him. He was hospitalized with severe dehydration and renal failure. The officials responsible for this crime have never been punished, nor have they so much as apologized to Chong.

The late Nick Christie likewise had every reason to put up resistance when he was taken into "protective" custody by Lee County, Florida sheriff's deputies in 2009. Christie, a resident of Cleveland, had gone to visit a brother in Florida. His wife was concerned that the 62-year-old man, who had been diagnosed with psychological problems, had left his medications behind. She made the familiar and reliably fatal mistake of calling the police for "help."

Christie, who was detained on a spurious "trespassing" change, was shackled for nearly two full days in a restraint chair. His captors hooded the victim and repeatedly attacked him with military-grade pepper spray. Christie begged for the jailers to remove the "spit mask" from his face, complaining that he couldn't breathe. When medical personnel were finally permitted to see Christie, they were overwhelmed by the pepper spray. When they attempted to treat him, the corrosive chemical residue was so potent it ate through their latex medical gloves.

This innocent man, who suffered from respiratory and heart disease, was tortured to death. His death was ruled a homicide. The State Attorney's office refused to indict the officials who kidnapped and fatally tortured Christie, insisting that there was no evidence of "criminal wrongdoing." (That prosecutor, Assistant State Attorney Dean R. Plattner, had a long history of indifference regarding criminal violence by police officers.)

Writing more than four decades ago, as efforts to repudiate the right to resist arrest were gaining momentum, Arthur Smith insisted: "Because of the evolution in criminal procedures, jail conditions, and the increased danger from resistance, an individual is less likely to be provoked at what he considers an unlawful arrest in 1967 than he would have been in 1767."

By 2013, it should be obvious to all honest and observant people that the only material difference between the medieval system Smith described and the one that confronts us now is the fact that British subjects had a legally recognized right to resist unlawful arrest.

Resistance may be dangerous, but submission is frequently fatal.

Welcome to Sulphur Springs, Arkansas—Where the Police Chief is a Murderer

Pro Libertate, March 27, 2013

Like many third-world countries, Arkansas is a beautiful place inhabited by lovely people who are burdened with an extravagantly corrupt ruling class. This helps explain, but by no means does it justify, the fact that the minuscule town of Sulphur Springs, Arkansas now has a convicted killer as its police chief.

In January 2010, Coleman Brackney, at the time an officer in the department that menaces nearby Bella Vista, murdered a man named James Ahern following a high-speed chase. After trapping Ahern's vehicle and then pounding on his window, Brackney shot him six times—the last time in the back. Brackney claimed that Ahern—who had a record of trivial and petty offenses, including the non-crime of "resisting arrest"—attempted to run him over after the chase had ended. This was a lie, of course: The dashcam video documented that Brackney was never in danger.

By any honest definition, this was an act of murder. Yet Brackney was prosecuted for "negligent homicide"—a charge that assumes that the officer, who shot Ahern six times at point-blank range, including once in the back, did not intend to kill the victim. He was sentenced to a single month in the Benton County Jail and fined $1,000. The families of the victim were given a $20,000 settlement by the county.

After Brackney was released, his criminal record was expunged. Last April, the Arkansas Commission on Law Enforcement—a regulatory body that enforces less rigorous professional standards than whatever body sanctions professional wrestling referees—reinstated Brackney's "peace officer" certification. All that he needed now was a job opening—and one was soon created in Sulphur Springs.

Between late 2010 and March 25 of this year, residents of Sulphur Springs had known the singular blessing of living in a community devoid of police. It is an abuse of language to refer to Sulphur Springs as a "town"; as of the last census, its population was about 500 people, and it had no measurable crime rate. There hasn't been a murder in Sulphur Springs in recent memory. By hiring a murderer as police chief, the people who presume to rule that tiny village

261

managed to handle both the supply and demand side of law enforcement, as it were.

"I told the guys the day I left I would be back," gloated Brackney in a local TV news interview, displaying the gift for self-preoccupation that typifies his caste. "You put the uniform back on and you look at yourself in the mirror, and you think, 'I'm back.'" Of course, the same cannot be said of Brackney's victim, for whom the newly enthroned police chief apparently cannot spare a thought.

Indeed, Brackney displays a sociopath's inability to recognize that he did anything wrong by murdering a man and then perjuring himself in an attempt to conceal the crime.

Like every other police officer who has committed criminal violence against a member of the public, Brackney takes refuge in the casual elitism that is commonplace among those in his profession: "Until you have actually rode [sic] with a police officer or have a family member or a friend that [sic] is a police officer, you don't really know what that job entails."

In other words: Until you have been licensed to perform acts of criminal aggression or unless you have a relative thus invested, you have no moral standing to criticize those who use that spurious sanction to commit criminal homicide.

To paraphrase Albert Nock's deathless insight, government police forces don't exist to eliminate crime, but rather to enforce a government monopoly on crime. Coleman Brackney embodies that principle with uncanny fidelity. This is to be expected of Arkansas, where there quite literally are no standards governing the qualifications and performance of police officers.

Practically any hominid who can drive a car, pull a trigger, and emit sounds that vaguely resemble the English language can be stuffed into a government-issued costume and exercise "authority" on behalf of the State of Arkansas.

Consider this: In order to become a licensed practicing cosmetologist in the State of Arkansas, an applicant must pass a state board examination and complete 2,000 hours of specialized training. After logging 600 hours an applicant can qualify to work as a manicurist or instructor.

The same state government that exercises such rigorous oversight of people who cut hair or paint nails in the private sector, it imposes no training or licensing standards on police officers. Practically anybody who asks for a job as a police officer in Arkansas can get a stinkin' badge; it's the *qualifications* that are unnecessary.

"The second night I ever put on a badge and gun I was riding in my own car," recalled Crittenden County Chief Deputy Tommy Martin. At the time, Martin was 21 years old and hadn't spent so much as a minute inside a police academy classroom.

"According to Arkansas state law, officers do not have to be certified for up to a year after they're hired," reported the Memphis Fox News affiliate in February 2010—just a few weeks after Officer Brackney murdered James Ahern. "The Commission on Law Enforcement Standards and Training says they can get an 8 month extension on top of that. So for almost 2 years, an officer can patrol the streets, by his or herself, and enforce the law without having any kind of training."

And, as we learned last April, that same Commission is eager to reinstate the certification of police officers who have served time behind bars for acts of criminal homicide.

Arkansas is riddled with tiny towns afflicted with police who are not merely corrupt, but demented.

In late 2009, Police Chief Greg Martin of Turrell, Arkansas (population roughly 900 people) was charged with aggravated assault after he broke into the home of City Council member Floyd Holmes and threatened the Councilman and his wife with a gun.

A similar confrontation a few months earlier in nearby Jericho actually resulted in an attempted homicide.

Until about 1990, the flyspeck town of Jericho (population circa 200 people) was blessedly devoid of police. This changed when the town received a grant to create its own police force—and the community has been suffering ever since.

Over the past two decades, Jericho acquired a richly deserved reputation as one of the most notorious speed traps in the South. But its police department doesn't just prey on unsuspecting visitors with out-of-state license plates: Persistent harassment by the police and a rising tide of official corruption drove many locals to leave the town.

A few years ago, Fire Chief Don Payne challenged a dubious speeding ticket in court. Later that day, he was hit with a second spurious citation as a transparent act of retaliation for challenging the first one. When he protested the second citation, Payne was mobbed in court by seven officers and then shot. This atrocity did have one salutary result: The police department was temporarily disbanded, and all outstanding citations were dismissed, while investigators tried to determine what had happened to the funds that had been mulcted from speed trap victims.

The town of Paragould has a population of 25,000, which makes it a major metropolis by Arkansas standards. This might explain the grandiose ambitions of Todd Stovall, the J.W. Pepper-grade living caricature who presides over the town's police department.

Last January, Stovall, who appears to be building his own little private army, announced that he would be deploying SWAT operators armed with AR-15s to harass people on the streets.

"The fear is what's given us the reason to do this," insisted Stovall as he announced that the city would be placed under martial law for the supposed purpose of deterring crime. "Once I have stats and people are saying they're scared, we can do this. It allows us to do what we're fixing to do."

There is no evidence that people in Paragould are in fear of anyone other than the bullet-headed dimwit who heads their police force, and the costumed adolescents under his command. The "stats" referred to by Stovall certainly don't justify the perception that the town is under siege. While Paragould historically has a high burglary rate, its violent crime rate is substantially below the national average: In 2010, the last year for which stats are available, there wasn't a single murder in the town.

Despite these facts, Stovall insists that a "crisis" exists that justifies the suspension of constitutional rules and the imposition of a city-wide curfew.

"I've got statistical reasons that say I've got a lot of crime right now, which gives me probable cause to ask what you're doing out," grunted Stovall at a town meeting at the West View Baptist Church. He admits that he didn't consult an attorney before reaching that conclusion, and that "I don't even know that there's ever been a difference" between what he's proposing and undisguised martial law. To those who might complain about being harassed by Stovall's minions, the chief offers an unqualified promise: "If you're out walking, we're going to stop you, ask why you're out walking, check for your ID. . . . We have a zero-tolerance. We are prepared to throw your hind-end in jail, okay? We are not going to take a lot of flack."

"We're going to do it to everybody," Stovall explained, anticipating objections. "Criminals don't like being talked to."

The same is true of citizens, of course. But like most members of his paramilitary tribe, Stovall divides the world between the Mundane population—which is to be intimidated into submission—and enlightened agents of State "authority" such as himself and the murderer who is the newly appointed police chief of Sulphur Springs.

The Persecution of Rita Hutchens

Pro Libertate, May 12, 2013

Sandpoint, Idaho resident Rita Hutchens is an opinionated 57-year-old quilt artist whose work has earned her international notoriety. Given that Hutchens is also an outspoken proponent of constitutionalist views, it's possible that some people have taken issue with her political opinions.

Hutchens has never harmed or threatened another human being. Yet local officials, led by Bonner County Deputy Prosecutor Shane Greenbank—an inventively dishonest official—are trying to make a criminal out of her. Failing that, they might simply seek to have her imprisoned indefinitely in a psych ward.

Around midnight on April 16, three Bonner County Sheriff's Deputies invaded Rita's home while she was asleep and half-clothed on her living room sofa. The deputies were enforcing a bench warrant issued several weeks earlier after Hutchens had failed to appear for a preliminary hearing on a misdemeanor charge.

In Idaho, as elsewhere, it is exceptionally rare for police to serve warrants after sundown. In its ruling in the 2011 case Idaho v. Skurlock, the Idaho Supreme Court recognized that at night time people "have a heightened expectation of privacy that should not be disturbed by a knock on the door and the presentation of a search warrant." In addition, executing a warrant at night "increases the likelihood of violence because nighttime searches cause an abrupt intrusion on sleeping occupants in a home, thus increasing the potential for a violent reaction from the occupants."

The bold and valiant deputies who kicked in Rita Hutchens' door at midnight acted in the serene confidence that they had no reason to expect a violent reaction on the part of their terrified victim.

The officials responsible for the Stasi-style midnight raid maintain that there was an element of urgency because she is suspected of a violent crime, to wit: battery on a city official at Sandpoint City Hall last August 12. If they are in a particularly creative mood, city authorities might embellish that charge by saying that it involved an impact weapon.

The implement of mayhem allegedly employed by Hutchens in the supposed assault on Deputy Clerk Melissa Ward was not a club, a set of brass knuckles, or throwing stars. It was a ballpoint pen.

No, really.

Furthermore, according to the sober and dutiful public servants who witnessed the attack, Hutchens did not hurl that potentially death-dealing projectile at Ward; instead, she threw it down on a tabletop, and the terrorized agent of the public weal was injured by a ricochet.

Somehow, Ward stoically fought through her trauma and finished her shift without being treated by paramedics. Significantly, although she did fill out a police report, Ward never swore out a criminal complaint.

Hutchens filed a subpoena demanding that Ward, the alleged victim, provide a sworn and signed criminal complaint.

Last November 14, the Idaho First District Court granted a motion by Sandpoint City Attorney Scott Campbell to quash that subpoena, ruling that "requiring Ms. Ward, the victim in this matter, to provide a signed complaint is unreasonable."

What this means is that there is no victim of record in the August 12 "battery" incident, and no criminal intent behind Hutchens' actions—unless, of course, Greenbank wants to pretend that this middle-aged woman deviously set up a bank-shot for the purpose of wounding the clerk. On the basis of his behavior toward Hutchens—another example of which we will examine anon— I'm convinced that Greenbank and his comrades possess sufficient cynicism to make that claim.

The patently spurious nature of the charge against Hutchens is brought into focus once it's understood why she had visited City Hall: She was there to review public records related to an incident in 2011 in which she was assaulted and illegally arrested by Sandpoint police officer Theresa Heberer.

At the time of her encounter with Officer Heberer, Hutchens was in the middle of evicting a deadbeat tenant (who, as it happened, had been arrested the previous day on outstanding warrants). She visited her property to determine if the power and water had been shut off. When Hutchens drove by the property— making two passes when she saw the renter talking with Officer Heberer—the tenant claimed that Hutchens had been "stalking" or "harassing" her. On the basis of that complaint from a manifestly unreliable source, Heberer got into her patrol vehicle and followed Hutchens to her home.

Heberer demanded that Hutchens submit to an interrogation. Hutchens, who didn't want to be bothered by a police officer—what decent and rational person would?—replied that she had nothing to say, invoked the Fifth Amendment, and turned to enter her home. Heberer responded by committing criminal trespass, then compounded that crime by seizing Hutchens and violently throwing her to the ground.

When her supervisor arrived on the scene, Heberer claimed that the encounter began with a traffic stop dealing with an expired registration. This was a lie, of course. Seeking to find some charge to justify the criminal violence inflicted on Hutchens, Heberer and her supervisor pored over the statute book and eventually decided to charge the victim with "resisting and obstructing" a police officer.

That charge was entirely without merit—a fact recognized by Magistrate Judge Barbara Buchanan when she threw it out of court.

"There was no reason to touch her," Judge Buchanan observed:

> She did not have to answer [Officer Heberer's] questions. She has a Fifth Amendment right not to do that. . . . You can't be charged with resisting and obstructing for exercising your Fifth Amendment right, and she did have every right to say, "I don't want to answer your questions, I want to go in my house." There is no basis for an arrest, there is no reason for a search warrant.

Unlike Melissa Ward, Hutchens was physically harmed by Heberer's assault, in addition to suffering the indelible injury of being handcuffed and unlawfully detained. She filed a $250,000 damage claim with the City of Sandpoint, which was rejected by Idaho Counties Risk Management Program. So she filed a notice of tort claim announcing her intention to sue the city for violating her civil rights.

It was in preparation for that lawsuit that Hutchens was researching public records at City Hall on August. As she did so, she was followed by a city official who carried a digital recorder and may well have been trying to bait her into some kind of actionable misconduct.

As Sgt. Riffel noted in his official report of the incident, "Rita Hutchens. . . has a fairly tense relationship with the City, and has pending lawsuits against them."

Had he possessed a particle of moral discernment and a rudimentary sense of honor, Riffel would have recognized that the battery complaint was an act of petty retaliation against a citizen regarded as an irritant. His reaction should have been to shake his head in disgust, put away his notebook, and tell the "victim" and her cronies to behave like adults. But this would have meant defending the rights of a Mundane, which would be impermissible.

Accordingly, Riffel—acting in the interests of Tax Feeder solidarity—filed his report and swore out the probable cause affidavit.

The criminal complaint against Hutchens, which was composed by Greenbank, is a masterpiece of bureaucratic hyperbole. It claims that Hutchens "did willfully and unlawfully use force or violence upon the person of Melissa Ward by striking Ward with a pen, or, in the alternative, did actually, intentionally, and unlawfully touch or strike the person of Melissa Ward against her will by striking Ward with a pen." This, sniffs Greenbank with the practiced pomposity of a pampered parasite, was a grave offense "against the peace and dignity of the State of Idaho."

Ward suffered no injury. There is no evidence that Hutchens intended to do her any harm. By way of contrast, judicial notice has been taken of the incontrovertible fact that Officer Theresa Heberer did "willfully and unlawfully use force or violence" upon the person of Rita Hutchens in an assault that did injure the victim.

It is precisely because Hutchens is seeking redress for the criminal violence she suffered at the hands of Heberer and her comrades that Greenbank—acting on behalf of the local political class—is seeking to imprison her.

As his florid description of Hutchens's purported offense demonstrates, Greenbank is a bit of a drama queen. This got him into trouble in his last gig, during which he afflicted the residents of neighboring Kootenai County. During opening arguments in a September 2008 domestic violence trial, Greenbank—who at the time was Deputy Prosecutor for Kootenai County—broke down in tears and theatrically asked for a tissue as he recounted the alleged crimes of the defendant.

This display left First District Judge Fred Gilber thoroughly unimpressed. Chastising Greenbank for trying to manipulate the jury, Gilber declared a mistrial. Predictably, Greenbank's initial reaction was to lie, insisting that he hadn't been crying and certainly had "no intent to appeal to the passions of the jury." However, the trial transcript documents that he admitted, "I did have tears running down my face, I did have snot running down my face."

Nor was this the first time that Greenbank or his colleagues had sought to manipulate a jury. As he declared a mistrial, Judge Gilber pointed out: "In [a] recent case the Court of Appeals has singled out the Kootenai County Prosecutor's Office for appealing to the passions or prejudice of the jury."

For the last six months, Hutchens has been acting as her own attorney. Greenbank, who has no appropriate credentials, claims that she has exhibited "unusually behaviors and affects—both in court and in her filings. It is evident that her mood is changeable, and her thoughts are disorganized." He filed, and was granted, a motion ordering Hutchens to undergo a mandatory psychological evaluation.

Embedded in that May 2 order is a remarkable claim that was introduced by Magistrate Judge Debra Heise without a particle of supporting evidence. Listed among the examples of Hutchens' "unusual behaviors and affects" was the act of "battering the assigned prosecuting attorney [Greenbank] outside of court when he served papers to her in the clerk's office. . . ."

That description would lead the untutored reader to assume that Rita Hutchens, a 57-year-old woman who stands about 5'1" and weighs all of 110 pounds, boldly attacked the intrepid paladin of the public weal in full view of witnesses, and somehow managed to avoid being dragged away in chains.

What actually happened was that Greenbank shoved a sheaf of legal papers in Hutchens' face—and she replied in kind by shoving them right back at him. In other words, just as she had "battered" Melissa Ward by accidentally striking her in the arm with a ballpoint pen, she "battered" Shane Greenbank by pushing papers at him. Although this would hardly be enough to injure a child, it should be acknowledged that on Greenbank's previous performance, trivial contact of this kind would be quite enough to make him cry.

It should also be noted that Greenbank's sense of moral outrage over crimes of violence is oddly adaptable. While he is treating Rita Hutchens as if she were a public menace, last August he agreed to a plea bargain by a man accused of hog-tying one handicapped 12-year-old child, and choking another one. The assailant in that case agreed to misdemeanor charges that led to a total of two weeks in jail.

The May 2 order for Hutchens to undergo a mental evaluation specifies that Dr. Carl Haugan, a "designated licensed psychiatrist," will file a report on Hutchens's mental condition by May 23. If she refuses to cooperate, the order explains, "the report shall so state and shall include, if possible, an opinion as to whether such unwillingness of the defendant was the result of mental disease or defect."

Judge Heise—whose trough is filled with a $107,043 annual salary plundered from more honest people in the private sector—clearly sought to prejudice the evaluation by imputing to Hutchens, as a matter of record, "unusual behaviors and affects" as well as a tendency toward "violence"—as supposedly demonstrated in the two instances of "battery." If, on the other hand, Hutchens refused to submit to an evaluation foreordained to find her incompetent, her refusal is to be taken as proof of her mental incapacity.

Not surprisingly, Hutchens has refused to play her scripted role in this cynical charade—in defiance of threats to have her arrested and jailed for defying the court order. If Hutchens were taken into state custody, it's entirely possible that Greenbank would seek to have her involuntarily committed for psychiatric treatment. While thus detained, she would be unable to pursue her lawsuit against the City of Sandpoint—which is almost certainly the point of this entire campaign of official persecution.

"Punishment Has Been Achieved"

Pro Libertate, August 11, 2013

"Punishment for this offense has been achieved."

With those words, which are found near the end of an August 8 motion to dismiss a spurious battery charge against Sandpoint, Idaho resident Rita Hutchens, the author—Bonner County Chief Deputy Prosecutor Shane Greenbank—incriminates himself.

For about a year, Greenbank tirelessly pursued a charge he knew to be entirely devoid of merit. His petulant motion to dismiss—a document littered with grammatical errors that occurred because the author's protruding lower lip obstructed his view of the computer screen—offers unambiguous proof that his objective was not to convict Hutchens of an actual crime. Instead, he sought to inflict punishment on her for seeking redress for criminal violence she suffered at the hands of a Sandpoint, Idaho police officer.

Rita Hutchens is a tiny 57-year-old internationally respected quilt artist who has never committed a violent act against anybody. She was accused of "criminal battery" because she allegedly threw a ballpoint pen at a desk in the Sandpoint City Hall while doing research for a potential lawsuit against the city.

That writing utensil supposedly ricocheted off the desktop and glanced harmlessly off the blouse of a deputy city clerk named Melissa Ward. The supposed victim suffered no injury and did not press charges. Yet his incident, insisted Greenbank in a complaint filed last October 5, was a violent assault and a "grave offense against the peace and dignity of the state of Idaho."

Greenbank, whose flair for rhetorical exaggeration would strike a hormonal adolescent girl as excessive, accused Hutchens of "willfully and unlawfully us[ing] force or violence upon the person of Melissa Ward." Bear in mind that this was not a case in which a pen was employed as a shank, as occurred in a previous episode here in Idaho, nor was the pen hurled like a javelin. It was tossed carelessly at a desk, which means that there was no criminal intent—an indispensable element of an actual crime.

The same cannot be said of the assault she endured at the hands of a Sandpoint police officer named Theresa Heberer, who attacked Hutchens in front of her home in November 2011. After jumping Hutchens from behind and handcuffing the victim, Heberer held a lengthy conference with her supervisor in an effort to contrive a charge that would justify an arrest. They eventually settled on "obstruction," a charge that was thrown out of court by Judge Barbara Buchanan several months later.

"There was no reason to touch her," Judge Buchanan observed:

> She did not have to answer [Officer Heberer's] questions. She has a Fifth Amendment right not to do that. . . . You can't be charged with resisting and obstructing for exercising your Fifth Amendment right, and she did have every right to say, "I don't want to answer your questions, I want to go in my house." There is no basis for an arrest, there is no reason for a search warrant.

After seeking medical treatment for the injuries she had suffered, Hutchens filed a damage claim with the City of Sandpoint. When that request was denied, she filed a notice of tort claim against the city. She was doing research into that claim on August 8, 2012, when the pen-throwing incident took place.

The existing audio record of the August 8, 2012 confrontation at Sandpoint City Hall was made by one of several city officials who had surrounded Hutchens while she was trying to examine records of her unlawful arrest. Her chief antagonist was city attorney Scott Campbell, whose office had turned down her damage claim several weeks earlier. The specific official who rejected that claim was Lori Meulenberg, who had prosecuted the obstruction charge against Hutchens.

Hutchens wanted to be left alone to examine the records without Campbell and others swarming her and looking over her shoulder. It should be recalled that she was the victim of a violent crime committed by one of their associates. She finally gave voice to her exasperation.

"I'm tired of you people! Just leave me alone!" she exclaimed. "I just want to look at the record, which I have a right to do, now, in private."

"Actually, you don't have a right to do [that] in private," Campbell said in a taunting voice that oozed condescension.

As Hutchens attempted to read the records, Campbell continued to violate her personal space in a fashion that he would have considered legally actionable if he had been on the receiving end. This could be considered a deliberate provocation, and if so it had the intended effect.

"Do not look over me!" she shouted at Campbell, who continued to behave like an adolescent bully.

"Is this a public place, Rita?" Campbell said, mockingly. "I have as much right to be here in a public place as you have."

At this point, Hutchens took the initiative to *de-escalate* the situation by saying that she would leave and "come back tomorrow with a witness."

What this means is that **Hutchens was not looking for a fight; she was looking to avoid one**. She was *never* the aggressor in any sense. Outnumbered, harassed, and mocked by city officials who had no respect for her rights, she withdrew from the office, allegedly throwing down a ballpoint pen as she left.

A few seconds after Hutchens departed, the silence was broken by Melissa Ward, the supposed victim.

"She just threw a pen at me," Ward snickered. Yes, the "victim" *laughed* at the incident.

"Should we prosecute her?" an audibly amused Campbell asked Ward.

Significantly, there is no indication that Ward—the identified "victim"—agreed that Hutchens should be prosecuted. Ward's giggling comment is the only indication that a pen was thrown by anyone. Hutchens adamantly insists that she didn't hurl the object, but simply left the building in disgust.

After Hutchens was charged with battery last November, she filed a subpoena demanding that Ward, the purported victim, provide a signed criminal complaint. Campbell, who instigated the persecution campaign against Hutchens, filed a motion to quash that subpoena.

That motion was granted by the Idaho First District Court, which ruled that "requiring Ms. Ward, the victim in this matter, to provide a signed complaint is unreasonable."

In what sense would it be "unreasonable" to require the alleged victim of criminal battery to sign a complaint? Ward didn't require medical treatment, and she's not functionally illiterate, so she is physically and intellectually capable of either writing or dictating a coherent narrative. The only way that the term "unreasonable" has relevance here is as a description of the charge itself—and Campbell's desire to prevent any critical scrutiny of the incident responsible for that charge.

The confected charge was a misdemeanor offense. Yet after Hutchens declined to appear at a pre-trial hearing late last year, an acting judge named Don Swanstrom (who is no longer in service, and might not have been authorized to act as a judge at the time) issued a day-or-night bench warrant for her arrest.

According a 2011 state Supreme Court ruling (Idaho v. Skurlock), a warrant of that kind is generally inappropriate because at night time people enjoy "a heightened expectation of privacy that should not be disturbed by a knock on the door and the presentation of a search warrant."

Nonetheless, three officers kicked in the front door to Hutchens' home on April 16 and dragged her away. In the course of this Gestapo-grade act of overkill, one of the officers discovered what was identified as "drug paraphernalia" under her sofa—which resulted in yet another charge being filed against her.

The judge who was originally tapped to hear the "paraphernalia" case was Lori Meulenberg—yes, the same Lori Meulenberg who prosecuted the obstruction charge and subsequently denied Hutchens' damage claim for the injury she suffered during her unlawful arrest in November 2011.

Finally, on July 23—more than three months after this case was reported in detail in this space—the Bonner County *Daily Bee* published a story offering a critical examination of the campaign to incarcerate Rita Hutchens.

"Despite being a low-level offense, the battery case against Rita Nancy Hutchens has some of the trappings of a high-stakes affair," observed the *Bee*. The article noted that the midnight arrest was questionable (at best), and that the treatment of Hutchens "stirred dismay by those in the community who contend law enforcement and the courts are running amok in Bonner County."

It was likewise notable that the case was "being closely followed by city officials. City Attorney Scot Campbell attended [the July 19] hearing, as did police Chief Corey Coon and Det. Derrick Hagstrom."

Why was the *crème de la scum* of Sandpoint's ruling clique so interested in this trivial case, and so perversely determined to see Rita Hutchens incarcerated? Why did Shane Greenbank insist on having her submit to a mental evaluation—a demand that resulted in her being arrested for contempt on two occasions?

Shortly after Hutchens was seized in her home in a midnight police raid, Greenbank filed a motion demanding that she be forced to undergo a psychological evaluation because of what he described as "unusual behaviors and affects—both in court and in her filings." He also made the remarkable claim—without providing a molecule of supporting evidence—that he had also been "battered" by Hutchens "outside of court when he served papers to her in the clerk's office. . . ."

The absence of any further description may lead the otherwise uninformed reader to assume that Rita Hutchens, who is 5'1" tall and weighs about 110 pounds, knocked Greenbank on his tax-fattened ass, which is something he richly deserves. What happened, in fact, is that Greenbank shoved a sheaf of legal documents into her face—and Hutchens shoved them right back. This, we are supposed to pretend, was an act of criminal "battery."

Greenbank's repeated demands that Hutchens undergo a psychiatric evaluation were similarly intended to prejudice the public against her. This is a violation of the ethical standards that govern prosecutors (yes, I was also surprised to learn that such guidelines exist, although they do nothing to inhibit the corrupt ambition of those who occupy the office).

Rule 3.8(f) of the ABA's ethical standards specifies that prosecutors must refrain from making "comments that have a substantial likelihood of heightening public condemnation of the accused"; Rule 3.6(a) forbids prosecutors to make comments that they know or reasonably should know "will be disseminated by means of public communication and will have a substantial likelihood of materially prejudicing an adjudicative proceeding in the matter."

Greenbank's untutored speculation about Hutchens' mental health was widely reported, echoed by camp-followers of the ruling municipal clique, and had a hugely damaging impact on her public reputation.

"They set out to destroy my reputation—really, to destroy me," Hutchens told Pro Libertate. "The claims they made about my mental health were in the paper all the time, and it's absolutely destroyed my business. If this had actually gone to trial, there's no way I could have been treated fairly by a jury after they had done so much to prejudice the community against me."

After being incarcerated for contempt of court in mid-July, Hutchens finally underwent the psychological evaluation, which resulted in a terse and unembellished statement that she was entirely sound of mind. This didn't deter the irrepressibly snotty Mr. Greenbank from using his motion to dismiss the charge to traduce his victim one last time.

"[W]hile it is unfortunate that the psychological evaluation did not result in some treatment recommendation that may benefit the defendant—and, by extension, the public—the State has done all it is able to do in order to minimize further risk to the public," sneered Greenbank. He neither explained why his judgment of Hutchens' psychological condition was superior to that of a credentialed mental health professor, nor did he provide any evidence that she *ever* posed a risk to the public.

The down-market Javert took some measure of comfort in the gratuitous suffering he had inflicted by incarcerating, impoverishing, and defaming an innocent and helpless woman whose "defiance" (his word) simply had to be punished.

Since Hutchens "has spent many more days in jail than she would have if she had actually been convicted of this offense," Greenbank gloated, "punishment for this offense has been achieved."

It is widely known, though rarely acknowledged, that prosecutors pursue punishment at the expense of both truth and justice. Bonner County is host to a specimen of that tribe in whom resides the distilled malice one so often finds in that occupation, untempered by the rudimentary intellectual discipline necessary to maintain the pretense of a commitment to principle. Greenbank's persecution of Rita Hutchens was nothing less than criminal, and if so much as a particle of justice still exists he will face the consequences of his actions.

Killing Without Consequences: "Counter-Insurgency" Warfare in Greenfield, California

Pro Libertate, August 22, 2013

After eluding the police for more than a week, Alejandro Gonzalez surrendered in San Jose on January 10, 2011. The 22-year-old was the suspect in a non-fatal shooting that had taken place on New Year's Day at a local bar called the Mucky Duck.

As should be expected, the police had done nothing useful to solve that crime. Their only contribution to the case was to stage a lethal SWAT raid against a man who had been nowhere near the bar when the shooting took place, and had nothing to do with it.

Four days after the Mucky Duck shooting—in which three people suffered non-life-threatening injuries—a multi-agency SWAT team invaded the home of 31-year-old Rogelio Serrato, Jr. Serrato, who was known as Roger to friends and family, was not a suspect in the shooting.

The search warrant issued for Serrato's house should have been executed by a small group of deputies. Although police contended that Serrato was "connected" in some way to Gonzalez, there was no reason to suspect that he was harboring the fugitive.

Serrato did have outstanding misdemeanor warrants, however, and apparently this was considered sufficient justification for sending in two dozen paramilitary drag queens who arrived in an armored convoy that included a Bearcat combat vehicle.

For about an hour, the invaders broadcast surrender demands via a "thunder-hailer" megaphone. One young female left the house and was taken into custody. Serrato—who, it is believed, was intoxicated and perhaps unconscious—didn't comply.

A three-member "break and rake" team approached the house, shattered a window, and threw in a flash-bang grenade, which lodged itself between two highly flammable polyurethane sofas that were next to an artificial Christmas tree. One of the sofas immediately ignited. The fire quickly propagated itself through the house, generating a dense black cloud of highly toxic smoke.

Roused by either the sound of the grenade or the subsequent fire, Serrato began screaming and trying to leave the house. The sight of the unarmed man, clad only in his underwear, threw a scare into Sergeant Joseph Banuelos, who had supervised the "break and rake" team.

"Suspect!" shrieked Banuelos. Rather than rushing into the home to arrest the suspect, the intrepid sergeant—acting in the interests of that holiest of all considerations, "officer safety"—ordered his team to retreat to the Bearcat vehicle. The SWAT team then trained its weapons on the house, which effectively prevented the victim from escaping from the burning building.

Significantly, the use of a flash-bang grenade as a "scare tactic" was part of the raid's tactical plan, rather than an improvised measure. Deputy Mark Sievers and Detective Al Martinez, who were part of the "break and rake" team, had previously ignited fires with flash-bang grenades, so they were aware of the potential fire risk involved in using that device. That the raid posed a potentially fatal fire danger is further demonstrated by the fact that the Greenfield Fire Department had been notified of the planned raid and was on standby.

The Fire Department responded quickly once fire enveloped Serrato's home—but the SWAT team held them at bay for nearly a half-hour while the screaming victim was trapped inside. By the time the firefighters could enter the home, Serrato was dead.

Just a few days ago, Monterey County agreed to a $2.6 million settlement with Serrato's family, which was paid by the county's insurance carrier and absolves the sheriff's office of legal responsibility. Speaking the language of institutional self-exculpation with remarkable fluency, County Attorney Charles McKee insisted that Serrato was to blame for his own death and that the officers should be "commended for trying to resolve a very tense situation."

It's often said that police are the country's most dangerous street gang. One significant distinction between police and their private sector counterparts is that street gangs don't expect to receive commendations when they kill innocent people.

It would be a wonderful thing if people could develop the intellectual equivalent of a computer utility that would remove uniforms, badges, and titles from news accounts of fatal police raids. Subtracting the indicia of "authority" would enhance the ability of people to see the truth about acts of aggressive violence, and recognize them as crimes irrespective of the claimed identity of those who commit them.

The killing of Roger Serrato was an act of murder through depraved indifference. The assailants had no justification to attack his home; they knew that their plan of attack posed the risk of a catastrophic fire; once that fire began, the assailants took no action to rescue the victim, and impeded the efforts of others to do so.

The SWAT raid was a specimen of police overkill born of opportunism: What's the use of having a SWAT team unless it can be deployed to arrest people with outstanding misdemeanor warrants?

It's possible, perhaps even likely, that police officials chose to attack Serrato's home simply because his location—unlike that of the actual suspect, Alejandro Gonzalez—was known. If the police had actually investigated the Mucky Duck shooting, rather than seizing on it as a chance to preen on camera in paramilitary attire, they would have learned that Gonzalez was not a threat to the public.

A lawsuit filed by Todd Graham, one of the shooting victims, claims that before he went to his car to get his gun, Gonzalez had seen several of his friends abused by a group of bouncers who had "escalated" a minor altercation into a life-threatening situation. At one point, a friend of Gonzalez named Mark Rosso, was thrown to the ground and pinned down by a bouncer and a bartender while another bouncer identified as "T.K." beat and kicked him.

In pre-trial testimony, Monterey police detective Michael Bruno admitted that witnesses had described that assault to him. Witnesses also claimed that Gonzalez went to his car and grabbed a gun while his friend was being beaten.

Graham, a bystander who was leaving the bar when the shooting began, insists that Gonzalez's decision to get his gun was made "in response to the actions of the bouncers." Graham and two of the bouncers were the only ones who were shot.

As Judge Pamela Butler acknowledged in Gonzalez's pre-trial hearing, the shooting was at least in part motivated by the desire to defend his friend, who was pleading for help and most likely in fear for his life. However, Judge Butler, a former gang prosecutor, insisted that Gonzalez's alleged affiliation with the Norteno street gang meant that the shooting was "gang-related."

This gave prosecutor Cristina Johnson a rationale for charging Gonzalez with ten felonies. The charges included not three, but four counts of attempted murder: One for the shooting of Graham, the innocent bystander; two for the bouncers who were attacking Rosso; and one more for the bartender who was helping to hold the victim down. While the bartender wasn't shot, Johnson insisted that he be treated as a victim because he was in the "kill zone."

The memory of man runneth not to an instance in which a police officer who used deadly force was charged for attempted murder because of the presence of an innocent victim in the "kill zone." Where "qualified immunity" ends in such cases, "professional courtesy" takes over.

Witness the case of Robert Shawn Richardson and Paul Bradley Rogers, who were convicted of second-degree manslaughter after shooting and killing a five-year-old boy in Noble, Oklahoma six years ago while trying to kill a poisonous snake. Because they received deferred sentences, the officers served no time in prison, and their records have been expunged. Where the "law" is concerned, the incident never happened, and the victim, Austin Haley, never existed.

"If the roles were reversed and I had shot the gun, it would be much different," observes Austin's mother, Renee Haley. "I would've been sent to jail and the sentence would have been done more harshly."

This is incontestably true. Austin wasn't a cop; he was one of the "little people." The same was true of Roger Serrato.

As Serrato's grandmother tearfully told a Greenfield City Council meeting, he was not a saint—but he was a human being who should not have been summarily executed.

In seeking to justify the murderous raid on Serrato's home, police applied the counter-insurgency template used by the military in Iraq and Afghanistan and applied it to "gang enforcement."

In Gonzalez's pre-trial hearing, Detective Bruno reported that a search of the suspect's home found "clothing and other items" indicating that he may have been associated with the Norteno street gang. While he admitted—under cross-examination—that the Mucky Duck shooting was at least in part motivated by self-defense, he insisted that it had the effect of enhancing the gang's image "by instilling fear in the community."

That sort of thing *never* happens when masked Berserkers in military attire lay siege to a residence, of course.

Shortly after his associates murdered Roger Serrato, Greenfield Police Department spokesliar Phil Penko told a local television station that "whether he was at the Mucky Duck is irrelevant" because "someone connected to the house" was allegedly there at the time of the shooting.

This is a specimen of what counter-insurgency experts call "pattern of life" analysis. All that is necessary to justify potentially lethal action against any individual is to create a "link" or "connection" between that person and a "suspected militant" (or, in this case, a suspected "gang associate") or an incident involving someone who meets that description.

In Afghanistan, "connections" of that kind have been used to justify midnight raids by kill teams. In Pakistan, the same analysis is used as the basis for drone strikes. We're seeing plentiful examples of the former here domestically, and we can expect to see the latter approach rolled out in the "Homeland" within the next few years.

Welcome to Deming, New Mexico—Where Police Rape is a Matter of "Protocol"

Pro Libertate, November 5, 2013

David Eckert was stopped by police in Deming, New Mexico without cause, subjected to an illegal search of his vehicle and person, and eventually forced to undergo what amounts to object rape in the form of multiple rectal probes, forced enemas, and a colonoscopy.

The purported reason for this treatment was suspicion of narcotics possession. A more credible explanation is that the police wanted to punish Eckert for politely asserting his rights during an encounter a few weeks earlier.

There is something at once infuriating and appropriate about the treatment inflicted on Eckert: If the beast called the Homeland Security State has a cloacal tract, is aperture might very well be located in Deming, New Mexico. The uniformed degenerates who kidnapped Eckert and subjected him to Gitmo-trade torture claimed to be working with a federally supervised narcotics task force. This part of their story is entirely plausible, given the extravagant and impenitent corruption that typifies federal counter-narcotics operations in the New Mexico border region.

On September 6, 2012, Eckert was stopped a few blocks from his home in Lordsburg by Hidalgo County Sheriff's Deputy Robert Rodriguez, who claimed to have noticed a cracked windshield on Eckert's car. When Rodriguez noticed that Eckert appeared nervous, he ordered the man out of his car. The deputy wrote a warning citation and then told Eckert he was free to leave. As Eckert turned to leave, the deputy—employing a tiresome and familiar tactic—continued to question him.

Eckert politely asked if he was free to leave, as he had been told. Feigning offense, the deputy claimed that this was "rude" and said that he suspected Eckert had narcotics in his vehicle. Eckert said that he wasn't interested in speaking with the deputy, and once again tried to leave. The deputy then seized the vehicle without probable cause and called Deputy Patrick Green, who deployed a drug-sniffing dog. The canine—as he was trained and expected to—"alerted" to the supposed presence of narcotics in the vehicle. A thorough search the following day failed to find any drug-related evidence.

However, to paraphrase the warning given to Dr. Zhivago by a Soviet Commissar, Eckert's attitude had been noticed.

On January 2, as he was leaving the parking lot of a Walmart in Deming, Eckert was stopped by Officer Robert Chavez for supposedly failing to come to a complete stop. Chavez did not witness the alleged infraction; he claimed to be acting on a report from a fellow Deming PD denizen named Bobby Orosco. Chavez ordered Eckert from the car and subjected him to a physical pat-down without probable cause or reasonable suspicion.

The assailant found Eckert's reaction to this criminal violation of his person to be suspicious: He claimed that the victim's posture was "erect and he kept his legs together."

After several other officers arrived—in response, once again, to an alleged traffic violation—Chavez wrote an extortion note (typically referred to as a "traffic citation") and the victim was told he was free to leave. This was a reprise of the tactic used in the previous traffic stop: Chavez continued to pester Eckert, who continued to assert his right to leave unmolested.

Chavez is a police officer, which means he is trained to lie, given social permission to lie, and will lie whenever it suits him. In his report he stated that Eckert gave consent for a search of his vehicle, which was untrue. While a drug-sniffing dog pawed through his car, Eckert was surrounded by police officers, two of whom—Hidalgo County Deputies David Arrendondo and Patrick Green—were acting as members of the Border Drug Task Force.

Arrendondo told Officer Chavez that Eckert was "known in Hidalgo County to insert drugs into his anal cavity." On the basis of what was either unsubstantiated gossip or a lie invented on the scene, Eckert was abducted and taken to the police station. When he demanded the right to make a phone call, Eckert was told he was not under arrest. His car was seized and searched—and, once again, no narcotics evidence was found.

A few hours after Eckert was seized by the Deming Police, Luna County Deputy District Attorney Daniel Dougherty obtained a warrant permitting officers ʼ ᵈuct a body cavity search. That warrant was valid only for the hᵉˑ ꞇ and 10:00 PM on January 2nd.

ʼs abductors took him to a local emergency room, the identified in Eckert's lawsuit only as "Dr. Ash," politely ꞇicers that what they were demanding was illegal and ᵉrs shrugged and, with the consent of prosecutor

Dougherty, drove the victim to another hospital in a different jurisdiction—Gila Regional Medical Center in Grant County.

Over the next 24 hours, Eckert endured an abdominal X-ray, multiple digital rectal inspections, three enemas, and a colonoscopy. None of these assaults on Eckert's bodily integrity yielded drug-related evidence of any kind— and if they had, that evidence almost certainly would have been inadmissible. Procuring evidence wasn't the point of this exercise; the primary objective was to punish an impudent Mundane.

All of those procedures took place outside the jurisdiction specified in the warrant; all but the abdominal X-ray were entirely unauthorized and took place after the time limit imposed in the warrant. More importantly, *none* of this was valid or licit in any sense: As Dr. Ash pointed out, subjecting an unwilling "patient" to invasive procedures was illegal and unethical.

Like their colleagues in the CIA—who enlisted physicians to collaborate in abuse of detainees at Gitmo—the officers in the Border Drug Task Force were able to suborn doctors into violating the law and their Hippocratic obligations in order to torture an innocent man.

On his way home from the hospital, Eckert had to endure the contemptuous mockery of his captors. The abuse has continued in the intervening months, as the hospital administrators have demanded that the victim pay for the privilege of being tortured on the orders of the police.

"We follow the law in every aspect and we follow policies and protocols that we have in place," recited Deming Police Commissar Brandon Gigante when he was asked by a local television reporter about the sexual torture committed by his officers against David Eckert. Indeed, judicially authorized object rape has become a familiar weapon in the Homeland Security State's arsenal.

What prompted police in the New Mexico border area to focus their sadistic attention on David Eckert? The irrepressible desire to punish a Mundane for "contempt of cop" plays a significant role in this abhorrent episode, to be sure. However, the lengths to which Eckert's tormentors went to invent a rationale for a drug investigation reflect the fact that drug prohibition is a hugely lucrative racket for the corrupt functionaries who afflict New Mexico's border region.

Deming, a city of about 14,000 people, hosts the headquarters of the New Mexico branch of the Homeland Security Investigations agency, which works hand-in-mailed fist with the New Mexico Border Operations High Intensity

Drug Trafficking Area Task Force (HIDTA). The HIDTA receives at least $8,000,000 a year in federal funding to conduct "counter-narcotics" operations. Many of those initiatives involve "controlled buys" and other sting operations—and nothing it does will abate drug trafficking in any way.

Like other federal entities of its kind, the HIDTA is a public works project for profligate sociopaths. Christopher DeSantis, who was employed as an agent of the Immigration and Customs Enforcement agent in Deming from 2001–2007, has described to Narco News how fellow agents in the HIDTA routinely divert tax funds and asset proceeds into "training" junkets to bars and strip clubs in Vegas, or to obtain unauthorized perks and personal benefits.

"They didn't give a sh*t," DeSantis recalls. "They just wanted to use up the money because the fiscal year was ending."

An internal audit conducted by the Department of Homeland Security confirmed that HIDTA funds were improperly used, and that official records were altered "to disguise how the funds were ultimately used."

Arguably the most serious finding in that audit was that "Confidential informants were improperly paid multiple times for the same information, service, or evidence by using alternate funding sources."

According to DeSantis, "it was common practice for the task force leadership to double count drug seizures," reports the Narco News. One of the ways it padded its statistics was to use a specific informant—identified as "SA-163"—to make controlled heroin buys each week, "like clockwork."

"We would meet someone who was bringing the drugs across the border, and we made the purchases in a parking lot or hotel," DeSantis attests. "Most of the time, we were just buying the drugs, and every once in a while, we would arrest a [low-level] mule."

Informant SA-163, as it turned out, "was getting paid by law enforcement and getting street value for his drugs with no risk," continues DeSantis. The drug dealer enjoyed protected profits, in *addition* to pay-offs drawn from multiple federal funding sources. His collaborators in the HIDTA were inflating their statistics and building career security—and embezzling federal funds to pay for drinking binges at "training" seminars.

DeSantis blew the whistle, and was promptly fired. The HIDTA continues to be a subsidized blight on New Mexico's border region, where it helps cultivate a law enforcement culture in which sexual torture of an innocent man is regarded as an appropriate "protocol."

California's Gun-Grabbing Einsatzgruppen

Pro Libertate, November 21, 2013

"When you are going to take their guns," observes Special Agent John Marsh, "they are not happy."

"They" are California residents who have been designated as "prohibited persons" by the state's Armed Prohibited Persons System (APPS). Those individuals are said to have "lost" their rights under the Second Amendment. Marsh leads a special APPS paramilitary task force dedicated exclusively to gun confiscation.

Using gun registration lists, and drawing information out of several other databases, APPS stormtroopers "regularly sweep through California cities" to seize firearms from people the state has designated "prohibited persons," reports the *Fresno Bee*. California Governor Jerry Brown recently signed a bill that will use a $24 million surplus from firearms purchase fees to hire 36 new jackboots for the squad.

As is always the case with "gun control" initiatives, APPS does nothing to abate violent crime, because criminally inclined people do not register their firearms. California gun owners who comply with the state's laws are subsidizing a program that is increasingly used to confiscate guns from innocent people on the whim of bureaucrats who aspire to disarm the public at large.

Speaking of the tens of thousands of Californians who have been classified as "prohibited persons," California's proto-Stalinist Attorney General (and presidential pinup) Kamala Harris insists: "They are those people who have been proven to violate the law, and present a threat to public safety." Harris insists that proactive disarmament of "dangerous, violent individuals . . . is smart and efficient law enforcement."

Harris, predictably enough, is lying through deliberate over-statement. Only a minority of "prohibited persons" are convicted criminals, and not everyone who meets that description is a felon—violent or otherwise.

A criminal conviction is not necessary for enrollment on the civilian disarmament register. All that is necessary is an official finding by the state's Welfare bureaucracy that the gun owner is "a danger to himself or others." This determination can come in the form of a restraining order issued *ex parte* in a domestic dispute, an involuntary "mental health" hold (a formal commitment proceeding is unnecessary), or conviction for a "violent" misdemeanor, including one issued for the non-crime of resisting arrest. It is estimated that at least 20 California residents are enrolled on the disarmament roster every day.

According to attorney Chuck Michel, who has represented gun owners in court, "there are 30 different ways you can be prohibited from owning a gun. Most of the people on the list aren't a threat, and don't even know they're on it."

Clad in black tactical gear and prominently displaying high-powered weaponry, Harris's firearms confiscation stormtroopers typically carry out raids late at night, or early in the morning. They arrive in overwhelming numbers and, without the benefit of a warrant, seek to intimidate targeted individuals into permitting searches of their property in order to confiscate any firearms that might be found. If the "prohibited persons" refuse to cooperate, the raiders will "seek a warrant and lock down the house until they get results," explains the *Bee*.

Commissarina Harris clearly sees California's gun confiscation program as a template for similar initiatives across the nation.

"California is leading the nation in a common-sense effort to protect public safety by taking guns away from dangerous, violent individuals who are prohibited by law from owning them," boasted Harris—who speaks exclusively in collectivist boilerplate, it appears—last January. In a letter to Vice President Biden, she urged him to use APPS as a national model. To that end, California Democratic Congressman Mike Thompson has sponsored the federal Armed Prohibited Persons Act of 2013, which thus far has failed to find traction in the house.

So far, California is the only state to deploy a dedicated gun confiscation team—but it isn't the only one to engage in preemptive civilian disarmament.

In 1999, the Connecticut legislature enacted a measure permitting police to confiscate firearms from any individual believed to pose "a risk of imminent personal injury to himself . . . or to other individuals." All that is necessary for the seizure to occur is a sworn complaint "by any state's attorney or assistant state's attorney or by any two police officers to any judge of the Superior Court." The confiscated firearms can be held for up to a year, without any criminal charges or civil action being taken against their owner. Thousands of firearms have been seized under that provision, which famously did not prevent the Sandy Hook Massacre.

No Quarter

In the Glorious Democratic Republic of Massachusetts, police and prosecutors didn't even bother pretending that they were enforcing a law permitting the preemptive disarmament of Gregory Girard, a resident of Manchester-by-the-Sea, after his estranged wife—who appears to be a temporally displaced subject of East Germany—called health and welfare officials to report that her husband held eccentric political views. Specifically, Mr. Girard believed that martial law, complete with gun confiscation, is imminent. Since it is impermissible for people to believe that government agents will carry out paramilitary raids to confiscate firearms, a paramilitary squad was sent to Girard's home to confiscate his firearms.

The Gun Control Act of 1968—which was largely modeled after the German civilian disarmament measures that proved so useful to the National Socialist Regime—prohibited the sale or transfer of firearms to anyone who is "adjudicated as a mental defective"—a term that itself savors of language that was in vogue in Germany circa 1938.

Germany's "Law on the Disarmament of the People" was enacted by the liberal Weimar Republic in 1920. It was followed in 1928 by another "common-sense" firearms law that centralized enforcement of gun laws. That 1928 law was employed by the successor regime to disarm those it sought to expropriate and, eventually, to annihilate.

The "purpose" and "goal" of the German gun law, explained the Weimar government's disarmament commissar in 1928, was "to get firearms that have done so much damage from the hands of unauthorized persons"—a statement that would be a serviceable German translation of Harris's rationale for California's APPS program.

Given that pedigree, it is appropriate to refer to Harris's "Gun Apprehension" units as *einsatzgruppen*—that is, paramilitary "special task forces" that operate outside of normal legal channels.

As is true of all similarly constituted "task forces," the purpose of the APPS *einsatzgruppen* is not to protect the public from violence, but rather to enforce the state's monopoly on aggressive violence. This fact was stated with remarkable clarity by a prominent spokesman for California's law enforcement rank-and-file: Emeryville Police Chief Ken James, who in 2012 was presented with what we're assured is the prestigious Joe Malloy Award for his tireless campaign to disarm everybody but the state's punitive priesthood.

"A gun is not a defensive weapon," insisted Chief James in a press conference earlier this year:

That is a myth. *A gun is an offensive weapon used to intimidate and used to show power.* Police officers do not carry a gun as a defensive weapon to defend themselves or their other [sic] officers. They carry a gun in order to do their job in a safe and effective manner, and face any oppositions [sic] that we may come upon. If it was a defensive measure, why did we lose 55 officers nationwide last year to gun violence—and unfortunately in just the two months of this year so far, we've lost two officers to gun violence in the State of California alone? We deal with gun violence on a daily basis. (Emphasis added.)

The substance of what this marginally verbal embodiment of arrogant privilege said is that police *deal out* gun violence on a daily basis—a vision neatly embodied by Harris's black-clad APPS *einsatzgruppen*, who are field-testing tactics that will soon be emulated by gun-grabbers nationwide.

Never Trust a Costumed Stranger

Pro Libertate, November 26, 2013

Within the space of seventy-two hours last weekend, three women were detained and sexually assaulted by armed strangers in official-looking costumes. Two of those incidents occurred in Texas, the other happened in Minnesota.

The first attack took place on a highway near Carrollton, Texas on Thursday, November 21. An unidentified man wearing what appeared to be a police uniform stopped a woman, handcuffed her, and assaulted her in the back seat of his car.

Early Sunday morning, a female student at the University of Minnesota was sexually assaulted by a man dressed like a police officer. The assailant, who was driving a black SUV, approached the woman and admonished her that she shouldn't be walking alone late at night. Beguiled by what appeared to be the stranger's official attire, the woman got into the vehicle. The driver locked the doors and conveyed the victim to a remote location, where he raped her.

Sandwiched between these episodes of sexual predation by ersatz police officers was one involving an actual cop. During a routine patrol on Friday, November 22, San Antonio Police Officer Jackie Len Neal allegedly stopped a 19-year-old girl, handcuffed her, and raped her in the back seat of his police cruiser. This was not the first time he has been accused of assaulting women during traffic stops.

Neal was arrested a few hours later, but released after making bail. He was immediately put on paid "administrative leave," and allowed to keep his firearms—professional courtesies that would not be extended to either of the other two accused roadside rapists if they were captured.

Following the attack by the police impersonator near Carrollton, police officials warned female drivers that if they are suspicious of the individual pulling them over, they should call 911 and then drive to a well-lit area before stopping.

This course of action might defeat the evil designs of a police impersonator. However, if the suspicious stranger is a police officer, a female driver who acts on that safety advice will probably find herself involved in a dangerous pursuit that could lead to criminal charges—assuming that she survives the encounter.

This is demonstrated by the cast of Arizona resident Dibor Roberts, who was attacked by a sheriff's deputy during a late-night traffic stop after she tried to find a safe and well-lit area to conduct unwanted business with the uniformed extortionist.

At roughly 10:45 PM on the evening of July 29, 2007, Mrs. Roberts, a 48-year-old nurse and naturalized U.S. citizen from Senegal, was returning from work when she noticed a car driving erratically in front of her.

After passing the dangerous driver, Roberts noticed police lights in her rear-view mirror. Her initial reaction was relief, since she believed the officer was going to pull over what she suspected was an impaired motorist. Her relief turned to puzzlement and then alarmed suspicion when she realized that she was the target.

Just a few days earlier, Dibor and her husband had discussed local incidents involving police impersonators. They were aware of advice given by police agencies to people being pulled over in dangerous circumstances: Drive carefully to a well-lit, preferably public area, and call 911 if possible to verify that it is a police officer. That was the official recommendation offered by the Yavapai County Sheriff's Office. That department's employees included Sgt. Jeff Newnum—who, ignoring another driver who was operating his vehicle erratically at unsafe speeds, had targeted Roberts for a revenue collection encounter on that dark July evening.

Roberts did nothing wrong. She acted in strict compliance with the Sheriff's official advice, slowing down and proceeding in the direction of a well-lit area. Her behavior was not that of someone trying to flee from the police.

Deputy Newnum, on the other hand, had already lost his composure, informing the dispatcher that he was in pursuit of a "black driver" who refused to stop. He pulled alongside Roberts and attempted a "pit maneuver" to force her off the road, which did nothing to allay the innocent woman's entirely proper suspicions. After Roberts came to a stop, Newnum erupted from his vehicle with a drawn gun because, he later testified, "I knew I had an angry driver."

Roberts, who by this time was terrified, frantically tried to explain that she was looking for a safe place to stop. Ignoring her desperate pleas, and no doubt eager to exploit an opportunity to inflict property damage, Newnum took out a baton and shattered the driver's side window, bellowing at her to "Open the f*****g door!" He then seized the terrified woman and dragged her out of the car. As he did so, Dibor's foot came off the brake and her car—which was still in gear—rolled forward over Newnum's foot.

Through her window, Dibor had repeatedly yelled "It's too dark; I'm afraid." She was dragged from her vehicle yelling "No, no, no, no," as Newnum threw her to the ground. Her cellphone was taken from her and thrown away as well.

"He pulled me out and the car jerked because I had my foot on the brakes," Dibor explained after the incident.

"She took it too far when she ran over my foot," insisted Newnum later under oath. This is a petulant lie of the kind that comes readily to the lips of tax-eaters of Newnum's ilk. He had needlessly escalated the encounter by threatening to use deadly force. Roberts made no effort to escape after supposedly assaulting Newnum.

Furthermore, Newnum's courtroom testimony that Roberts clearly intended to run over his foot contradicted his official report from six months earlier, in which he said it wasn't clear whether this was a mishap or an act of malicious intent. He likewise equivocated on the witness stand as to whether or not he was injured in that "attack."

Another key contradiction in Newnum's testimony dealt with his concerns over Robert's "threat" to his safety. The deputy claimed that he was worried that he couldn't see Roberts's hands, which supposedly justified his decision to approach the car with a drawn gun at the "low ready" position. However, he also testified that when he reached Roberts's vehicle he saw her hands plainly, and that they were gripping her steering wheel "firmly"—which he said justified suspicions that she might have been impaired.

In his closing arguments during the trial, Yavapai County Prosecutor Glen Hammond insisted that the driver's crime was that "she did not stop"—which would mean that Sheriff Waugh had abetted the crime by instructing motorists uncertain of the identity of their pursuer not to stop until they reached a well-lit area. Hammond's position was that *Roberts was a criminal because she had obeyed the instructions offered by the Sheriff,* and that it was not necessary to prove that she had willfully tried to flee or injure Newnum.

The jury, which apparently was populated entirely by punitive populists, ratified that claim after less than two hours' deliberation, finding Roberts guilty of two felonies—resisting arrest (which isn't a crime) and unlawful flight. (Significantly, the initial traffic violation was dismissed outright, as was a charge of "assaulting" Newnum for supposedly running over his foot.) The trial judge, in what he probably thought was an act of tremendous generosity, dismissed the first conviction and sentenced Roberts to six months' supervised probation. This left an undeserved felony conviction on her record, which meant an end to her nursing career.

Not content to ruin Roberts's professional life and inflict substantial financial and emotional hardship on this innocent woman and her family, Hammond—offering the last full measure of prosecutorial malice—tried to depict the terrified nurse as the bully in this encounter.

"All he [Newnum] wanted from the very beginning was an apology and [he] left it up to the County Attorney what to do with this case," whined Hammond. "It was a misunderstanding. It has been really tough on him and his family due to a lot of press, a lot of hate mail. He has been called a racist. . . . He just wants everyone to move forward and"—at this point, dear reader, you may want to find a receptacle for your rebellious gorge—"let the healing begin."

Bobbing in this slurry of insipid clichés is an unintended confession by Hammond that he had committed malfeasance of office: If this incident was a "misunderstanding," then it wasn't a crime, and shouldn't have been prosecuted as such. In addition, if Newnum really wanted nothing more than an apology "from the very beginning," he should have complied with Dibor's reasonable and lawful request to find a well-lit area to conduct the traffic stop.

An actual peace officer (who wouldn't be involved in roadside shakedowns in the first place) would have cleared up that "misunderstanding," rather than escalating it. Jeff Newnum, like practically everybody else in his profession, is a law enforcer who impersonates a peace officer. Such people are immeasurably more dangerous than their imitators.

About the author

William Norman Grigg (1963-2017) was the managing editor of The Libertarian Institute. He was an independent, award-winning investigative journalist and author of five books, including *Liberty in Eclipse: The War on Terror and the Rise of the Homeland Security State* and wrote at his blog Pro Libertate. Will was a loving husband and doting father to six children.

Note from the publisher

William Norman Grigg died far too young in the spring of 2017. He was one of the most talented writers and eloquent voices for liberty in our society.

I had been a huge fan of Will's writing since the mid-1990s, but thinking back to the turn of the century, one thing really stands out. Just after the attacks of September 11, 2001, when President George W. Bush's approval rating was soaring above 90 percent as he vowed revenge, and the vast majority of the American right was embracing authoritarianism and war, Will Grigg, editor of the John Birch Society's magazine, *The New American*, wrote a feature examining the arguments for an invasion of Afghanistan in light of the Christian Just War doctrine of Saint Thomas Aquinas.

By that standard, Will said, the administration's case for war against Afghanistan failed on all but one of the 14 criteria. For example, he wrote that while people had been attacked on American soil, revenge was far from a good enough excuse for war, which would be certain to kill more innocent people. Besides, terrorism is a crime, not a military action. The attack on the Twin Towers had been committed by a group of bandits, not a foreign state. The Taliban government of Afghanistan had signaled it was willing to negotiate the handover of Osama bin Laden and al Qaeda, but the administration was choosing to ignore the offer. The U.S. Congress did not have the authority to pass an overly broad Authorization for Use of Military Force which diffused their proper responsibility in place of a constitutional declaration of war or letter of marque and reprisal.

Though without question the perpetrators had to be brought to justice, Grigg wrote, by the standards of his Christian faith and the U.S. Constitution, the United States must refrain from war against Afghanistan.

For antiwar conservatives and libertarians like me, this brave stance by Will and *The New American* helped to reinforce what we already knew: Bush's "War on Terror" was an unnecessary evil that demanded our opposition. He had also handed us a great rhetorical shield and cudgel for our fight with the pro-war right.

Whatever their faults, the members and leaders of the Birch Society unquestionably were American patriots to their core. Always at the heart of their doctrine was the preservation of the Constitution and its Bill of Rights, the

American flag, the Christian religion, and Western Civilization, broadly conceived.

There was not and could not have been any confusion about it. William Norman Grigg was not taking the side of our country's enemies; he simply knew better than to believe in the false reality the government and media were constructing. The administration claimed that "everything changed" on September 11, and that they now had carte blanche to remake all of human civilization—to "create [their] own reality"—with military violence whenever and wherever they saw fit in order to fight against "terror." Afghanistan was to be just the beginning of a new era of American war in the name of ridding the world of tyranny and evil.

In two separate articles in late 2001, Will was one of the first journalists to deeply examine the failure of the U.S. government to stop al Qaeda's attack. Even more important, Will explained that America was not being assaulted by "radical Islam" due to jealousy or hatred of our freedom, as the president claimed, but by the government's own former Arab mercenaries, left over from the 1980s war in Afghanistan against the Soviets. They had turned against their American patrons in reaction to specific U.S. policies, such as the stationing of U.S. troops in Saudi Arabia to bomb and blockade Iraq all through the 1990s, supporting dictatorships in Egypt and Saudi Arabia and backing Israel's occupations of Palestine and Lebanon.

The terrorists had killed thousands of Americans with the express purpose of provoking an *overreaction* in order to bog America down in a war of attrition in far-off Afghanistan, just as the Carter and Reagan administrations had helped them to do to the old USSR a generation before, hastening its collapse and eventual total withdrawal from the region.

Thus, Will warned the last thing the administration should do was to take advantage of the crisis to expand further into the Middle East—which was exactly what al Qaeda wanted and expected the U.S. government to do.

This should be quite obvious to everyone by now, but to state it all so plainly within just a few weeks of the attack was a measure of Will's brilliance as an analyst as well as his fearlessness in declaring the truth in the pages of what was arguably the most conservative publication in America.

It certainly meant everything to me at the time.

Though I never met him in person, we had become friends by the mid-2000s, and I'm grateful I had the chance to talk to Will more than 70 times over the years on my radio show. These interviews included discussions about his previous book, *Liberty in Eclipse*, and many of his great original reports on local police and prosecutorial abuse of innocent people.

As shown in this book, Will's later specialization in stories about local police violence and false convictions in state courts was some of the most important work done in the libertarian movement in the early 21st century. He set such a great example and represented our movement so well that he made us all look good by association with him.

One reason I started the Libertarian Institute with Will and Sheldon Richman in 2016 was to try to provide Will with a platform to promote his great work and with a way to support his struggling family of eight.

In addition to this book, we have created an archive of much of Will's work at LibertarianInstitute.org/Will. It includes old newspaper columns from the early 1990s, some entries from the Birch Blog, articles he wrote for the Institute and everything from his own blog, *Pro Libertate*. It also includes the audio archives of his great *Freedom Zealot* podcast, *Liberty Minute* radio spots and even a few sermons.

Will Grigg will be long remembered as a great man and a good man. He was a proud husband and loving father.

He was a heroic champion of freedom in our time.

Scott Horton, May 2019

Made in the USA
Columbia, SC
21 October 2021

47624529R00176